Tehrik-e-Taliban
PAKISTAN

Tehrik-e-Taliban
PAKISTAN

Origin, Evolution and Future Portents

Ashok K. Behuria

KW
KNOWLEDGE WORLD

KW Publishers Pvt Ltd
New Delhi

MANOHAR PARRIKAR
idsa
MANOHAR PARRIKAR INSTITUTE FOR
DEFENCE STUDIES AND ANALYSES
मनोहर पर्रिकर रक्षा अध्ययन एवं विश्लेषण संस्थान

Manohar Parrikar Institute for Defence Studies and Analyses
No. 1, Development Enclave, Delhi Cantt.
New Delhi 110 010
Phone: +91-11-26717983
Website: www.idsa.in

ISBN   978-93-91490-02-7   Hardback

Published in India by Kalpana Shukla

KW Publishers Pvt Ltd
4676/21, First Floor, Ansari Road
Daryaganj, New Delhi 110 002
Phone: +91 11 43528107
Marketing: kw@kwpub.in
Editorial: production@kwpub.in
Website: www.kwpub.in

Contents

Preface

While interacting with tribal elders in Mir Ali in, North Waziristan on 2 March 2021, the army chief of Pakistan, General Qamar Javed Bajwa referred to "an uptick in violence and deadly clashes" and emphasised on the need "to remain vigilant and steadfast to thwart hostile attempts to create chaos and reverse the gains of Operation Radd-ul-Fasaad".[1] General Bajwa spent an entire day with forward troops in Asman Manza, South Waziristan and Mir Ali in North Waziristan. It was days after the claim by Inter Services Public Relations (ISPR) on the occasion of anniversary of Operation Radd-ul-Fassad (which was launched in 22 February 2017), that over the last four years, the Army had conducted as many as 750,000 intelligence based operations (IBOs) throughout the country with the help of intelligence agencies including the ISI, the MI, the IB as well as the police and other law enforcement agencies.[2]

The very day the ISPR was claiming success of operations, the media reported that militants on motorbikes shot four women aid-workers in Mir Ali while in the Shewa area of North Waziristan, gunmen killed one person and abducted at least eight others. On everyday basis since then, the Tehrik-e-Taliban Pakistan (TTP) has put out claims in social media about conducting attacks on security forces in different parts of the tribal areas—in Bannu, Dera Ismail Khan, Lakki Marwat, Bajaur, North and South Waziristan and Mohmand.

These claims and counter-claims point to a disturbing disquiet among the military of Pakistan about the state of internal security situation in Pakistan because of the continuing threat the armed forces of Pakistan have encountered from TTP, a conglomerate of radical Islamist groups formed in December 2007. It appears to stage a come-back after nearly seven years of concerted army action in the tribal areas starting with Operation Zarb-e-Azb (ZeA) in June 2014 and continuing with Operation Radd-ul-Fassad (RuF) since February 2017. After losing its firebrand and pathological militant Amir, Mullah Fazlullah, also infamous as Mullah Radio, in an American drone attack in Afghanistan in June 2018, it is gathering its strength all over again with its new leader Abu Mansoor Asim investing in mergers of various splinter groups to turn TTP into a dreaded terror machine it used to be. It seems to be undertaking a well-directed social-media campaign to regain its image it has lost among the people of Pakistan, after conducting a heinous attack on the Army Public School of Peshawar on 16 December 2016. All in all, amid myriad Islamist groups operating in the Af-Pak region, TTP has managed to hold its sway as a regional and local Islamist outfit, much like Taliban, seeking to bring about an armed Islamic revolution and displace the Pakistani army in Pakistan, while retaining its interest in global Islamic issues.

The run of the Islamist groups in Pakistan has always been an engaging area of study for researchers focussing on the future of Pakistan worldwide. What makes the subject even more fascinating is the agency as well as autonomy with which these groups operate, and the invisible umbilical cord that connects them to the shadowy and murky realm of intelligence games planned by powerful agencies and factions within the Pakistani state system, which plays a significant role in the permutations and combinations that the groups work out among themselves. All this makes it daunting for a researcher to track and corelate events, incidents, personalities and outfits and arrive at a conclusive opinion about the subject of study.

As a student of Pakistani society and politics, when the first signs of Taliban-like onslaught emerged in the horizon in the late 1990s in the Pakistan-Afghanistan borderlands, incidentally brought to my attention by my good friend Vishal Chandra, who is a student of Afghan politics, I started tracking the phenomenon with all the constraints that an Indian researcher working on Pakistan is likely to have. One had to court criticism and even ridicule while pointing out politely even in early 2002 that jihadi elements that Pakistani agencies had enabled, through their entanglements in Kashmir and Afghanistan, had started coalescing into a force that the Pakistani state would find it difficult to handle. Many Pakistan-watchers in India would refuse to believe that there can ever be an entity called Pakistani Taliban and would deem it as an extension of Afghan Taliban and hence unworthy of scholarly merely attention. The effort to pull out some early articles on the theme partly, in the wake of TTP's emergence in 2007, succeeded in drawing the attention of analyst in India to this phenomenon. The work on TTP by this researcher went on till it hit another bend on the road in the shape of the attack on Army Public School (APS), Peshawar, and massive army action in the tribal areas. It seemed as if Pakistan had found a way of completely eliminating this menace once and for all time to come. However, seven years hence, through dismantling of the terror infrastructure in the tribal areas and merger of the tribal areas with Khyber Pakhtunkhwa province, the resilience shown by the entity called TTP demanded refocusing of attention on the theme.

The present work is a result of an abiding interest in the phenomenon of radical Islamist terror that haunts Pakistan today. Through this work, an attempt has been made to understand the phenomenon through study of its origin, evolution and growth. The research questions that it seeks to answer are: Why does the tribal areas remain a problem area for rulers and administrators throughout history? How and why radical Islamism embedded itself in the terrain? Was it influenced by overall emphasis on Islam in Pakistani state politics? What is the role of history and politics in fuelling religious passions in the area? What has led to the survival of TTP despite humongous efforts of the Pakistan army to decimate it? What are the future portents of such a movement? What impact it is likely to have on Pakistani society and politics?

This work would not have been possible without the charitable help of my friends across the border, who would like to remain anonymous, given the nature of relations that the two countries have. The vast body of literature available in the cyberspace/internet was very helpful, although it took away a lot of my time trying to isolate wheat from the chaff. My colleagues in the South Asia Centre at the Institute deserve special thanks for their constant persuasion and encouragement, especially Dr Smruti S Pattanaik, Dr Muhammad Eisa, Dr Zainab ul Akhter, Dr Mir Ahmad Nazir and my ex-colleagues, Dr Yaqoob-ul-Hassan and Manzoor. I fondly remember the hours of debate and discussions we have had over the issue, which helped me a great deal in putting my thoughts into perspective and overcoming my own prejudices. I owe a debt of gratitude to the library staff of the Institute, especially Mukesh Jha and Vikrant Kumar, who were always there to dig out information and articles from various sources making my efforts easier and more manageable. I would also like to thank Col Vivek Chadha and Vivek Kaushik for their constant words of encouragement through my lean days, pepping me up to be up and doing, when my morale was down.

I do not claim to have unearthed anything new in this work, but I have most certainly tried to collate as much information as I could use, rather than gather, and look at the issue in all its dimensions. As an evolving issue, as with any other issue in the socio-political domain, TTP-related Islamist assertion as well as the Pakistani state's response to it, will remain dynamic, and I would be happy to be proved wrong in some of my pessimistic assertions I make here. I hope this work will be a helpful addition to the existing pile of works on the theme, aiding researchers to develop a holistic view on the phenomenon called Tehrik-e-Taliban of Pakistan and its impact on the regional security situation.

March 2021
New Delhi

Ashok Behuria

Abbreviations

AeH	Ahl-e-Hadith
ANP	Awami National Party
APS	Army Public School
AQIS	Al Qaeda in Indian Subcontinent
ASWJ	Ahle Sunnat Wal Jamat
CID	Crime Investigation Department
CII	Council of Islamic Ideology
CT	Counter Terrorism
CTD	Counter Terrorism Department
DIG	Deputy Inspector General
ECP	Election Commission of Pakistan
ETIM	East Turkestan Islamic Movement
FATA	Federally Administered Tribal Areas
FC	Frontier Corps
FCR	Frontier Crimes Regulations
FIR	First Information Report
FR	Frontier Regions
FRC	FATA Reforms Commission
HUJI	Harkat-ul-Jihad-al-Islami
HuM	Harkat-ul-Mujahideen
IED	Improvised Explosive Device
IJI	Islami Jumhoori Ittehad
ISI	Inter-Services Intelligence
ISIS	Islamic State in Iraq and Syria (Islamic State of Iraq and al-Sham)
ISPR	Inter Services Public Relations
JeM	Jaish-e-Muhammad

JIT	Joint Investigation Team
JuA	Jamiat-ul-Ahrar
JUI-F	Jamiat-ul-Ulema-i-Islam-Fazlur Rahman
KP	Khyber Pakhtunkhwa
LeI	Lashkar-e-Islam
LeJ	Lashkar-e-Jhangvi
LeT	Lashkar-e-Taiba
MI	Military Intelligence
MMA	Muttahida Majlis-e-Amal
MML	Milli Muslim League
MNA	Member of National Assembly
MQM	Muttahida
MSG	Mujahideen Special Group
NACTA	National Counter-Terrorism Authority
NAP	National Action Plan
NWA	North Waziristan Agency
NWFP	North West Frontier Province
PATA	Provincially Administered Tribal Areas
PCNA	Post Crises Needs Assessment
PDM	Pakistan Democratic Movement
PIPS	Pakistan Institute for Peace Studies
PKR	Pakistan Rupee
PML-N	Pakistan Muslim League-Nawaz
PPP	Pakistan People's Party
PTI	Pakistan Tehrik-e-Insaf
PTM	Pakistan Tahaffuz Movement
QWP	Quami Watan Party
RuF	Radd-ul-Fassad
SATP	South Asia Terrorism Portal
SNAR	Sharia Nazam-e-Adl Regulation
SSG	Special Services Group
SSP	Senior Superintendent of Police
SWA	South Waziristan Agency
TLP	Tehreek-i-Labbaik Pakistan
TLYRAP	Tehreek-i-Labbaik Ya Rasool Allah Pakistan
TNSM	Tehrik-e-Nifaz-e-Shariat-e-Muhammadi

TSG	Taliban Special Group
TTP	Tehrik-e-Taliban Pakistan
UNESCO	United Nations Educational, Scientific and Cultural Organization
ZeA	Zarb-e-Azb

Introduction

The post-9/11 developments had a profound effect on the militant groups operating in the tribal borderlands of Pakistan. The growth of Taliban-inspired groups in this terrain was too obvious to be missed, even before 9/11. But such groups were largely ignored by Pakistan and their demands for imposition of Sharia in areas controlled by them were treated with sympathy rather than concern. The tribal areas did not beg too much attention at the political and administrative levels. When Sufi Muhammad (1933-2019), who was jailed in Pakistan for sending his followers as volunteers to Afghanistan to fight the Americans in 2001, established his Tehrik-e-Nifaz-e-Shariat-e-Muhammadi[3] (TNSM) in 1992 in the Malakand Division and launched his black turban movement in 1994 to demand Islamic rule in the region, the Pakistan authorities conceded the demands in December that year. The Governor of North West Frontier Province (NWFP) introduced the Nizam-e-Shariat Regulation to placate these forces, perhaps thinking such concessions at the peripheries of the Pakistan state, would help quarantine the virus locally and stop its spread elsewhere.

Similarly, the local administration in Orakzai let off the militant groups calling themselves Tehrik-e-Tulaba (or Taliban) Pakistan in December 1998 after a tame warning. The prospect of a few hotheaded mullahs imposing their version of Sharia-based Islamic rule in different pockets of the tribal areas did not ruffle the feathers much in Islamabad. It was at best treated as natural, and at the worst, as a tolerable and manageable aberration. Moreover, Pakistani rulers were aware of the fact that there was a steady outflow of tribal mujahideen into Afghanistan to fight alongside Taliban in

Afghanistan with the implicit or explicit approval of its intelligence agencies, and therefore, the left-over militants in the tribal areas posed no existential threat to the Pakistani state. They could rather be used as assets both to secure 'strategic depth' in Afghanistan and reserves for subversive low-intensity engagement with India.

The 9/11 changed all this as the militant-chickens came home to roost. As US-led operations dislodged the Taliban from Kabul, these militants came back home along with their transnational mentors and collaborators. The tribal areas witnessed a surplus of multinational jihadi elements of all hues shadowed by American intelligence. Pakistan was predictably soft with most of these groups because of the strategic alliance that it had struck with most of them in its aborted Afghan-Taliban enterprise. But the situation was unlikely to remain so especially when the US goaded the Pakistan military into action. The devastation caused by B12 stealth bombers in Afghanistan warned Pakistan of the consequences of neglecting American pressures and the veiled threat from US, to bomb Pakistan to stone-age if it did not oblige,[4] kept Pakistan gasping for breath as local Afghanistan-returned tribal militants girded their loins to turn the area into a safe-house/sanctuary for international jihadi groups relocating themselves to the tribal areas of Pakistan.

As the Pakistan army entered the terrain under US pressure in its quest for Al Qaeda heavy-weights like Osama Bin Laden and Ayman al-Zawairi, it had to contend with local militants who shielded the so called 'foreign fighters'—Uzbeks, Chechens, Arabs, Africans, etc. As the Pakistan army tried to persuade the tribal warlords to surrender some of these foreigners, it came face to face with stiff resistance which culminated in an all-out armed resistance, soon enough, against the Pakistani state.

The developments surrounding this military-militant interaction in the tribal belt against the larger setting of the grand war on terror led by the Americans were covered in the international media with aplomb. As instances of local militant groups imposing Taliban-like administration and justice systems grew, there was a sense that Pakistan was facing a looming threat of Talibanisation. When this phenomenon was isolated by this author in early 2002-2003, it was dismissed by peer-Pakistan-watchers as an Afghanistan-focussed one and as an exaggerated account of the developments taking place in the region unworthy of scholarly attention.

However, towards the close of 2005, the worst nightmares of Pakistan were coming true. A group calling itself "Pakistani Taliban"[5] slowly emerged in the tribal areas seeking to replicate the (Afghan) Taliban experiment in the tribal areas as media reports of militant excesses poured in from the area in December 2005. In Miramshah—also written as Miranshah (named after Timur Lane's son Miran Shah) and nerve centre of Pashtun resistance under the leadership of Mirza Ali Khan better known as Faqir of Ipi in the 1950s—the headquarter of the North Waziristan agency, the local militant group calling itself Taliban executed alleged "criminals, drug pushers, bootleggers and extortionists", with their bodies hung from poles, eyes gouged out, and cash stuffed into their mouth.[6] The video footage of it was circulated later bringing back memories of Mullah Omar and his men when they hung some rapists in Kandahar from abandoned Soviet tanks in 1994. While this Miramshah incident was the goriest and widely reported, many other similar assertions by local mullahs went unreported. The local militants—very much like Taliban in Afghanistan—sought to impose a puritanical version of Islam on the populace by banning music and dance, cutting of beard and by imposing Quranic punishments for crimes. A new generation of clerics and militants was ready to push for a "Taliban movement" in the tribal belt of Pakistan. These groups finally came together in the face of attack by Pakistani security forces to form Tehrik-e-Taliban Pakistan (TTP) in December 2007. The TTP has had a bloody presence in Pakistan ever since making its presence felt even outside the tribal belt in the hinterland of Pakistan.

Over a decade since its first assertions in Pakistan—after nearly two decades of high-pitched military operations (2002-till date)[7] in the areas susceptible to Taliban influence—as we reassess the effect of such a movement, we notice that the phenomenon has come to stay in Pakistan. It has threatened internal security and posed an existential threat to Pakistan, despite years of military operations, intelligence penetration, US-aided drone strikes and steady elimination of high-value militants. The resolve of the militants has grown rather than flagged over the years and shows no sign of wilting under heaviest of pressures. The close and complex interactions among Al-Qaeda, TTP and its allied local Taliban groups in the tribal areas, various Afghan Taliban factions and the Islamic State of Khorasan, slowly raising its head in the region, have posed a critical challenge for Pakistani security establishment despite its all-out efforts to eliminate the threat. With the appearance of *Da'esh* or Islamic State of Iraq and Syria (ISIS)—an ultra-radical Islamic group in the neighbouring West Asian region—since 2014, a new jihadi context has emerged in the Pak-Af region.

In order to understand the socio-political dynamics that fueled Islamist militancy of the most persistent kind in Pakistan, one has to understand the very complex relationship that has come into play since the US attack of Afghanistan following 9/11, among (i) Pakistan army and intelligence; (ii) Afghan Taliban; (iii) local Pakistani militant leaders who were inspired by and had fought alongside Taliban; (iv) Al-Qaeda—consisting of a hotchpotch of foreign militants from different Arab countries, Chechnya, Uzbekistan, China (Xinjiang or Eastern Turkestan), diasporic elements from within Muslim communities residing in Europe as well as very few new converts from the West; and (v) the Islamic State-Khorasan. To understand the context, within which the TTP came into being and operated over the years, the policies of the Western countries towards the region in the aftermath of 9/11, the approach of the Pakistan military towards Islamist jihadi groups as well as its temptation to use terrorism as an element of its security policy, its complex and complicated relations with India and Afghanistan, the role of the post-Bonn Afghan political system and its response to Pakistan's pro-Taliban policy need to be explored and analysed in a dispassionate manner.

The present volume seeks to understand the context in which Pakistani Taliban or TTP, as it is called now, came into being, the enabling factors that made the growth of TTP possible, the formation and growth of TTP as a militant organisation, its leadership and its activities over the years, its ideological orientation and its worldview, its aims and objectives, its relationship with other militant groups in and outside Pakistan and the efforts of Pakistani establishment to come to terms with such a phenomenon. There is an attempt to analyse the process and study its implications for Pakistan and the region.

Notes

1. "Normalcy in tribal areas to be set in stone by its people: COAS", *The Express Tribune*, 3 March 2021 at https://tribune.com.pk/story/2287152/army-chief-cautions-against-hostile-attempt-to-sow-chaos-in-erstwhile-tribal-regions

2. "Army dismisses speculations on DG ISI's replacement", *The Express Tribune*, 23 February 2021 at https://tribune.com.pk/story/2285521/army-dismisses-speculations-on-dg-isis-replacement

3. Tehreek-e-Nafaz-e-Shariat-e-Mohammadi (loosely translated as Movement for Enforcement of Muhammad's Sharia) was established in 1992 by Maulana Sufi Muhammad who was earlier with Jamat-i-Islami, Pakistan.

4. Pervez Musharraf (2006). *In the Line of Fire: A Memoir*, Simon & Schuster Ltd, UK, p. 201.

5. The media reports on the self-proclaimed group called Pakistani Taliban flowed in since early 2006. Some of them are Zahid Hussain, "Terror in Miramshah", *Newsline*, April 2006 and Declan Walsh, "Pakistani Taliban take control of unruly tribal belt", *The Guardian*, 21 March 2006.

6. Syed Saleem Shahzad, "The Taliban's Bloody Foothold in Pakistan", *Asia Times* online, 8 February 2006 and also see Zahid Hussain, quoting eyewitness account, "Terror in Miramshah", *Newsline*, April 2006.

7. These included Operations *Al-Mizan* (2002-2006), *Zalzala* (2008) and *Rah-e-Nijat* (2009) in Waziristan area, *Operations Rah-e-Haq* (2007-2009) and *Rah-e-Rast* (2009) in Swat, *Op Sirat-i-Mustaqeem* (2008) in Khyber, *Op Zarb-e-Kaleem* (2008) in Hangu district, *Op Sherdil* (2009) in Bajaur, *Koh-e-Sufaid* (2009) in Kurram, *Op Zarb-e-Azb* (2014-2017) and *Op Radd-ul-Fasad* (2017-2019).

1.   The Terrain and People

When you approach an Afghan to make terms with him ... you find the more he gets the more he wants.... They have the character of being avaricious, mercenary, treacherous, and predatory ... [and] among the Afghans especially, fanaticism is much more political than religious....

—George Campbell[1]

Various Accounts

One of the most famous modern accounts of history and politics of the people inhabiting the rugged terrain[2] straddling Pakistan and Afghanistan, known until 2018 as Federally Administered Tribal Areas (FATA), is that of the British Historian Mountstuart Elphinstone (1779-1859). He would consider them combative and fiercely independent. He would sum up by saying—"their vices are revenge, envy, avarice, rapacity, and obstinacy; on the other hand, they are fond of liberty, faithful to their friends, kind to their dependents, hospitable, brave, hardy, frugal, laborious, and prudent; and they are less disposed than the nations in their neighbourhood to falsehood, intrigue and deceit."[3] Indicating their aversion for control and rebellious spirit, Elphinstone would quote laboriously from various poets during the rule of the Mughal ruler Aurangzeb, during the late 17th century, and particularly mention Khushal Khan Khattak who spent his life "in struggles against the great Moghul" and wrote eloquently:

The Afghan youth have reddened their hands,
As a falcon dyes its talons in the blood of its quarry.
They have made their white swords rosy with blood,
As a bed of tulips blooming in summer.

Almost half a century later, Winston Churchill sent brilliant dispatches (in 1896-97) about the people in the tribal areas north of Peshawar as a 23-year-old journalist attached to the Malakand Field Force in the Swat Valley which was fighting the rebellious Pashtuns in the region. His letters/dispatches were later compiled in the form of a book[4] where he made some perceptive observations about the terrain and its people. He wrote that it was a terrain full of "many tribes, but of similar character and condition", and in "a continual state of feud and strife" and "warlike leisure", where "every man's hand is against the other, and all against the stranger". In full display is the "strength of civilisation without its mercy" and "the weapons of the nineteenth century are in the hands of the savages of the stone age".

Various Accounts

Churchill characterised the inhabitants of this terrain as "hardy and martial people, well-armed, brave, and trained by constant war", who "embark on war with careless levity", "fight without passion, and kill one another without loss of temper" with "an absolute lack of reverence for all forms of law and authority". These people have "a strong aboriginal zeal to kill"—an instinct "preserved in unexampled strength and vigour" and tempered by religious passion stimulating "wild and merciless fanaticism". Churchill would further state that their "system of ethics, which regards treachery and violence as virtues rather than vices, has produced a code of honour so strange and inconsistent, that it is incomprehensible to a logical mind". Coming to their religious disposition, he would warn that all of them "are held in the grip of miserable superstition" and such superstition "exposes them to the rapacity and tyranny of a numerous priesthood—"Mullahs," "Sahibzadas," "Akhundzadas," "Fakirs,"—and a host of wandering Talib-ul-ilms, who ... live free at the expense of the people" and "no man's wife or daughter is safe from them".[5]

If Churchill was describing the Pathans of Swat, Bajaur and Mohmand, accounts by military officials (during the 1919-20 Waziristan operations) of Waziris and Mehsuds of Waziristan (both North and South) are no less unflattering.

> Their character, organization and instincts have made them independent and strongly democratic, so much so that even their own *mlaliks* (or elders) have little real control over the unruly spirits ... *the Waziristan tribesmen carry their lives in their hands and finding that the natural resources of their country do not favour them enough, they eke out their existence by plundering their more peaceful neighbours.* This mode of life has in their men a fine physique and a free and independent manner, and in their women a remarkable power of resisting fatigue and of nurturing their children under the most adverse conditions and circumstances.... Both Wazirs and Mahsuds are notorious for their raiding propensities, and for the rapidity with which they remove their plunder to the security of the inner hills of their country.[6]

After pointing out that Mehsuds and Waziris often fought with each other, the readers are cautioned that it was "important to remember, however, that a wave of fanaticism or the rise to power of some commanding personality may at any time cause Mahsuds and Waziris to sink their differences and effect a formidable combination against us" (*read invaders*).[7] There is also mention of Mullah Powindah among the Mehsuds who was termed by Lord Kitchner as the "Pestilential Priest". In 1900, this mullah was wooed by the British with an offer of a monthly allowance of Rs 100 and a grant of land in 1906. But such offers could not placate the mullah who became a constant thorn in the side of the British government.

The entire region was under the sway of notorious outlaws and fanatic mullahs during the British rule. The British inflicted severest punishments on many of them from time to time. One of the notorious outlaws, Hakim Khan, with a following of twenty-nine, was attacked near the village of Charsada on 28 February 1911. Hakim and 20 of his accomplices were killed, and the rest were captured and put to death by hanging. Early in 1907 one Sufi Sahib, accompanied by a Shinwari from Deh Sarak, Abdul Karim, preached jihad in Tirah valley, while Lala Pir, a secret agent from Kabul, was engaged in stirring up the tribes in Khost and Waziristan, and holding communication with Mullah Powindah. Other known rebels in the first decade of twentieth century were Gud Mullah and Hazrat Sahib of Chaharbagh among the Mohmands, Mullah Saiyid Akbar among the Afridis.[8] It was interesting to find the mullah retiring to Afghan territory after being repulsed by the British army and reappearing again the moment the emphasis on security of the place declined.

One of the most empathetic portrayals of the Pathans of the terrain came from Lieutenant Enriquez, who held that these tribes were yet to settle down during their 300 years of existence in the areas hemmed in by the Suleiman and Safed Koh ranges. He would argue that they behaved exactly like the English tribes during the early centuries in England. He would say that it was unjust to judge Pathans by twentieth century standards for they lived in tenth century. There were many among them like those recruited in Khyber Rifles who displayed exemplary loyalty. Admiring the confidence of the Pathans, another observer Oliver would say grudgingly that even if a Pathan might be filthy and ragged, he would "saunter into a Viceregal durbar as proud as Lucifer, and with an air of unconcern a diplomatist might envy".[9] There is also interesting mention of tribal heads or Khans and Maliks wielding influence rather than power, while the mullahs having entire villages and clans under their control.[10] In such circumstances, wrote Sir George Campbell, Secretary of State for India (1868-1874), "the difficulties and expense of any attempt to meddle with that country far outweigh the advantages" and "the passion for independence of a people occupying such a country is the best safeguard of our frontier".[11] There was also a realisation that the Afghan country would require lot of money to make its ruler run it peacefully.[12]

Most of these assessments which follow Elphinstone's account of 1815 have a very critical view of the Pashtun people and their instinctive aversion for control. Moreover, the days following

Elphinstone's trip to Kabul (which he spelt as Caubul) were particularly tumultuous in the Pashtun areas. In the post-Sepoy mutiny (1857) days the anti-colonial resistance of the Mullahs with overt religious and ethnic overtones must have been pretty much worrying for the British rulers. Moreover, the British observers must be closely following the incidents in the region with great interest. In this connection the Wahabite revolt against Sikh rule in Punjab stands out, which started in 1826, and culminated in the death of Sayid Ahmad Barelvi (1786-1831), a mullah from heartland of India, under influence of Shah Waliullah's interpretation of Islam (which was akin to Wahabism). He had teamed up with Shah Ismail (1779-1831), grandson of Waliullah (1703-1762) and some tribal Pashtun mullahs, chief among whom was one named Akhund Abdul Ghaffur or Saidu Baba (1793-1878) of Swat. In the late 19th century, the British adopted an aggressive "forward policy", and occupied the strategic areas like the Khyber Pass, Gomal Zam and the Tochi Valley in 1889-90, Samana in 1891 and Kurram Valley in 1892. The British intentions were clear—to defend the Empire from any possible Russian advance by creating a "buffer zone". The British were only motivated by strategic considerations and had no interest in altering the way of life of the tribes in what came to be known in Pakistan as Federally Administered Tribal Areas (FATA).

Anti-Sikh Sentiments turn against the British

Against this backdrop, when the British displayed greater interest and enthusiasm than the Sikhs in pushing their sphere of influence westward, the anti-Sikh tempo of the Wahabi movement initiated by Sayid Ahmed Barelvi soon transformed into an anti-colonial one and militated against British rule once the British defeated the Sikhs in 1849, seized control of the tribal areas west of Punjab and extended the boundaries of the empire till Afghanistan. The situation worsened following the drawing of the Durrand Line in 1893 vide an agreement between Sir Mortimer Durand, a British civil servant and diplomat, and the Afghan Amir, Abdur Rahman Khan, to settle the boundary between British India and Afghanistan. The line ran through the terrain inhabited by the Pashtun and Baloch and divided them between the two countries.[13] The Amir of Afghanistan signed the agreement—a one page note with seven articles—under pressure and was not happy with it. His sense of dissatisfaction with the arbitrarily-drawn artificial line and the fond hope that the line will be altered someday correcting the historical wrong committed in 1893 continue to characterise the approach of the rulers in Kabul till today. Even the Taliban leaders, known for their strategic dependence on Pakistan, refused to be persuaded by their Pakistani interlocutors that it was in their interest to recognise the Durand line and settle the boundary between the two countries forever.

It was natural, therefore, that in the aftermath of the boundary agreement in 1893, the Pashtuns of the areas under British control, ceded to them by the Sikhs in 1849, would rise in revolt under active and/or passive support from Kabul. It is well known that Saidu Baba's disciple Mullah Hadda (mentioned in Churchill's accounts, died in December 1902) enjoyed the patronage of the Afghan Amir Habibullah. Similarly, the Mad Fakir of Swat, Saidullah,[14] responsible for the uprising in Malakand in 1897 is also believed to have enjoyed the support of the Afghan Amir. The British managed to establish their control through imposition of very strict criminal laws like the Murderous Outrages Regulations in Punjab in 1867 to suppress outrageous crimes committed by murderous tribes. The law was further modified in 1877 and imposed specifically on the tribal areas to ensure peace in the terrain.[15]

Pashtun Areas Separated

In 1901, five settled districts—Bannu, Dera Ismail Khan, Hazara, Kohat and Peshawar—were separated out from the province of Punjab and five tribal agencies—Dir-Swat-Chitral, Khyber, Kurram, North Waziristan and South Waziristan—were added to it to carve out a new province which was named North Western Frontier Province (NWFP). The province was placed under the control of a chief commissioner who reported directly to the Governor General. Keeping the rebelliousness of the people of this terrain, British Indian government introduced the Frontier Crimes Regulations (FCR) in the province even before the creation of the province. This act built upon the Murderous Outrages Regulations earlier specifically dealt with the frontier areas and aimed at maintaining tight control over the Pashtun population in the tribal areas. The FCR prescribed special procedures for the tribal areas. These were different from the criminal and civil laws that were in force in rest of British India. These regulations were based on the concept of 'collective territorial responsibility', and permitted dispute resolution through a tribal Jirga (council of elders), a customary practice in the tribal areas. The FCR act expanded the scope of earlier criminal regulations and invested wide-ranging powers, including judicial authority in the local administrative officials. During this time, the British administrators also introduced the institution of the Political Agent who was provided funds and vested with wide powers to secure the loyalties of influential people in the area. The Maliki system was introduced during this period with a view to roping in the local elite and using them as levers to exercise control over the tribes. Under this system, the local tribal elders (now known as Maliks) were designated as intermediaries between the members of individual tribes and the colonial authorities. They also helped the government to implement its policies.[16]

In spite of all this, the British could not quite control the terrain and continued to station large amount of troops in the area to engage various armed groups challenging the might of the British Empire. There was a recognition amongst the British rulers that the people of the terrain were too rebellious and uncontrollable to be amenable to modern system of governance. Therefore, they would rather choose not to devote too much attention towards the areas inhabited by the Pathans and/or Afghans and allow them some measure of independence as much as it would not jeopardise their colonial and imperial interests. They were quite happy about their characterisation of some areas as settled where they introduced rule of law and rest as unsettled which were largely left to the people to rule as per their own traditional norms, but under strict criminal laws imposed on them by the British to ensure that the Pashtun tribes of the frontier did not act against the interest of the empire. These unsettled borderlands were this mostly used as a buffer against both unruly Pathans of Afghanistan and the allegedly expansionist designs of Tsarist Russia.

The British rulers were not interested in mainstreaming this area and bequeathing the legacy of representative rule to the people inhabiting this difficult terrain. The British observers created a lasting myth of invincibility of the people and impossibility of transforming their behaviour to suit the needs of modern systems of governance, which survives to this day. In fact, when the demands for greater representative system of administration came from the people of NWFP, in the wake of the Government of India Acts of 1909 and 1919 which introduced representative rule in rest of India, the British ignored such demands. However, in response to the civil disobedience (red Shirt) movement of the Khudai Khidmatgars—which was raging in the settled areas while the tribal political agencies were plagued by violence—the then British Prime Minister Ramsay MacDonald announced the elevation of NWFP's status to a governor's province like other provinces of India at the concluding session of Second Round Table Conference in 1932. This representative system was limited to the settled areas and the legislative council of NWFP, elected through a restricted franchise (only three to four percent of the people eligible for votes could exercise their franchise, based on their social and economic status) were not granted any say in the administration of the tribal areas and tribal policy remained a central subject under the direct control of the governor of NWFP who served as the Agent to the Governor-General.

Tribal Areas under Pakistan

Soon after partition and formation of Pakistan in 1947, various tribes in the region entered into agreements with the Government of Pakistan pledging allegiance to the new state. The Government of Pakistan signed some 30 instruments of agreement with local rulers, strengthening this arrangement further. Mohmand Agency was included in FATA in 1951, and Bajaur and Orakzai in 1973. Apart from seven agencies—Khyber, Kurram, Bajaur, Mohmand, Orakzai, North and South Waziristan—FATA also had six Frontier Regions (FR), i.e., FR Peshawar, FR Kohat, FR Tank, FR Banuu,

FR Lakki and FR Dera Ismail Khan. Apart from FATA, Pakistan also designated some other areas (designated so by Article 246-b of the Constitution) inhabited by tribes regarded as less amenable to democratic system of governance as Provincially Administered Tribal Areas (PATA). These areas consisted of four former princely states and some districts inhabited by tribes difficult to control.[17] Some of the PATA districts were in Balochistan and most of them are dominated by Pashtuns and together with FATA, the areas form a contiguous terrain stretching from Chitral in the north to Chaman in the south which is home to radical Islamist insurgency today.

Various constitutions of Pakistan granted the tribal areas special status and the area covered by the so-called 'Tribal Areas' grew steadily until it attained the shape in 1973 covering both FATA and PATA, consisting some of the former princely states. The first Constitution of Pakistan in 1956 not only guaranteed the rights and privileges of the princes but the Frontier states and agencies were granted special status by retaining their status as a "Special Area" under Article 104 which provided that the executive authority of the province of West Pakistan was empowered to act in the area subject to the President's concurrence. Under 1962 Constitution, the tribal agencies and princely states in the frontier region were declared Tribal Areas, and under Article 223 of the Constitution no central or provincial law applied to these areas unless the President and the Governor respectively, so directed.[18] Under the 1973 Constitution of Pakistan, FATA fell within the 'territories of Pakistan" (Article 1). It was granted representation in the Pakistan National Assembly (vide Article 51) and the Senate (vide Article 59) but remained under the direct executive authority of the President (Article 247). Laws framed by the National Assembly did not apply to FATA, unless ordered by the President, who was also empowered to issue regulations for the peace and good government of the tribal areas. It was administered by the Governor of the erstwhile North Western Frontier Province (NWFP) renamed in 2010 as Khyber Pakhtunkhwa (KP) in his capacity as an agent of the President of Pakistan, under the overall supervision of the Ministry of States and Frontier Regions in Islamabad.

The Constitution of Pakistan governed FATA through the same rules, which were imposed by the British in 1901 as Frontier Crimes Regulations (FCR). The Jurisdiction of Supreme Court and High Court of Pakistan did not extend to FATA and PATA, according to Article 247 and Article 248 of the 1973 Constitution of Pakistan. The KP Provincial Assembly had no power to legislate on FATA, and could only exercise its powers in PATA that were part of KP. The assembly could implement the law directly as it could do in other parts of the province or Settled Areas of KP. This created a political vacuum in FATA, Frontier Regions and PATA. Such lawless conditions were said to serve the interests of terrorists, as there was absence of various government departments like police, judiciary, local governments, and civic amenities. The jurisdictions of the High Courts and Supreme Courts of Pakistan did not extend to the Tribal Areas.

Tribal Areas Treated with Neglect

Pakistani central government used the tribal areas, which included the FATA and PATA regions, as its strategic backyard. The entire region was 'in' Pakistan but not 'of' it. As per the Article 246 of the 1973 Constitution, the Pakistani Parliament had no authority over these areas. The article defined the territorial extent of the Tribal Areas and as has been discussed above the following Article (247) dealt with the administration of the tribal areas. The article stated clearly that the laws passed by Majlis-e-shoora (the national Parliament) or the Provincial Assemblies would not run there. The Supreme Court and High Courts of Pakistan also did not have any jurisdiction over these areas. However, this was not to deny that constitutionally speaking, "the executive authority of the Federation" and "the executive authority of a Province" extended to these areas, which meant that the authority of the President and Governor ran in the tribal areas known as FATA and PATA. While FATA was under direct control of the President of Pakistan, as regards the PATA, the Governor had to have the prior approval of the President for introducing any regulation in the PATA, which was under his direct control.

The FATA area was traditionally left to be controlled either by local tribal elders or ambitious mullahs. The state presence was limited to political agents, who were low level bureaucrats, holding a parallel line of authority along with local collaborators called *maliks* and *lungi-holders* or *lungidars,* patronised by the state. The policing of the area was done through *khasadars*, levies and scouts, raised from the local populace, who were grossly underpaid and undertrained. Based on the principle of patronage, under the '*Maliki*' system, the *Malik* of each clan or the *lungidar* of each sub-clan and tribe was made responsible for maintaining peace in his area. He was also responsible for providing protection to government interests and received recognition and material benefits in return. The main objective of the FCR was the suppression of crime and protection of the interests of the Government of Pakistan (earlier that of the British Empire); including keeping lines of communications open with Afghanistan. All administrative and judicial powers were thus invested in the Deputy Commissioner (Political Agent), who usually dealt with civil and criminal disputes through tribal Jirga, which functioned like a 'council of elders'. The Political Agent, however, retained the authority to make final decisions in all cases. It is also important to note that the decisions of the Jirga were not legally binding on the Political Agent in any manner. The political agents wielded unbridled powers and were regarded as corrupt and did not in any way either represented or respected peoples' will. The political agent of each agency, depending on its size, had two or three assistant political agents, three or four tehsildars and between four and nine naib tehsildars with the requisite supporting staff. In 1976, Governor of KP, then NWFP, the then Major General (Retd.) Naseerullah Babar set up a committee to suggest measures for final merger of the tribal areas into NWFP. The recommendations of the report of the committee advocating merger could not be acted upon both because of fear of reprisal from the entrenched elite in the terrain (by the Zulfikar Ali Bhutto government) and military take-over in 1977. Bhutto had stalled the issue and decided to take it up after March 1977 elections, but he could not do that because he was removed in a coup on 5 July 1977.

These agents along with local *maliks* and *lungidaars* were effective in maintaining order and protecting the interests of the state until the 1980s when a new socio-political dynamic set in, in the tribal areas, because of the frontline status Pakistan gained since the Soviet army entered Afghanistan in December 1979 in aid of the communist government in Kabul. The Islamist mujahideen warriors challenging the communist dispensation, to begin with, and confronted with the might of the Soviet forces, in the changing circumstances, were regarded as "freedom fighters" by the US and supplied covert military aid through Pakistani intelligence agencies to defeat the former Soviet Union. In the process, in order to keep the jihad going and both to mobilise greater support for it and keep indoctrinating the young and impressionable refugee children pouring into Pakistani tribal borderlands, hundreds of madrassas were constructed in the area as well as in the hinterland and specially designed school textbooks preaching jihad were produced in the US and supplied free of cost to the children in these madrassas.[19] As per Pakistan interior ministry's figures, the number of madrassas grew in the country from 246 in 1947 to 2886 by 1988 and most of these dotted the Afghan-Pakistan frontier. Their number increased to 28,982 by 2010 according to some public survey; however, the interior ministry put the figure at about 20,000.[20] Thus, both state and international sponsorship further radicalised the already radical socio-cultural landscape in the tribal areas. According to some accounts, by 2003, there were at least 600,000 youths in Pakistan who had passed out of the madrassas, received training for waging armed jihad and fought in Afghanistan and Kashmir. At least 100,000 of them were active cadres of different Jihadi outfits and over one million students were still enrolled in various Islamic seminaries, while there were several hundred thousand supporters of various Pakistan's Islamic religious parties.[21]

Jihadi Transformation[22]

The Afghan jihad years (1980-1989) transformed the socio-cultural landscape in the tribal areas of Pakistan. The religious forces patronised by the state emerged as alternate centres of authority in the region. Local mullahs gained tremendous informal power in the area through the 1980s and 1990s. However, there was a period of peaceful cohabitation and no apparent clash of interest when one group (the existing power-elite in the terrain, working with the governments at the federal and provincial levels) served as an agent of the centre and the other was pampered by the state to wage jihad across the Durand Line. With the rise of Taliban in Afghanistan in the mid-1990s, midwifed by the Pakistani intelligence and army, the mullahs of the region fed with the success of Afghan jihad started dreaming of Islamic emirates in their own areas, if not entire Pakistan. In 1994, Sufi Muhammad of Tehrik-e-Nifaz-e-Shariat-e-Muhammadi (TNSM) forced the governor of NWFP to concede his outfit's rule by Islamic sharia in Malkand division with Nifaz-i-Nizam-i-Sharia Regulation of 1994, and later the NWFP government promulgated Shariah Nizam-i-Adl Regulations, 1999, in the Malakand Division and Shariah Nizam-i-Adl Ordinance, 1999, in Kohistan district to introduce [a] "real" Islamic system in these areas. This particular ordinance provided the blueprint for Nizam-e-Adl regulation of 13 April 2009, a decade later.[23]

Concessions to Islamists

It deserves mention here that the process of Islamic radicalisation struck deep roots in Pakistan over almost two decades (1978-1999)— tentatively from the coup by Zia-ul-Haq through the years of democracy marked by bitter political rivalries and poor governance till yet another coup by Pervez Musharraf. During these years, both the prime political parties—Peoples' Party of Pakistan (PPP) and Pakistan Muslim League-Nawaz (PML-N)—did nothing to reverse the trend of radicalisation in Pakistan in general and the Pashtun tribal areas in particular, even if it was increasingly recognized in Pakistan that the jihadis had a serious impact on the internal security situation. The then Army Chief Jehangir Karamat went on to admit that Pakistan's internal security was 'the most important facet of national security'.[24] During Nawaz Sharif's second tenure as Prime Minister (1997-1999) his cabinet even appointed a committee to take stock of the internal security situation in November 1997, which submitted its report in May 1998. The report held that 'it was imperative for intelligence agencies to keep track of the possible linkages between the militant training imparted by various political groups for jihad in Kashmir and Afghanistan, and acts of terrorism committed in Pakistan'.[25]

Despite this, various governments ignored the phenomenon of Islamist assertion at what they would regard as 'the peripheries' and buy peace through concessions, hoping that such gestures would quarantine it at the margins without affecting Pakistan's body politic. As an example, Benazir Bhutto's government (1993-1996) conceded Sufi Muhammad's demand for Sharia rule in Dir and Malakand in December 1994.

It is also strange that while Nawaz Sharif was getting familiar with the corrosive effect of radicalisation at one level, he was seeking to capitalise on the perceived pro-Islamic sentiments at another, by bringing about 15th Amendment in August 1998 to further Islamicise the constitution and offering a handle to the pro-Sharia campaigners all over the country. The amendment bill introduced by Nawaz Sharif government and passed by two thirds majority in the lower house stated:

> "In view of the fact that the Objectives Resolution is now substantive part of the Constitution, it is necessary that Quran and Sunnah are declared to be the supreme law of Pakistan, and the Government is empowered to take necessary steps to enforce Shariah." It made it obligatory on the part of the federal government to "to take steps to enforce the *Shariah*, to establish *salat*, to administer *zakat*, to promote *amr bil ma'roof* and *nahi anil munkar* (to prescribe what is right and to forbid what is wrong), to eradicate corruption at all levels and to provide substantial socio-economic justice, in accordance with the principles of Islam, as laid down in the Holy Quran and Sunnah."[26]

TNSM chief Maulana Sufi Mohammad backed the bill with all his might and in October 1998, he ordered his followers to kill journalists who opposed the implementation of the bill, termed as "Shariah bill".[27]

The power elite in Pakistan did not think it necessary, therefore, to bring the terrain to the political mainstream and introduce a uniform legal and administrative system in the tribal areas. After years of restricted franchise, the need for introducing universal franchise in FATA was felt not by any mainstream political party of Pakistan but by the caretaker govt of Meraj Khalid in 1996, after Benazir Bhutto's govt was dismissed by then President Farooq Leghari. However, the elections subsequently held in 1997 elections were on non-party basis. Political parties' participation Act was modified later in 2002 to make it possible for parties to field candidates in FATA, but it could not be implemented without amendment of the FCR provisions. In 2002, an attempt was made to introduce local representative bodies in FATA and in 2004 some members were nominated by political agents into local councils because the council had no powers and the nominated ones were not regarded with respect by the local populace. Attempts at administrative reforms were made by a Committee on legal reforms, headed by Justice (Retd.) Mian Mohammad Ajmal, in 2005 to recommend modifications in FCR after public consultation across FATA. Some of the recommendations of the committee were implemented in 2011. Another set of reforms suggested by a special committee, headed by Sahibzada Imtiaz Ahmad in 2006 were implemented granting some independence to the FATA secretariat. In 2012, 'FATA Local Government Regulation 2012' was developed to introduce local bodies in FATA, however, the Regulation was never promulgated. The amendment of FCR under Zardari government in August 2011 finally made it possible for political parties to contest elections from FATA and in 2013, they fielded candidates for the first time on party basis. As it was quite obvious, women of FATA were granted right to vote only in 1996. However, tribal customs stood in their way of participating in the elections in an uninhibited manner. As militancy gathered momentum in 2013, a Political Parties Joint Committee on FATA Reforms, comprising of 10 political parties (PML-N, ANP, JI, JUI-F, MQM, NP, PML-Q, PPP, PTI, QWP), was formed "which adopted and endorsed an 11-point FATA reforms plan in July

2013. The proposed reforms by this joint committee included, amendment of Article 247 to guarantee fundamental rights to all tribal citizens and shift legislative power from the President of Pakistan to the Parliament; the importance of holding local body elections; the need for a comprehensive package for FATA with focus on infrastructure development, health, education and employment and separation of executive and judicial powers in FATA."[28]

Costs of Neglect

The state ignored the hold of militants in the tribal areas and rather chose to use militant groups to strengthen and consolidate the position of Taliban in Afghanistan. Many volunteers from these regions went across the border into Afghanistan to join the Taliban and fight against the northern alliance and international forces. On the eve of the attack on Afghanistan in 2001, Sufi Muhammad (1933-2019) of Swat sent thousands of his supporters to fight the Western forces in support of Taliban, under the military's watch. Sufi was arrested upon his return from Afghanistan in 2002, after the Taliban were made to flee by the US forces.[29] TNSM was banned in 2002. There was a shift in state policy after 9/11 under acute pressure from the US. When Pakistan joined the War on Terror, it was forced to withdraw its contacts with the local mullahs. It sought to extend its control through the *maliks* and tribal elders. Initially, the amount of force used was quite nominal. This was mainly through the local *khasadars*.

However, Pakistan soon discovered that the effective control of the whole region had passed on to a new generation of Islamic radicals, who had the will and ability to take on the Pakistani state, its past-sponsors, without any hesitation. Indeed, Pakistani state had made huge cache of arms available to them earlier for Afghan jihad, which continued throughout the Taliban years. It ignored the private weapons factories coming up in areas like Darra Adam Khel and oversaw the process of militarisation of the entire belt. There were jokes in Pakistan that even Pakistan army had to buy weapons at a cheaper rate from Darra Adam Khel.

The Pakistani army was forced to station itself around the tribal belt by the close of 2002. Between 2002 and 2006, the army conducted its Operation *Al-Mizan* (Justice) leading to a series of armed campaigns in different areas of FATA, assisted by US special operation forces, who were looking for Al-Qaeda operatives fleeing Afghanistan in this area, as was reported later. Pakistan also brought in infantry battalions, Special Force units, the elite SSG (Special Services Group) as a show of its sincerity. As per the data gathered by two scholars from RAND Corporation "approximately 17 infantry brigades 45 infantry battalions, and some 58 Frontier Corps wings"[30] (a wing is roughly equal to a battalion) were involved in this operation. The same sources held that the number of the forces grew to somewhat fewer than 120,000 regular army, Frontier Corps, and Frontier Constabulary troops ... in FATA and NWFP between March 2008 and March 2009". Operation Kalosha II, which was launched in 2004 in South Waziristan, was part of this operation. Initially, the army suffered unexpected setbacks in South Waziristan at Baghar, Wana and Kalosha between 2002 and early 2004. Musharraf would characterise the impassioned resistance put up by the tribal insurgents as of "last-man-last-bullet" type. However, in Op Kalosha II, with heavy reinforcement and use of Cobra helicopters and fighter jets and 13-day cordon and search operation in an area spread over a 50 km stretch south-west of Wana, the Pakistan army declared victory, which proved pyrrhic at best and fleeting at the worst.

The main operations of the army, during this period, were conducted through the local *khasadars*. Wholesale army operations were only episodic in nature. They were ordered only when the local militants flouted the instructions of the army. There was an unwritten understanding between the local militants and the army that they will not provoke each other unnecessarily. The army, under Musharraf, made several attempts to buy peace in the area. It bribed local Taliban leaders like Nek Muhammad, Baitullah Mehshud, Mullah Nazir, Mangal Bagh and many others and signed peace deals with them. However, none of them succeeded at the end. By 2006-

07, the operations became more frequent indicating the inability of the Pakistani state to establish its writ in the area. The local militants regrouped as Pakistani Taliban and more actively colluded with the Taliban of Afghanistan on the one hand and Al-Qaeda on the other. This was bad news for Pakistan.[31]

Galloping Talibanisation

By June 2007, the National Security Council of Pakistan headed by President Musharraf took due note and held that the following areas were affected by the virus of Talibanisation in varying degrees—the districts and frontier regions of Tank, Lakki Marwat, Bannu, Kohat as well as the settled districts of Hangu, Dera Ismail Khan in southern NWFP, Peshawar, Mardan and Charsada in the central NWFP and Mansehra, Swat, Malakand and Dir in the northern NWFP.[32] In December 2007, the Pakistani Taliban calling itself Tehrik-e-Taliban announced its formation. By the close of 2008, Sunni radical groups of all hues had come together in these areas. They were also seen to be operating in a much more coordinated manner than ever before. Pakistani state underwent a democratic transition in March 2008. Musharraf was forced to leave by September 2008. The number of army operations increased in 2008 under the new army chief. The US forces were granted greater freedom in their aerial operations in the tribal areas.

By 2009, Ahmed Rashid would argue that there was no "creeping Talibanisation" in Pakistan, it was a galloping Talibanisation.... The leadership of the Taliban is now in Pakistan and they have stated their intention of overthrowing the government here. The Taliban are linking up with groups in Pakistan and the Pakistani Taliban movement is turning into a multiethnic movement. Groups cultivated to fight in Kashmir have joined up with the Pakistani Taliban, and include Punjabis having previous association with organisations such as Lashkar-e-Taiba, Harkatul Mujahideen, Jaish-e-Muhammad and others. Now, some 40 groups in Pakistan are loosely affiliated with the Pakistan Taliban—the several years of progressive diplomacy with India exacerbated the rise of different Taliban-affiliated factions."[33]

The army operations (which have been dealt with in detail in subsequent chapters) did reverse the tide of Talibanisation to some extent, but the phenomenon has remained in the tribal belt as a marked feature of tribal society and politics and kept on bothering the Pakistani government, which has led it to look for political options in addition to overwhelming use of kinetic power in response to militant assertion by TTP, primarily basing itself in the tribal belt. With the launch of military operations in the area in June 2014, there was a dominant view that this had to be followed up with political measures to bring FATA into the political mainstream and years of political and administrative ambivalence must end. The Governor of Khyber Pakhtunkhwa constituted a FATA Reforms Commission (FRC) in 2014, the mandate of which was to propose reforms for FATA. A report was submitted by the FRC to the Governor KP in April 2015. It suggested establishment of representative councils the Tribal Agencies and FRs and also creation of a Governor's Advisory Council comprising of these members in a bid to introduce responsible governance, apart from suggesting other measures to tighten security of the terrain. There was also a 2015 FATA Long Term Governance Action Plan 2015-2025 developed by erstwhile FATA Secretariat in collaboration with Post Crises Needs Assessment (PCNA) FATA unit in 2015 which focused on 5 reform areas: political, institutional, justice, counter radicalisation and fostering reconciliation, and social cohesion, which forms the basis for administrative and political reforms that were suggested later. In September 2015, as many as 19 elected representatives from FATA (MNAs and Senators), in an unprecedented show of unity, called upon the government to abolish the tribal areas and merge them with Khyber Pakhtunkhwa province and said that they had drafted a bill to this effect to stop the 'half citizen' status of the people of FATA.[34] Shortly afterwards, in November 2015, the Nawaz Sharif government set up a six-member committee headed by Sartaj Aziz, which came out with a report in ten months in August 2016.[35] The report of this committee was prepared after consultations with 3,525 tribesmen during the process, including 3,096 Maliks and tribal elders and 429 lawyers, youths, traders and members of civil society.[36] It recognised that the "events of last decade had greatly enhanced the urgency of fundamental reforms in FATA" mostly because the "region suffered substantially after the emergence of militant groups in the region after 2001". There were protests by some groups like Jamat-ul-Ulema-i-Islam-Fazlur (JUI-F) and Pakhtunkhwa Milli Awami Party (PMAP) opposed merger, while the MQM called for a separate province for FATA. The rest including Jamat-i-Islami (JI), Awami National Party (ANP), Qaumi Watan Party(QWP), Pakistan Tehreek-i-Insaf (PTI) and the Pakistan People's Party (PPP) demanded immediate merger.

On 2 March 2017, Nawaz Sharif presented the case before his cabinet which approved of the recommendations to mainstream FATA.[37] However, certain decisions of the cabinet like introducing a Riwaj Act to replace FCR and lack of clarity about the phased reforms in FATA administration, especially rumours of a serving General to be appointed as the chief operating officer under KP governor to oversee implementation of the reforms, evoked widespread criticism. The government agreed to withdraw Riwaz act in September 2017 and went on to introduce the 30th Amendment bill 2017, to effect the merger and this was suitably modified as 31st Amendment bill 2018 later. On 24 May 2018, the bill was passed as Amendment in the National Assembly (229 in favour 1 against) and on 25 May, the Senate passed with 71 votes in favour and 5 against (all PMAP Senators walked out). It was sent to the provincial assembly, as per constitutional requirement, and the bill was passed there on 27 May with 87 votes in favour. Finally, the President signed it into law on 31 May 2018.

With the amendment bill passed in both houses, the government brought in FATA Interim Governance Regulation, 2018, on 28 May 2018, to replace FCR and fill in the vacuum created by the repeal of Article 247 of the constitution which laid down process of administration in the area. The regulation was criticised because it contained provisions which were there in both FCR and Riwaj Act that it sought to replace.[38] In October 2018, Peshawar High Court declared many provisions of the act (like assigning judicial powers to civil administrative officers) unconstitutional and illegal and went on to restrain Assistant Commissioner of Bara Tehsil from using judicial power in a civil case.[39] To overcome such issue in administration, the provincial government brought in a bill called "Khyber Pakhtunkhwa Continuation of Laws in the Erstwhile Provincially Administered Tribal Areas Act, 2018" and later in August 2019, an ordinance called KP Actions (in aid of civil power) Ordinance, 2019 was brought in which was an exact copy of two earlier regulations promulgated by the president in 2011 for FATA and PATA, which offered legal cover to several detention centres set up during the military operations in different regions. These regulations assign extensive powers to the armed forces and authorised officers and gives interning authority power to detain a suspect until the action in aid of civil power by the armed forces kicks in. On 17 October 2019, Peshawar High Court scrapped the ordinance and declared in null and void.[40] This ordinance was criticised widely.[41] However, subsequently the matter was taken to the Supreme Court and in November after suspending the order till 15 November 2019, on 21 November chided the federal government by saying "We must satisfy ourselves about the constitutionality of the law pertaining to the KP government's Action in Aid of Civil Power Regulation Ordinance 2019".[42]

While the judgment on the case remains inconclusive, there is widespread concern amongst the people of the erstwhile FATA and PATA regarding their constitutional rights, which should have accrued to them after the passing of the 25th Amendment (31st Amendment Act 2018) to the constitution which sought to mainstream FATA and PATA by removing the provisions in the constitution that gave the government sweeping powers to intervene in the region. The cases of forced disappearances, target killing, harassment of people criticising the government which fuels popular protests under a civil society group which calls itself Pashtun Tahafuz Movement (PTM) threatens to disturb the peace of the region and has given rise to an assertive Pashtun nationalism, which has already started characterising the pronouncements of not only the PTM followers, but also that of the hardline TTP leaders, even if they are at the two opposite ends of the spectrum of resistance against the Pakistani state. The unintended consequence of this is the disaffection such hurried, under-planned move for merger has engendered, which is likely to increase, if the whole issue is not addressed empathetically. The incumbent government of Imran Khan, always in a haste to attribute everything to lapses by the previous government(s), has in fact made the situation worse providing an opportunity for the TTP to bounce back, which will be discussed in detail in subsequent chapters.

Notes

1. George Campbell, *Afghan Frontier: the substance of a speech not delivered*, Edward Stanford, London, 1879, pp. 4, 24.

2. In his famous verse, "The Ballad of East and West", published in 1889, Rudyard Kipling (1865-1936) depicts the terrain as "rock to the left, and rock to the right, and low lean thorn between".

3. He would divide the people into Eastern and Western Afghans and consider Eastern Afghans inhabiting the rugged land drained by the Indus on its western banks as being Agricultural unlike their Western cousins who were pastoral and accounted for the ruling families of Afghanistan. See Mountstuart Elphinstone, *An Account of the Kingdom of Caubul, and Its Dependencies in Persia*, Tartary, and India, Longman, Hurst, London, 1815, p. 253.

4. Winston Churchill, *The Story of the Malakand Field Force: An Episode of Frontier War*, Thomas Nelson and Sons, London (Cheap Edition), 1916.

5. Ibid., pp. 23-29.

6. Army, General Staff Branch, *India, Operations in Waziristan, 1919-1920*, Superintendent Government Printing, Calcutta, 1921, p. 3.

7. Ibid., p. 5.

8. Arnold Keppel, *Gun-Running And The Indian North-West Frontier*, John Murray, London, 1912, pp. 25-26.

9. Enriquez and Oliver, cited in H. C. Willy, *From Black Mountain to Waziristan*, MacMillan, London, 1912, pp. 35-37.

10. Ibid., p. 39.

11. George Campbell, *Afghan Frontier: the substance of a speech not delivered*, Edward Stanford, London, 1879, p. 4.

12. Campbell goes on to write, "in Afghanistan the only chance of exercising a considerable authority is when power falls into the hands of a very strong and wise man with money at his command. Without plenty of money, not an angel from heaven could rule that country", Ibid., p. 14.

13. In case of the Baloch the boundary lines the British drew up with Persia/Iran (Goldsmith Line) and Afghanistan (Durrand Line) in 1893.

14. See for details David B. Edwards, *Heroes of the Age, Moral Fault Lines on the Afghan Frontier*, University of California Press, Berkeley, 1996.

15. See for details, Brandon Marsh, *Ramparts of Empire: British Imperialism and India's Afghan Frontier, 1918-1948 (Britain and the World)*, Palgrave Macmillan, 2014.

16. http://fata.gov.pk/Global.php?iId=28&fid=2&pId=23&mId=13

17. See Article 246 of Pakistan Constitution to find out how the tribal areas are defined and which are the areas designated as PATA and FATA.

18. Navid Iqbal Khan, "Malakand Division (Khyber Pakhtunkhwa: A Case Study of the Process of "State Inversion"", *Pakistan Journal of History and Culture*, Vol. XXXI, No. 1, 2010, p. 134.

19. Joe Stephens and David B. Ottaway, "The Abc's of Jihad in Afghanistan, Courtesy, USA", *Washington Post*, 23 March 2002 at http://emperors-clothes.com/news/abc.htm. See also detailed discussion by Abid Ullah Jan, *Afghanistan: The Genesis of the Final Crusade*, Pragmatic Publishing, Canada, 2006, pp. 117-120.

20. Ali Chisti, "Punjab: the new FATA", *Daily Times*, 7 June 2010 at http://archives.dailytimes.com.pk/editorial/07-Jun-2010/comment-punjab-the-new-fata-ali-k-chishti

21. Syed Sleem Shahzad, *Inside Al Qaeda and Taliban, Beyond Bin Laden and 9/11*, Pluto Press, London, 2011, p. 8.

22. Hassan Abbas provides a discursive analysis of the processes that led to the rise of Taliban and its consolidation as a powerful jihadi-political entity during 1979-2001 in his recent work, *The Talliban Revival: Violence and Extremism on the Pakistan-Afghanistan Frontier*, Yale University Press, New Haven, 2014, in Chapter 3, titled "The Afghan Jihad and the chaotic rise of the Taliban (1979-2001)".

23. Muhammad Amir Rana, *A to Z of Jehadi Organizations in Pakistan*, Mashal Publications, Lahore, 2011, pp. 182-191, Asad Munir, "Law and Disorder", *The Friday Times*, 30 November-6 December 2012 Vol. XXIV, No. 42 at http://www.thefridaytimes.com/beta3/tft/article.php?issue=20121130&page=6.1

24. Quoted in *The News*, 6 October 1998.

25. Ejaz Haider, 'Price of Kashmir-Afghanistan Policies', *The Friday Times*, Lahore, 3-9 June 1998.

26. See "The Constitution (Fifteenth Amendment) Bill, 1998" at http://pakistanconstitutionlaw.com/15th-amendment-bill/

27. See report by European Country of Origin Information Network, at https://www.ecoi.net/local_link/190011/293529_en.html

28. Report of the Committee on FATA Reforms 2016", August 2016, p. 29 at https://www.safron.gov.pk/SiteImage/Downloads/Report%20of%20%20Committee%20on%20FATA%20Reforms%202016.pdf.

29. He remained in prison till 2008 when his services were sought to bring the situation in Malakand under control. He negotiated a deal with the then Awami National Party government in then NWFP whereby Shariah was implemented in the area. Then President Asif Ali Zardari signed the Nizam-e-Adl Regulation law for Swat, paving way for the implementation of Sharia law in the Malakand region on 19 April 2009. However, this deal did not last because he took a radical stand that democracy was *haram* and the decision taken by Islamic courts in Malakand could not be appealed in Pakistani courts. His son-in-law, the infamous radio-mullah, Maulana Fazlullah continued with his aggressive policy to control Swat inviting army action (Operation Black Thunderstorm) and an agreement that all charges against Sufi and his associates would be withdrawn. However, the government pursued the cases against Fazlullah and the agreement broke down. Maulana was rearrested in 2009 and stayed in prison till January 2018, when he was released as per the orders of the Peshawar High Court. Soon after the TTP attack on Army Public School in Peshawar, Sufi Muhammad issued an informal decree against TTP then led by his Fazlullah and said that members of the banned outfit "lacked the traits essential for a Muslim....They [TTP] do not come up to the definition of Momin and Muslim set by the Holy Prophet (PBUH)," he stated in a written 'will'. He even accused his son-in-law of "bringing a bad name to the TNSM, killing a number of its leaders, and inflicting colossal loss on seminaries". Ali Akbar, "TNSM chief Maulana Sufi Muhammad released after 8 years in jail", *Dawn*, 15 January 2008 at https://www.dawn.com/news/1383097

30. Seth G Jones and C Christine Fair, Counterinsurgency in Pakistan, National Security Research Division, RAND Corporation, Santa Monica, 2010, pp. 46-47.

31. Abubakar Siddique, *The Pashtun Question: The Unresolved Key to the Future of Pakistan and Afghanistan*, C Hurst & Co Publishers Ltd, 2014.

32. See Ismail Khan, "Talibanisation imperils security, NSC warned: Immediate action urged", The Dawn, 23 June 2007 at http://www.dawn.com/news/253069/talibanisation-imperils-security-nsc-warned-immediate-action-urged.

33. Huma Yusuf, "Pakistan is facing galloping Talibanisation: Ahmed Rashid", *The Dawn*, 4 May 2009 at http://www.dawn.com/news/812897/pakistan-is-facing-galloping-talibanisation-ahmed-rashid.

34. "Tribal lawmakers ask govt to make Fata part of KP – Pakistan", *Dawn*, 8 September 2015 at https://www.dawn.com/news/1205571/tribal-lawmakers-ask-govt-to-make-fata-part-of-kp.

35. The report titled "Report of the Committee on FATA Reforms 2016", August 2016 at https://www.safron.gov.pk/SiteImage/Downloads/Report%20of%20%20Committee%20on%20FATA%20Reforms%20 2016.pdf.

36. "Ministry defends report on Fata reforms", *Dawn*, 26 January 2015 at https://www.dawn.com/news/1310829/ministry-defends-report-on-fata-reforms.

37. "Federal cabinet approves recommendations to 'mainstream' Fata", *Dawn*, 2 March 2017 at https://www.dawn.com/news/1317961.

38. Ismail Khan, "Mainstreaming Fata with interim governance law", *Dawn*, 31 May 2018 at https://www.dawn.com/news/1411061.

39. Sohail Khan, "PHC restrains Bara AC from using judicial powers", *The News*, 27 December 2018 at https://www.thenews.com.pk/print/411195-phc-restrains-bara-ac-from-using-judicial-powers.

40. "PHC scraps 'action in aid of civil power' ordinance", *The Express Tribune*, 18 October 2019 at https://tribune.com.pk/story/2081969/phc-scraps-action-aid-civil-power-ordinance.

41. "ICJ chided Pak for new ordinance in Khyber Pakhtunkhwa, says will 'lead to human rights violations'", *Business Statndard*, 28 September 2019 at https://www.business-standard.com/article/news-ani/icj-chided-pak-for-new-ordinance-in-khyber-pakhtunkhwa-says-will-lead-to-human-rights-violations-119092800201_1.html.

42. Sohail Khan, "Constitutionality of KP internment centres must be established: SC", *The News*, 21 November 2019 at https://www.thenews.com.pk/print/572151-constitutionality-of-kp-internment-centres-must-be-established-sc.

2. Tribal Areas in Tumult (2001-2007)

The Pashtun dominated areas in Pakistan, earlier known as Federally Administered Tribal Areas (FATA) and Provincially Administered Tribal Areas (PATA) of Pakistan, in the Pakistan-Afghanistan borderlands, straddling the Durand Line, have historically acted as the nerve-centre of militancy throughout history. In fact, the region—peopled by hardy and fiercely independent tribal community,[1] overwhelmingly Pashtun and rooted in tribal customary law of Pashtunwali—has traditionally posed serious challenges for all invaders passing through the terrain, including Alexander the Great, the Mongols, the Mughals and the British colonialists. During the post-colonial days too, the Pakistan government, drawing upon the colonial legacy of treating the region as a buffer, treated the region as an autonomous entity in practice, even if it was under direct control of the federal administration in theory. Since the Pak-Afghan border is porous and the writ of the government does not run that effectively in the terrain, this region, regarded as a vanishing point of jurisprudence, has become an attractive sanctuary for outlaws from rest of Pakistan, consisting of sectarian militants, proclaimed offenders wanted by police, as well as militants from across the border from Afghanistan.

During the days of the Afghan Jihad (1979-1989), the tribal belt, extending from FATA till northern Balochistan in Pakistan, acted as a natural destination for refugees and *mujahideen* (religious fighters) from Afghanistan. The socio-political engineering engendered by the US in liaison with Pakistani intelligence during the 1980s led to mushrooming of madrassas in the terrain, which provided recruits for filling the ranks of the Islamist *mujahideen* fighting the communist forces in Afghanistan. The Pashtuns of Pakistan from this terrain also joined the *mujahideen* ranks and fought against the infidel communists in Afghanistan. There were, of course, recruits from other provinces of Pakistan, who had transited through the *Deobandi*[2] madrassas, dotting the border areas. According to Pakistani intelligence sources quoted by Pakistani commentators, as many as 500,000 young men,[3] primarily Pashtun from NWFP and the FATA, but also from other areas of Pakistan, were indoctrinated in the philosophy of Islamic jihad during the years of Afghan resistance. Overwhelmingly Pashtun, bound by tribal codes of honor, loyalty and revenge, these elements also had a deeply Islamist facet to their personality.

Following Soviet pull-out in 1989, not much information was available on the Pakistani component of the mujahideen excepting their alleged involvement in sectarian conflicts in Pakistan and militancy in Kashmir. But the rise of Taliban in 1994 changed the scenario. Students from religious seminaries in Pakistan flocked to Afghanistan to join the Taliban efforts in Afghanistan. Taliban, which initially intended to bring back monarchical rule by inviting Zahir Shah, soon allied itself with Osama Bin Laden, the wealthy Saudi, one of the most fervent sponsors of Afghan Jihad, known for his radical Wahabi orientation, and founder of the Al-Qaeda (the Base) to take on the West.

After their alliance with Al-Qaeda, Taliban were lost in a renewed enthusiasm to establish chaste and pure Islamic rule in Afghanistan. As Taliban consolidated their position, militant groups, operating in Kashmir, Sunni sectarian outfits operating within Pakistan and rebel groups from Uzbekistan, Tajikistan, Xinjiang, Chechnya and Arab countries poured into Afghanistan to receive training in Al-Qaeda-run training camps and to join Taliban in its war of consolidation. The frontier between Pakistan and Afghanistan was left unguarded and open during the Taliban rule in Afghanistan, with thousands of Pakistani tribesmen joining Taliban war efforts with active encouragement from the Inter Services Intelligence (ISI) of Pakistan.[4]

The relatively younger leadership of the Taliban had a strong Pakistani connection unlike the top rung *mujahideen* of the Afghan Jihad years. Most of the top Taliban leaders had received their education in Pakistani madrassas and retained their links with the fellow Pashtun leaders and mujahideen.[5] As the Pakistani elements joined Taliban, their influence grew and some of them rose to prominence in the Taliban hierarchy. The Pakistani State facilitated their participation in Taliban's factional wars for increasing its stakes in Afghanistan and considered such efforts as part of its policy of ensuring a 'strategic depth' in Afghanistan.[6]

However, as some commentators have pointed out, Pakistan-Afghanistan relations during Taliban period only ensured a "reverse strategic depth" for Taliban and various pro-Taliban groups emerged in the tribal belt and entrenched themselves in the local terrain since late 1990s.

The attack on World Trade Centre on 11 September 2001 changed all this. Pakistan reversed its policy and joined the US sponsored Global War on Terror. As the US led attack on Afghanistan began in October 2001, and the Taliban fled from Kabul, steady streams of Taliban and Al-Qaeda militants trickled into the tribal areas of Pakistan bordering Afghanistan. These militants were multinational in character—Afghan, Arab, Pakistani, Chechen, Uzbek, Uyghur, etc.—who had fought in support of Taliban in Afghanistan. Afghans and Pakistanis constituted majority of these forces pouring into Pakistan, however. While Al-Qaeda elements spread across length and breadth of Pakistan, the Taliban forces as well as many Central Asian and Arab supporters of Al-Qaeda chose to remain in the tribal areas.

While natural Pashtun ethnic linkages explain the spontaneous support that the Taliban receive in the terrain, there are other reasons which provided incentives to the people to shelter non-Pashtun Taliban or Al-Qaeda forces that moved into the region after the US assault. During the last about 26 years of jihadi turbulence, the region played host to co-mujahideen from all parts of the world, notably the Arabs and the Central Asians, many of whom married into the local community and stayed on. Even then, when Al-Qaeda fighters crossed into Pakistan (some estimates suggested that about 2000 of them), tribesmen of the area initially captured some of them and sold them over to the US for hefty prices. However, the tribal temptation for money was soon neutralised by the Al-Qaeda strategy of providing much more lucrative and lasting monetary support to people working for them. They distributed millions of dollars among the tribal elders in return for shelter. Pakistani tribal fighters, working for Al-Qaida, received up to US$ 250 each as monthly wages, which was higher than the monthly wages of a Pakistani soldier.[7] The Al-Qaeda also set up training camps by taking up mud-walled compounds from the locals on hire. A close observer of the Taliban in Pakistan, would say "at least 15 camps had operated under the protection of sympathetic tribesmen, mostly around Wana and Shakai" and "in the early spring of 2004, senior Al-Qaida leaders had gathered there for a terror summit".[8]

FATA and the continued Impulse for Rebellion

As the TTP made the tribal belt its home, it was suggested by many analysts that the government would have to introduce wide-ranging reforms to own up the terrain and its people and dispense with the British practice of buffering off the space for security reasons. The Zardari government (2008-2013) made some efforts to amend the FCR and allow political parties to operate out of the terrain, but the suggested reforms remained rudimentary and the pace of change was inordinately slow. Some observers called it "too little too late"[9] and held that there were far more serious issues of making the system representative by bringing administrative and economic reforms in line with the system prevalent in other areas of the country. In line with the demands of the political parties, it was long felt that the representatives from FATA must be given powers to legislate for their own region.[10] There is a general perception, even today, that the trend favouring militancy in the area can be reversed only if the region will be successfully mainstreamed in a wholesome manner keeping political, economic and administrative issues in mind. In view of the popular appetite for change, the opportunity needed to be seized and reforms introduced to change the character of control system in place that had outlived its utility. Since the earlier system with its emphasis on control and collective responsibility enforced from outside had failed to stem the tide of militancy, it was felt necessary to introduce changes in line with the demands emanating from the people of the region and promote local representative systems in the region. Such institutions by ensuring "peaceful political activism" could provide a "constructive alternative" to jihadist militancy, it was argued. [11]

9/11 Before and After: A Brief Overview

The days following 9/11 were particularly painful for Musharraf government in Pakistan. After grooming the Taliban as a strategic ally for nearly seven years, it was time for the military leadership to take a hard call—whether to be with the Americans or against them. Pakistan had nurtured the Taliban to the chagrin of its mujahideen proxies who had defeated the Soviet forces but failed to unite to offer stable administration to the Afghan people. Despite the Taliban's medieval ideological orientation, Pakistan preferred them as a disciplined force and backed their assaults against former mujahideen forces aligned against the Taliban.

The Taliban captured Kabul in 1996 and by then, it had made substantial inroads into areas traditionally controlled by the Tajiks, Uzbeks and Hazaras. The arrival of Osama Bin Laden in Afghanistan in May 1996 under invitation from the mujahideen government, few months before Kabul fell to the Taliban, and his loyalty towards Mullah Omar and Taliban played a role in both hardening the Islamist line toed by the Taliban and adding to its fighting capability by drafting Arab, Uzbek, Chechen, Uyghur and many other foreign militants into the Taliban fold. Pakistan guided Taliban to the best of its ability by deputing both serving and retired army officers and resources and allowed Islamic groups from its territory to make common cause with Taliban. Through diplomatic efforts, Pakistan could even muster tacit support of countries like the US and China for the Taliban regime. There were even efforts by the Taliban to placate the West and the world was getting used to the Taliban phenomenon and trying to bring moderation into its behaviour and mainstream it.

However, Al-Qaeda's overreach in the form of 9/11 destroyed all hopes of Pakistan to make the Taliban regime acceptable to the West. After the failure of tentative efforts made by Pakistan to convince Mullah Omar to surrender Osama Bin Laden to the US authorities, when the attack on Afghanistan looked certain, Pakistan was forced to take a U-turn and join the US efforts to dislodge the Taliban government in Kabul for fear of losing out to especially India, which expressed its solidarity with the US efforts given its long experience with cross-border Islamic militancy. The then military ruler of Pakistan, Musharraf, who was facing international opprobrium for having come to power through a coup, also saw a God-given opportunity to end his regime's isolation by joining the international effort against terror. In a strange turn of history, this time round the international community chose to work with a dictator with secular credentials (who had no scruples to be photographed with his dogs) unlike the case with his predecessor Zia-ul-Haq, an enthusiast of Islamic rule. Back in December 1979, when Soviet forces walked into Afghanistan, Zia was labouring under international boycott, and the US had discovered a potent ally in him for his Islamic credentials. The jihad against erst-while Soviet Union altered irreversibly the socio-political landscape in the Pakistan-Afghanistan region leading to forces like the Taliban, necessitating yet another intervention by the West.

Pakistan Army's Entry into Tribal Areas

The tale that followed the US-led attack on Afghanistan on 7 October 2001, as part of its global war on terror, in the tribal borderlands of Pakistan, has thrown the entire country and the region into a tailspin ever since. Pakistan has found it difficult to negotiate with this reality it helped create over the years. The FATA region as well as bordering areas in Pakistan has undergone a radical jihadi transformation which has been very difficult on the part of Pakistan state to diagnose and counter. The radical Islamist conglomerate called Tehrik-e-Taliban Pakistan (Movement of the Taliban in Pakistan) has posed a serious challenge to Pakistan and threatened to infect rest of Pakistan and the neighbouring region with its stubborn conservative and orthodox Islamic world view. Its determination to not only uphold such an ideology but also to materialise it in Pakistan by all means (as the Peshawar tragedy of 16 December 2014 would indicate) and then take it to other regions of the world has attracted many other fringe radical elements into the fold of this 'movement' and sent shivers through the spine of the security community in Pakistan. How and why such a phenomenon surfaced in Pakistan and gathered momentum despite its regressive world view, and also despite the assertion in many quarters that the power elite in Pakistan is of a liberal persuasion, begs critical scrutiny. Some preliminary observations are made in the following discussion on this theme.

Interestingly, in his address to the nation on 12 January 2002, Musharraf outlined his policy shift in favour of US-led war on terror. This address clearly revealed the concern among Pakistani policy makers regarding the impact of the militant Islamist approach the Taliban was taking across the border on Pakistani society. He revealed that Pakistan had sealed the border in January 2001 and made it compulsory for Pakistani *talibs* (students) crossing over to Afghanistan to fight alongside the Taliban to produce relevant documents for travel. In a way, this was in recognition of the reverse strategic depth that the Taliban had started developing in Pakistan. In February 2001, the government promulgated an ordinance to deweaponise people in Pakistan. In August 2001, the military government led by Musharraf banned sectarian outfits like Lashkar-e-Jhangvi (known for its rabid sectarian, anti-Shia views) and Sipah-e-Muhammad (a militant outfit raised in 1993 by Shias to target Sunni sectarian leaders) and placed Sipah-e-Sahaba (a sectarian Sunni outfit formed in 1985 out of which LeJ emerged in 1996, now known as Millat-e-Islamia or Rah-e-Haq) and Tehrik-e-Jafria Pakistan (TJP)—initially known as Tehrik-e-NIfaz-e-Fiqh-e-Jafaria (TNFJ), a Shia outfit formed in 1979 in response to controversial laws imposed on Shias by military dictator Zia-ul-Haq—under observation. By January 2002, these two organisations were banned too along with Tehrik-e-Nifaz-e-Shariat-e-Muhammadi (TNSM)[12] and in addition Sunni Tehrik was—a Barelvi outfit, raised in 1990, to protect the interests of the Barelvis in the face of growing attacks on them by militant Deobandi groups—placed under observation. The Musharraf government also banned Jaish-e-Mohammad and Lashkar-e-Taiba and as it was mentioned in the address, no organization was allowed to form Lashkar, Sipah or Jaish and incite people to violence "either in internal or external contexts".[13]

The Pakistan army entered tribal areas under US pressure in October 2001. The security landscape of the region changed beyond recognition after this according to Pakistani media observers.[14] In fact, the Pakistan army entered Shawal Valley for the first time ever. The valley runs from Datta Khel westward and extends across the Durand Line into Afghanistan, covering both FATA and Paktia province of Afghanistan. It is a difficult terrain hemmed in by hills on all sides. The Afghan Shawal area is even more intractable. Following 9/11, many high value foreign terrorists were suspected to be hiding in this Pakistan-Afghanistan area. Therefore, Pakistan army was asked to enter into the valley for the first time in October 2001.[15] The valley, inhabited mostly by Datta khel and Zaki khel tribes, is known to have provided shelter to rebels historically. Faqir of Ippi (1897-1960) (alias Mirza Ali Khan) was one such rebel who fought against the might of the British empire assisted for some time by intelligence agencies of the Axis countries, especially of Italy and Germany, during the second world war.[16] Pakistan establishment set up a tribal lashkar (group) in Pakistan's Shawal area and asked them to apprehend and hand over all Taliban, Al-Qaeda and Afghan figures who had fled Afghanistan entered the tribal areas of Pakistan. However, the performance of the laskhar was not up to mark, and the tribal leaders lost their shine once the area was flooded with militants from Afghanistan.

The situation was quite similar in the two Waziristan agencies.[17] Pakistan army entered South Waziristan in May 2002 based on reports that many high-value militants were escaping into this area from Afghanistan. Previously, Tochi and Waziristan Scouts used to take care of the security of this region. As soon as it entered it sought to throw a security cordon stretching from Shawal valley in North Waziristan till Angoor Adda in South Waziristan. If Pakistan army entered the terrain for the first time to fight out foreign militants, the local militants also attacked the army installations for the first time in this area. Rockets and mortars were hurled at South Waziristan Scouts camps in Wana and Brigade headquarters at Zaire Noor camp. Refusal of local pro-Al-Qaeda tribal elements to surrender foreign militants despite a Jirga decision to that effect in South Waziristan, indicated the first instance of fundamental feature of the tribal system crumbling down in the area now trudged by Al-Qaeda elements.

The army also deployed units of Special Services Group (SSG) and crack commando units of Quick reaction in both the agencies (NWA and SWA). The army stationed two brigades and several check posts along the route from Ghulam Khan border crossing through Datta Khel and Shawal in NWA till Angoor Adda border crossing in SWA. This was mainly done to stop the flow of foreign Al-Qaeda elements from across the Durand Line especially from the provinces of Khost and Paktika. The intelligence network was also strengthened with dozens of operatives from the three main agencies—IB, MI and ISI—scouring the area and reporting back to their regional heads in Bannu and Dera Ismail Khan. Several top military officers were posted in both Miramshah and Wana to oversee the activities of these operatives. Based on human intelligence network that these agents activated complemented by technical intelligence enabled by the US forces across the border, the military conducted several raids, cordon-and-search operations, and regular vehicle checks in the region, giving the local people a taste of police state for the first time.

Failure to Convince the Local Population

The reaction of the locals was that for almost three decades the state had taught the tribal population in the region to accommodate the foreign militants from Arab countries—Chechnya, Eastern Turkestan, Uzbekistan and other central Asian republics—as fellow mujahids and suddenly they were asked to "unlearn that lesson".[18] They were reluctant to accept that these jihadis, who had become legends for them, were terrorists. Some of these mujahideen had even married into local tribes, and were regarded as locals. Apart from marital bond, through religious exhortations, lure of money that

Al-Qaeda could provide in return for local hospitality and provision of security, and at times through threats of dire consequences, these foreign elements escaping the Afghan theatre of conflict had created enormous stakes among the local population for which they felt it almost their duty to defy the diktats of the Pakistani state, which was largely absent till then from this terrain.

Some of the operations by the Pakistan military in early 2002, therefore, failed miserably. For example, in June 2002, the Al-Qaeda militants surprised the well-trained Pakistani forces during a raid they conducted in Azam Warsak, west of Wana in South Waziristan. Some 30 high value militants fled the scene with their entire families—with women and children, resisting the attack quite successfully. The army lost 10 soldiers while the militants lost only two. The army learnt its lesson from such experiences and its raid in Baghar in October 2003 was relatively successful with the killing of eight suspected militants, mostly residents of the area. Interestingly, among the dead were Arab and Uzbek militants as well as Hassan Mahsun, a leader of the Eastern Turkestan Islamic Movement (ETIM), which reconfirmed the army's suspicion about the presence of foreign elements in the terrain.[19] However, immediately after Baghar operations, the army suffered reverses in January and February 2004 in the same area. The retreating soldiers were ambushed by the militants in January while on 27 and 29 February 2004, military check-posts in Zam China, north of Razmak, and Dre-Nishtar in Shawal valley in NWA came under heavy fire from the militants.

In South Waziristan in particular, frequent military-militant encounters/clashes virtually disabled whatever nominal civilian administrative machinery was there in the area and antagonised the local population who started suspecting every move by the Pakistani state as directed unnecessarily against them at the behest of the USA, which was declared as the great Satan by Al-Qaeda leadership. Moreover, the tribal jirga system—which enforced discipline at the local level and maintained order quite effectively over the years— was progressively regarded as illegitimate, once its decisions echoed the directives issued from Islamabad. The confrontation between the Al-Qaeda operatives and Pakistan army ruined the local economy which thrived on legal and illegal trade across Durand Line leading to impoverishment of the local population setting off a favourable dynamics for resistance which was tapped by Al-Qaeda quite well. While the army made its presence felt contravening the FCR, it invoked the same rules to impose heavy fines on local population— for example, the fine of about 5.4 million Pakistan Rupees (PKR) was imposed on the Ahmadzai tribe as a whole in the wake of the February 2004 attacks on military camps. Every time an Al-Qaeda operative was captured the local tribes would be asked to cough up 1 million PKR. As per tribal customs, the burden is shared equally among families and thus the poor suffers the most.

Policy of Double-dealing

The differentiated approach of the Pakistan army towards the two principal militant groups—the Taliban and Al-Qaeda—also added to the consternation at the local levels regarding the duplicity of Pakistani behaviour. As news reports suggested, the ground level functionaries of the Pakistan army would turn a blind eye to Taliban operating in the area and even facilitate their movement across the border even when it knew that these elements were targeting Afghan and foreign forces across the border. In one such incidents in February 2004,[20] the Taliban operatives sped down the Miramshah-Ghulam Khan road and reached the Bangi Dar border crossing and passed the Pakistan army check posts unobstructed, went across the Durand Line, and fired at Afghan soldiers. This was reported in the media and there was extra-pressure on Musharraf, then smarting under the assassination attempts in December 2003, to account for such laxity on the part of the Pakistan army. Musharraf's despair could be gauged from his reported admonishment to the Pakistan army officers at National Defence College on 12 February 2004, when he said: "On the western border, certainly, everything is not happening from Pakistan, but certainly something is happening from Pakistan.... Let us not bluff ourselves ... whatever is happening from Pakistan must be stopped".[21] Analysts suggested in the media that even if the top leadership wanted to oblige the Americans, such message could not "trickle down to the institutional grassroots", with the result that powerful sections within the army sought to circumvent the direction coming from above.

Stratfor analysts recognised during this time that the mountainous border region of the Afghan-Pakistani border region was "porous, relatively unguarded and home to the Pushtun ethnic group that straddles national boundaries" and "Al-Qaeda, unhobbled by state loyalties, [could have] moved its core personnel into this region, where it is more complicated for US forces to operate".[22] Moreover, the reality on the ground isolated quite early in October-November 2001 was that the Pakistan army, especially its notorious spy agency, Inter-Services Intelligence, or ISI, was *a state within a state, with independent, and worrying, political tendencies* (italicised by the author) and it was playing both sides of the game, hunting with the American hound and running with the Taliban hare.[23] Due to overbearing pressure from the American side (encapsulated in much-cited Richard Armitage's threat to stay prepared to be bombed into stone-age) and the unwelcome prospect of India exploiting the situation to its advantage (as was made clear in Musharraf's address to the nation on 19 September 2001[24]), Musharraf had chosen to join the US in its Afghan adventure. However, the then ISI Chief, Lieutenant General Mahmood Ahmad did everything possible to persuade the Taliban not to surrender Osama Bin Laden and even supply men and material to the Taliban army to defend itself against the US attack.[25] Moreover, Lt Gen Mahmood reportedly encouraged Jalaluddin Haqqani—who was in control of the border province of Khost, never formed the core of the Talban team, and was given a rather unimportant ministry of border affairs—not to leave Taliban and switch his loyalty towards the Americans during his October 2001 trip to Islamabad supposedly to take cues from ISI about his future strategy when the war became imminent.[26] Another close observer of the emerging situation observes that Musharraf believed that the Americans would be in Afghanistan for five years at best and he would have to deal with the Taliban after American withdrawal.

Hence, the Pakistani establishment continued to maintain links with the Taliban leadership and offered them sanctuary in the borderlands away from the gaze of the American intelligence officials who flocked to Pakistan both to keep a tab on the foreign militants fleeing the Afghan war theatre as well as Pakistan army's behaviour in the changed situation. While Pakistan army was forced to move into the tribal areas, guided by both human and technical intelligence supplied by the Americans, it made a clear distinction between the Afghan Taliban and the Al-Qaeda elements.

Temptation to Privilege Taliban over Al-Qaeda

At the ground level, the army sought to flush out Al-Qaeda cadres by nurturing the Taliban and the local population. At first it wanted to tolerate them unless they confronted the army till about 2003, largely because the military continued to employ both serving and retired army and intelligence officials well-versed in Afghan mujahideen politics, to deal with the Taliban militants. Given their familiarity with many Taliban leaders, they were not only soft towards the Taliban but also towards Al-Qaeda. However, by early 2004, the army started modifying its position and tolerated the Taliban but sought to push non-Afghan foreign elements across the border expecting Afghan and the international security forces to deal with them. What worried the Musharraf administration the most was the fact that radical Islamist militant groups had not been able to comprehend his government's differentiated policy towards the Taliban and Al-Qaeda and considered both as natural friends who deserved their hospitality and protection.

Pakistan army's hobnobbing with the Afghan Taliban was noted by many Pakistani reporters. During 2003-2004, Pakistani agencies were manoeuvering to install friendly governments in the border provinces in Afghanistan. Khost and Paktika were in a way awarded to Jalaluddin Haqqani and his sons. Mullah Ruhullah, son of famous mujahideen Jamilur Rehman of Laghman was given charge of Nuristan and asked to collect arms for resistance. Similarly, the Taliban were encouraged to re-consolidate their hold along the border areas. Saifur Rahman Mansoor, son of Mullah Mansoor of Shah-i-kot in Paktia province, was asked to organise resistance within Afghanistan. All this while, the propaganda machinery in the shape of the vernacular Urdu media in Pakistan was kept alive by Pakistan to defend Afghan Taliban and its world-view. The commentators in the vernacular media continued to take a pronounced pro-militant position in Pakistan and criticised, in a subdued manner of course, the policy somersault by the military government of Musharraf under American pressure.

Attempt on Musharraf: Army goes After the Jihadis

The Musharraf administration gradually realised the disastrous fall out of its policy in the shape of deep radicalisation of the entire Pashtun borderland stretching from Chitral in the north to Quetta in the South. Other developments like attack on Indian parliament on 13 December 2001 which compelled Musharraf's to ban India-focussed terror groups like Lashkar-e-Taiba (LeT) and Jaish-e-Muhammad (JeM) led to a revolt in the jihadi ranks against the government. Some of the jihadi leaders like Illyas Kashmiri, one-time favourite of Gen Musharraf for having presented him with the head of an Indian soldier, migrated to the tribal areas with a determination to confront the Pakistan army. Around this time in early September 2003, Ayman Al-Zawahiri, the deputy of Osama Bin Laden and top Al-Qaeda leader urged the soldiers of Pakistan to "revolt against him [Musharraf] and topple him before he turns you into servants to the Hindus and Crusaders.... Man should not obey any creature if there is disobedience to the Crusader".[27] Musharraf would continue to remain a jihadi target and Ayman Al-Zawahiri would again repeat his appeal on 4 March 2004 few days before the military attacked Kaloosha and justify his stand by arguing that

> Musharraf is the one who enabled the United States to topple the Islamic Emirate in Afghanistan. Without his great help, the United States would not have been able to do this.... Who stifled the jihad of the Kashmiri people, went back on their right to self-determination, and considered the mujahideen in Palestine as terrorists and feverishly seeks to recognize Israel?[28]

In early 2006, Zawahiri would call upon all Pakistanis to topple President General Pervez Musharraf as soon as possible, called him "a bribe-taking, treacherous criminal" and asked the Pakistani army to mutiny against Musharraf[29] and went on to say:

> Without a doubt, Pakistan is one of the most important of the countries targeted by this new colonialist crusade which seeks to weaken Pakistan and fragment it into entities under the control of India, which is allied with the Americans and Jews ... the anti-Islamic American/Crusader/Zionist plan has no place for the presence of Pakistan as a strong, powerful, able state in South Asia, because this plan doesn't forgive Pakistan for separating from India in the name of Islam, and doesn't forgive it for including the largest Islamic schools with wide influence among the Muslims of South and Central Asia, and doesn't forgive it for the flourishing of the popular jihadi movements in it against the Indians in Kashmir and first the Russians and then the Americans in Afghanistan, and doesn't forgive it the favorable response of its people, scholars, students, mujahideen and tribes to the Islamic emirate in Afghanistan—since its founding and to this very day—and to its amir the lion of Islam, Mullah Mohammed Omar.... In this context, India appears to be the best candidate to implement the Zionist/Crusader plan to humiliate Pakistan and weaken it and tear it apart.[30]

In the same address, Zawahiri betrays his concerns about Musharraf's policies, even if the army under him was playing a double game of targeting select Al-Qaeda leaders while leaving the jihadi infrastructure alive at home and nurturing Taliban of Afghanistan to field them as a sympathetic ally in the Afghan war theatre. Zawahiri would say:

> ... Musharraf is the one who is seeking to change the combat doctrine of the Pakistani army by repeating that the real danger to Pakistan is from within and not foreign: i.e., he is inciting the Pakistani army to fight its people and brothers and turn a blind eye to the Indian threat. And if the combat doctrine of any army becomes corrupted, and its fighting turns into fighting for the sake

of salary and position alone, then this army will run away from the battlefield whenever fighting breaks out.... I call on every officer and soldier in the Pakistani army to disobey the orders of his commanders to kill Muslims in Pakistan and Afghanistan, or otherwise he will be confronted by the mujahideen who repelled the British and Russians before. The Truth—Exalted is He—[who] says, "Say to those who have disbelieved, if they cease [from disbelief], their past will be forgiven".

The jihadi aversion for Musharraf even became more prominent following assassination attempts on him in 2003. The first attack on Musharraf took place on 26 April 2003 when a car packed with explosives was blown off at the Falak Naz Centre near Shara-e Faisal mosque in Karachi, after his vehicle passed by. Later investigations revealed that eight cadres of the Harkat-ul-Mujahideen Al Alami (HuMA) group led by one Asadullah had conducted this attack when Musharraf was scheduled to visit the Army House from the airport. However, the remote control to set-off the device failed and importantly, an Inspector named Wasim of the Rangers had abetted the accused in their attempt and was subsequently arrested.[31] The second attack was on 14 December, at Jhanda Chichi bridge near 10 Corps Headquarters in Rawalpindi. An estimated 250 kg of explosives were used in the blast. Few days later, on 25 December, two suicide bombers tried to ram cars packed with explosives into Musharraf's car not too far from the place where the attack on 14 December took place. Two suicide bombers were soon identified as Mohammed Jamil, a JeM activist from Azad Kashmir who had returned from Afghanistan after US attack and Hazir Sultan a Harkat-ul-Jihad-i-Islami activist from Afghanistan who was operating in South Waziristan following US attack. A loose alliance of members from five militant organisations—JeM, HUJI, LeJ, LeT and HuM-Al Alami[32]—known as Brigade 313 came up immediately after US bombing of Afghanistan. Qari Saifullah Akhtar, one of the founders of HUJI, who also came back to Pakistan in 1981 and Ilyas Kashmiri belonged to this new group.

Army Operations in 2004 Ruffles the Tribes

Till 2004, the Pakistan army suspected Osama Bin Laden's presence in and around Ghund Raghzai area of Shakai in South Waziristan. According to reports, the US bases in Paktika, bordering SWA, were regularly fired upon by Al-Qaeda forces. As early as in February 2004, then Taliban spokesman, Saiful Adel had told media that there were indeed dozens of "volunteers" in its ranks and most of them were Arab. Intelligence inputs also confirmed that a large chunk of foreign Al-Qaeda affiliated militants fleeing the battle zone in Afghanistan had entered the area and were sheltered mostly by local tribesmen in South Waziristan. These militants were moving relatively freely between the two parts of Waziristan, North and South. This led to a nine-month long military operation from January till September 2004, which was called *Operation Al-Mizan*. The objective of such operation was either to arrest militants or push them across the border. In the encounters that followed, many civilians perished due to what media and Human Rights organisations called excessive and indiscriminate use of force. Official estimates suggested at least 500 people dead—202 militants, 150 soldiers, and 148 civilians. This was the period when Pakistan witnessed its first drone attack killing one of the most notorious militants from the area—Nek Mohammad (1975-2004), on 18 June 2004 in his hideout in Doag village, just outside Wana. The subsequent military operations in North and South Waziristan, were resisted by the militants as well as the local population and the resultant violence peaked between June and September 2004.

Because of its geographical contiguity with Afghan province of Paktia through which most of the Afghan militants entered Pakistan, South Waziristan was the natural focus of US-Pakistan security forces and as early as from January 2002, Pakistan had sent in its military to set up local check-posts to monitor the evolving situation in the region. As reports later suggested, the Pakistani intelligence actively colluded with the local forces to facilitate migration of a number of high value militants escaping Afghanistan in the wake of Operation Anaconda launched by the US in Paktia. But coming under increasing US pressure, there was some effort made by Pakistan to at least show some solidarity with the Americans by capturing some of the foreign militants while ensuring that it retained its control over the Waziristan. The whole purpose of Pakistani troops-presence in the tribal terrain during that time was not so much to stop the tide as to manage it—to use largescale influx of militants from Afghanistan to its advantage.

Eye of the Storm: South Waziristan

The evolving politics in South Waziristan against the backdrop of war in Afghanistan posed a critical challenge to Pakistani leadership. While South Waziristan is largely inhabited by Mehsuds in the central and eastern highlands, some sub-branches of the Ahmadzai Waziris dominate the fertile valley west of Wana bordering Afghanistan. The Mehsuds were relatively better exposed to Pakistani system than these Waziris. Nevertheless, Ahmadzai Waziris, dominating the Waziri community in the tribal areas, mostly in Waziristan, were known as being "soft and tractable" and not given to conflict during the British rule. Among the Ahmadzai sub-tribes, the Yargulkhel sub-branch of the Shaikh Khel sub-tribe, known for its wealth and bloodline, dominated the socio-political landscape west of Wana in South Waziristan. Some of the famous Yargulkhel militants asserting themselves then were Nek Muhammad (1975-2004), Haji Omar (1951-2008) and his brothers, Haji Sharif and Noor Islam. Other important local leaders like Abdul Aziz and Maulvi Abbas, not from the same tribe, came to their support. Most of them had links with Maulana Fazlur Rahman's JUI at one point of time, but the turmoil following US attack had compelled JUI-F leadership to distance itself from their indulgence in local adventurism to rescue and shelter foreign militants and earn a good buck in the bargain.

By March 2004, Nek Muhammad had established a reputation as a saviour of the Al-Qaeda-affiliated foreign elements in the South Waziristan area. Hailing from Kalosha, near Wana, born in 1975, son of a local malik and khasdar, Nek was characterised as "a hard-headed boy, endowed with an impenetrable soul and an obstinate determination to carry out his will no matter how mindless it might be".[33] He had found his life's mission at the age of 19 when he joined the Taliban forces around 1994 and fought with them quite ably to rise to the level of a local commander in Kargha military base near Kabul in 2001, when the US attacked Afghanistan. By then, he had established contact with foreign militants and when he returned to his native place fleeing Afghanistan under US attack, he took it upon himself to provide shelter to these militants in South Waziristan. In the bargain, he earned lot of money from Al-Qaeda and established himself as the leading militant in the area and even senior mujahid leaders like Haji Omar, who had risen to the level of adviser to Mullah Omar of Taliban, as well as his influential brothers Haji Sharif and Noor Islam, acknowledged his leadership.

For Pakistani agencies, not all high-value Taliban and Al-Qaeda operatives sneaking into Pakistan were regarded as useful. Moreover, the prospect of local militia hobnobbing with the foreign elements establishing their writ and control was not quite welcome for the military. The operation they conducted near Baghar China village area in October 2003 had alerted them to the nuisance potential of the foreign militants and the challenge they could pose to the military if they were to confront them militarily. The presence of Uyghur militants among the foreign militants must have been particularly worrying for the military, as one of the main leaders of East Turkestan Islamic Movement (ETIM), Hasan Masum, was found dead in the Baghar operations (mentioned in Musharraf's memoir too). Therefore, it was natural for the Pakistan military to pressurise the tribes in South Waziristan to surrender the foreign militants under their protection to the Pakistani state.

However, this was not acceptable to the local militant leaders. Most of the prominent tribal militant leaders from the region cutting across different tribes had participated in the Afghan jihad of the 1980s and later in favour of Taliban after it made its appearance in 1994. While militants from Kalosha-based Yargulkhel tribe held sway around Wana, another important leader in the area west of Kalosha was Mullah Nazir, who came from a rather less known Ahmadzai sub-tribe of Ghulam Khel, and controlled the important border crossing area of Angoor Adda. When the foreign militants including the Afghan Taliban, the Arab Al-Qaeda, and their affiliates—Chechens, Tajiks, Uyghurs and Uzbeks[34]—sneaked into Waziristan area in droves under the protection of important Taliban leaders like Jalaluddin Haqqani and Saifur Rahman Mansoor, they passed inevitably through Shah-i-kot in (Paktia), Afghanistan, to enter Pakistan through South Waziristan. As the Battle of Shah-i-Kot (part of Operation of Anaconda launched by the US in March 2002 to dislodge Al-Qaeda elements around Gardez area, capital of Paktia) intensified, by late February 2004, the trickle of foreign Al-Qaeda militants into Pakistan became a torrent. By March 2004, the army entered Waziristan to respond to local resistance building up around the issue of providing asylum or refuge (*Nanawati*), in line with the Pashtun tradition of *Melmastiya* (hospitality), to foreign mujahideen fleeing Afghanistan.

Tolerate Taliban, Go After Al Qaeda

These foreign militants did enjoy empathy of the local population as well as the sympathy of the Pakistan military and intelligence officials at the lower levels, who could not entirely accept the policy reversal decided at the highest level. By all accounts, it is they who might have allowed these militants fleeing the war in Afghanistan to escape into Pakistani territory, without being fully aware of the future consequences. The Taliban-Al-Qaeda distinction that Musharraf articulated later was yet to percolate to the ground level. Moreover, Musharraf's bid to track down hardcore Al-Qaeda operatives and going soft on Taliban was not received well in the tribal areas, who had fought with the Taliban in Afghanistan intoxicated with the dream of enforcing Islam in the region through jihad. Moreover, the money that the Al-Qaeda and foreign militant groups affiliated to it offered to the local warlords/militant leaders in the tribal agencies of Pakistan for granting shelter and protection to their cadres added a material dimension to their spiritual leaning in favour of helping out like-minded groups wedded to jihad for the sake of ushering Allah's rule into the earth. Pakistan army's strategy of tolerating Taliban as a lever or an asset for their future game plans in Afghanistan played havoc with their overall policy of siding with the US for decimating Al-Qaeda. As Farhat Taj[35] mentions in her book (*Taliban Anti-Taliban*) some of the top military leaders had told her quite clearly that it was strategically important for Pakistan to keep the US bogged down in Afghanistan. Taj says that even the Pakistani intelligence had its role to play in the formation of the Tehrik-e-Taliban Pakistan!

Be that as it may, the army operations that were conducted in the tribal areas as a whole during 2002-2004 do suggest that the Pakistan army did not want to concede control of this area to the militants on the one hand and wanted to convey to the international community that it was quite serious about its purported role in the ongoing war on terror, on the other. Going by the evidence, the Pakistan army did want to put pressure on the Nek Muhammad-led local militant group operating in and around Wana to surrender foreign militants by 16 March 2004. When the local tribal Jirga could not persuade Nek Muhammad to oblige the Pakistani military, Kalosha near Wana, became the theatre for the first major standoff between the Frontier Corps (FC) and Nek Mohammad's militia. The FC surrounded the houses of Nek Muhammad, Haji Sharif and Noor Islam before dawn on 16 March 2004 and as they were contemplating to enter the houses, Nek Muhammad suddenly sprang up a surprise on them and "hurled his bullet-proof truck right up against the cordon of security forces, throwing the [soldiers] in disarray and cruising his prized guest Tahir Yuldashev to safety".[36] Even if the army continued with its operation and claimed it a success on 26 March 2004, the reverses it suffered in terms of men and materials alerted it to the strength of the militants in such an unfamiliar terrain. The militants, the media reports suggested, had elaborate communication network, bullet proof vehicles, watchtowers, tunnels, trenches and sophisticated arms which baffled the army. In the face of this challenge, it became an ego issue for the military to try its best to keep things under control, even if it did not mean to oblige the Americans.

The army was even more surprised by the attacks it had to confront after the Kalosha encounter, away from the Yargulkhel dominated territory in South Waziristan. The firing of rockets on army posts in the Mehsud dominated areas of South Waziristan, in many areas in North Waziristan, Kurram and Khyber suggested that diverse militant groups present in the entire terrain had started reacting violently to the army's presence in the area. What had perplexed the Pakistani military even more was the seeping influence of these militant Islamist groups to settled areas in the immediate neighbourhood of FATA in then North western Frontier Province (NWFP). Moreover, these groups shared the Islamic world-view of the Taliban and sought to implement it in respective areas under their control. A case in point was the tribal court in Orakzai agency executing eight suspected criminals on 14 March 2004, (the suspects were lined up and shot by a tribal firing squad) in clear disregard of the laws of the land and the request by the local administration to hand them over.[37] The army's clear lack of strategy and determination added to the strength of the militants. The army operations were at best episodic, lacking in determination to hold forth and 'stay' in the areas under control after confronting the militants and ensure complete flushing out of militants from the area. There was no attempt to back it up with revival of the administration that the militants had destroyed and sought to replace. Moreover, Musharraf's statements[38] that the efforts were backed by US intelligence agencies succeeded in inflaming local passions especially when the army had resorted to heavy shelling in areas of confrontation levelling up whole bazars and villages in some places.

Shortly after the attack, a defiant Nek Muhammad vowed to take on the army with even greater vehemence but very soon the army resorted to the policy of orchestrating a deal to ensure the tribal militants conformed to the strategy adopted by the Pakistan military. In fact, on 24 April 2004, Pakistani state entered into an agreement, in a place called Shakai north of Wana, with Nek Muhammad Wazir—who had assumed leadership of the tribes despite his Waziri descent in an overwhelmingly Mehsud-inhabited South Waziristan and his young age (only 29 years of age by then). This deal was alternately known as 'Wana Five' deal as five militants, i.e., Nek Muhammad, Sharif Khan, Noor Islam, Maulana Mohammad Abbas and Maulana Abdul Aziz, were granted amnesty.

The deal was negotiated by two pro-MMA MNAs from South Waziristan, Maulana Merajuddin Qureshi and Maulana Abdul Malik Wazir. Aware of the sensitivities of the tribal militants, the then Peshawar Corps Commander Lt. Gen. Safdar Hussain agreed not to refer to the Shakai Jirga as 'surrender' and instead described it as "reconciliation." The militants did not lay down arms. Rather, they presented an array of gifts, including an old sword, Waziristani daggers, prayer mats, *meswak* (wooden tooth brush) and *tasbeeh* (prayer beads) to the corps commander and other civil and military officers who accompanied him to Shakai.[39]

Nek agreed to stop support to the foreign jihadists and get all the foreigners living in the area registered with the government. In a video that did the rounds subsequently, Nek Muhammad was seen to be garlanding Lieutenant General Safdar Husain, head of Pakistan's XI corps and saying that "the most important thing is that we are Pakistani soldiers, too. The tribal people are Pakistan's atomic bomb. When India attacks Pakistan, you will see the tribal people defending 14,000 kilometres of the border."[40] General Husain representing the government agreed to release all prisoners, pay compensation to those dead and injured; and those who lost their houses and shops during the operation, and allow foreign militants to stay peacefully in the area after registration. The government allegedly paid about Rs 50 million to the tribal militants who wanted to pay up their debt to Al-Qaeda and return to the path of peace.[41] It should also be mentioned here that Gen Safdar got carried away during his speech and whether it was to placate the tribal sentiment or letting out the best-kept secret of the Pakistan army, he questioned US attack on Afghanistan by saying that when none of the twin tower attackers was an Afghan, it was not right on the part of the US to attack the Afghans!

The Shakai agreement was dishonoured in practice and Nek Muhammad refused to hand over foreign jihadists. Nek was too deeply engaged in the Al-Qaeda and Taliban network to recoil so fast so soon. He had, after his return from Afghanistan in 2001, set up training camps for Taliban in the suburb of Wana and amassed a grand fortune for himself. Unable to stick to the terms of the agreement that he would help the government in registering foreign operatives, he declared war on Pakistan in June. He began assassinating traditional tribal leaders to cut down government (read army) penetration into the area. On 18 June 2004, barely two months after the deal, Nek was to be the target of the first ever drone attack (by an American Predator UAV) in Pakistan. The army claimed the attack to hide the fact that it was acting in collusion with the US while tracking elements wanted by the US. But it did not remain secret for too long when commentators in the US, unready to leave the credit to the Pakistanis, spilled the beans about it soon afterwards, even if Pakistani agencies continued to claim the attack and deny any link with the US and called any such claim as "absolutely absurd".[42] A year later, when yet another drone attack on 3 December 2005 killed Abu Hamza Rabia, an Egyptian believed to be a senior Al-Qaeda operative in-charge of Al-Qaeda's external operations in Miramshah, North Waziristan, the Pakistani military continued to claim that it was the result of an explosion. It tried its best to hide the US connection. In fact, a local journalist Hayat Ullah Khan[43] was reportedly kidnapped two days later on 5 December 2005 by the agencies for having shot photographs of the remains of the US missile that targeted Rabia. His bullet-ridden body was found near Miramshah on 16 June 2006. Strangely, shortly before that the Pakistani authorities went public with their protest against US drone strikes at three houses in Damadola, Bajaur on 13 January 2006, which had resulted in the death of about 18 people. Apparently, the Americans were acting on information that Al-Qaeda leader Ayman al-Zawahiri was hiding there. Zawahiri was not there and the US claimed to have killed some Al-Qaeda operatives. However, exposure of US drone attack at this stage did not spare Hayat Ullah his life. It is quite another thing that the Pakistanis tamely covered up and supported similar drone attacks on Damadola in October 2006 and May 2008.

Interestingly, all this while since 9/11, there were several reports of ISI rescuing militants of all shades from Tora Bora following the October 2001 attack. One of them was especially telling in that it was based on the boastful confessions of an ISI agent who was apprehended by Afghan intelligence while spying on Indian agents in Kabul and kept in Pul-i-Charki prison, outside Kabul since

2007. The report appeared in 2011, where he claimed that he was a civilian employee of the ISI, recruited mainly for his knowledge of the mountain tracks through which he had led many militants—Pakistanis, Uzbeks, Chechens and many Arabs—into Pakistan from camps even belonging to Al-Qaeda in Afghanistan.[44] However, by 2004, the Pakistan army had started projecting itself as being too sincere in its attempts to haul up Al-Qaeda militants. The arrests of Sheikh Omar involved in the Daniel Pearl murder case in 2002, Al-Qaeda's No. 3 Abu Zubaida in March 2002 and top Al-Qaeda operative Khalid Sheikh Mahmood in March 2003 indicated that Pakistan was ready to oblige the Americans to some extent. However, in its efforts to retain its links with the Taliban, Pakistani army and intelligence were carefully selective in their approach towards the militants operating in the tribal areas.

Pakistani Taliban raises it Head

In South Waziristan, as in other areas of FATA, the army was guided more by its own sense of defeat than any promise made to the Americans to hunt down the bad-jihadi Al-Qaeda elements. Moreover, there must have been a creeping sense of insecurity among the army officials visiting the terrain more frequently since 2001-2002, keeping in view the assertion of the Islamist radical elements seeking to displace whatever rudimentary state administrative structure present in the terrain with an overtly Taliban-like system in the tribal areas.

Against this backdrop, Pakistan media reported about a video footage shot in Miramshah in late 2005, which alerted the Pakistanis to the reality of the Talibanisation of the tribal areas and the propensity of the people to bring in a Taliban-like system of governance in the area. The video footage was that of a public execution of some purported "criminals, drug pushers, bootleggers and extortionists", and gory scenes of their bodies hung from poles, eyes gouged out, and cash stuffed into their mouth, brought back the memories of Taliban in Afghanistan in 1994, when Kandahar witnessed the spectacle of some sodomisers hung from abandoned Soviet tanks by the roadside.[45]

This incident suggested that militant Islamism of the Taliban variety had come of age in Pakistan. Islamists like Sufi Muhammad (leader of Tehrik-e-Nifaz-e-Shariat-e-Muhammadi or TNSM) had started imposing Sharia on the people of Malakand division since 1992, even before Taliban emerged as a political force in Afghanistan. His campaign gained momentum after Taliban's success in Afghanistan. TNSM had under its sway Dir, Swat, Malakand and Bajaur. Similarly, Maulana Shami-ul-Haq (leader of his own faction of Jamiat-ul-Ulema-i-Islam) had been demanding Sharia-based Islamic rule since early 1990s. He had, in fact, prepared the Taliban foot-soldiers for Islamic militancy in his seminary at Akora Khatttak, i.e., Dar-ul-Uloom Haqania, which was the *alma mater* for most of the top Taliban leadership in Afghanistan.

There were also others like Mufti Shamzai of Binori mosque of Karachi, the ideological mentor of the Taliban and many such religious zealots in Pakistan who would subscribe to the idea of Islamicising politics in Pakistan. After Taliban overran Kabul in 1996, this constituency became restive and some of them sent their followers to Afghanistan to fight in support of Taliban. Interestingly, at least nine years before Tehrik-e-Taliban Pakistan (TTP) announced its formation in the Tribal areas, a local outfit calling itself Tehrik-e-Tulaba Pakistan (but also reported in the media as Tehrik-e-Taliban Pakistan) had started making its presence felt in Orakzai, and in clear disregard of the system in place in the area, this outfit had apprehended some criminals who were allegedly involved in some acts of murder and robbery and put them to justice in a Kangaroo court run by the local ulema and executed them in public in December 1998.[46] The inspiration for this had certainly come from the Taliban and TNSM, three years before 9/11.

The successful rise of Taliban in Afghanistan had also infused in the Islamists of Pakistan fond hopes of taking over Pakistan one day like the Taliban. Even Sufi Naqsbandi Maulana Akram Awan of Chakwal had made an attempt to march on Rawalpindi in March 2001, of course not in a militant way, with his demand of imposition of Sharia in Pakistan. General Musharraf had tough time persuading him to stop his sit-in demonstration in front of the Army General Headquarters

(GHQ) in Rawalpindi. After the fall of Taliban in late 2001, Pakistani militants siding with Taliban came back home to experiment with the Taliban precepts in the tribal hinterland and successfully made their writ run in local pockets in Waziristan, Bajaur, Malakand, Swat and even in Khyber. All this came to the fore in 2004-2005 with the resurgence of Taliban in Afghanistan and militant assertions of local Pakistani Taliban like the one in Miramshah described above. The assertion of the Ghazi brothers (Abdul Rashid Ghazi and Abdul Aziz) of the Lal Mosque at the heart of Islamabad since late 2005 made General Musharraf realise that forces sympathetic to Taliban were no longer localised in the tribal terrain. They had started spreading to other areas threatening the internal security of Pakistan and had challenged the writ of the Pakistani state.

Notes

1. There are several accounts of the fiercely independent and control-averse population of the tribal borderlands straddling British India and Afghanistan by English historians, administrators, journalists and soldiers written especially during the period stretching from the last decade of 19th century till the 1940s. There is a recurrence of views about the people and their disposition. A review of major writings on the theme has been provided later in Chapter ... in this book.

2. A puritanical version of Islam named after its place of origin, Deoband, in India. Many of the leading clerics in Pakistan, including Mufti Mahmud the father of the present leader of MMA, Maulana Fazlur Rehman, and Mufti Abdul Haq, the father of Shami-ul-Haq had graduated from this religious seminary.

3. Syed Saleem Shahzad, "Fighting talk from Osama and the Taliban", *Asia Times Online*, 25 April 2006.

4. Zahid Hussain, *Frontline Pakistan: The Struggle with Militant Islam*, I.B. Tauris, distributed by Palgrave Macmillan, 2006.

5. Many of the top leaders came from one madrassa, i.e., Darul Uloom Haqqania in Akora Khattak in the Manshra district of North West Frontier Province (NWFP) in Pakistan, which was run by Maulana Shamiul Haq.

6. Pakistani help often determined the stature of a group among other factions. The faction that was patronised by the Pakistani establishment usually attracted the largest share of Pakistani mujahideen. If it was Gulbuddin Hekmatyr's Hizb-e-Islami during the anti-Soviet jihad, it was certainly Taliban during the post-1994 days.

7. Zahid Hussain, "Pakistan's wild western faultline", *The Australian*, 31 March 2007.

8. Ibid.

9. Salem Safi, "Too little too late", *The News*, 24 August 2011.

10. "Parties reject FATA Reforms Commission proposals", 18 May 2015 at http://fatareforms.org/2015/05/18/parties-reject-fata-reforms-commission-proposals/

11. In the year 2006, the US National Intelligence estimate suggested in this vein that See "Trends in Global Terrorism: Implications for United States, April 2006 at http://www.dni.gov/press_releases/Declassified_NIE_Key_Judgments.pdf

12. TNSM was founded by Maulana Sufi Muhammad in May 1989 in Dir, after he left Jamat-i-Islami. It was responsible for a popular insurrection in favour of immediate imposition of Sharia in Malakand division in 1994 forcing the then governor of NWFP to come out with an ordinance to this effect. In 2001, on the eve of US attack on Afghanistan, the Maulana had mobilized thousands of volunteers from madrassas in Dir, Swat, Bajaur and Chitral to go across the border and join the ranks of the Taliban. The Maulana was arrested in November 2001 following the infamous Kunduz airlift which brought back some of the Pakistani volunteers along with their ISI handlers. Out of about six thousand recruits, only seventy returned with Sufi Muhammad. See Muhammad Amir Rana, *A to Z of Jehadi Organizations in Pakistan*, Mashal Books, Lahore, 2011, p. 183 and Ahmed Rashid, *Descent into Chaos: The United States and the Failure of Nation Building in Pakistan, Afghanistan, and Central Asia*, Viking Press, 2008, p. 160.

13. Pervez Musharraf, "Address to the Nation", 12 January 2002 at http://www.satp.org/satporgtp/countries/pakistan/document/papers/2002Jan12.htm

14. Report, "Descent into Anarchy", *The Herald*, March 2004, p. 61.

15. Syed Saleem Shahzad, "Beseiged in Shawal", *Asia Times online*, 1 May 2004 at http://www.atimes.com/atimes/South_Asia/FE01Df04.html

16. See Milan Hauner, "One Man against the Empire: The Faqir of Ipi and the British in Central Asia on the Eve of and during the Second World War", *Journal of Contemporary History*, Vol. 16, No. 1; The Second World War: Part 1, January 1981, pp. 183-212 at http://www.khyber.org/publications/021-025/faqiripi.shtml

17. See discussions on Talibanisation in North and South Waziristan in Anand Gopal, Mansur Khan Masud and Brian Fishman, "The Taliban in North Waziristan", (pp. 128-163) and Mansur Khan Masud, "The Taliban in South Waziristan", (pp. 164-201) in Peter Bergen, Katherine Tiedemann, eds., *Talibanistan: Negotiating the Borders Between Terror, Politics, and Religion*, Oxford University Press, New York, 2013.

18. Maulana Abdul Malik, local MNA from Muttahida Majlis-e-Amal (MMA) cited in Herald Report, "Descent into Anarchy", *The Herald*, March 2004, p. 62.

19. M. Ilyas Khan, "Who are these people?", *The Herald*, April 2004, p. 64.

20. Ibid., p. 67.

21. "Pakistan trying to stop attacks inside Afghanistan: Musharraf", *The Dawn*, 13 February 2004 at http://www.dawn.com/news/403858/pakistan-trying-to-stop-attacks-inside-afghanistan-musharraf

22. "Pakistan Braces for the American Storm", *Geopolitical Weekly*, Stratfor, 13 February 2004 at https://www.stratfor.com/weekly/pakistan_braces_american_storm

23. Douglas Frantz, "Pakistan Ended Aid to Taliban Only Hesitantly", *The New York Times*, 8 December 2001 at http://www.nytimes.com/2001/12/08/international/asia/08STAN.html?pagewanted=print

24. Musharraf stated: "Our critical concerns are our sovereignty, second our economy, third our strategic assets (nuclear and missiles), and forth our Kashmir cause. All four will be harmed if we make the wrong decision. When we make these decisions they must be according to Islam.... At this moment, we have to foil the designs of the enemy and to protect the interests of the country.... Pakistan is considered to be the fortress of Islam and if this fortress is harmed, Islam will be harmed ... at http://news.bbc.co.uk/2/hi/not_in_website/syndication/monitoring/media_reports/1553542.stm & https://presidentmusharraf.wordpress.com/2006/07/13/address-19-september-2001/)

25. Ahmed Rashid, "The U.S. Will Act Like a Wounded Bear: Pakistan's Long Search for Its Soul", *Descent into Chaos: The U.S. and the Disaster in Pakistan, Afghanistan, and Central Asia*, Viking, 2008, pp. 74-79.

26. See Kathy Gannon, *I Is for Infidel: From Holy War to Holy Terror: 18 Years Inside Afghanistan*, Public Affairs, New York, 2005, p. 94. Gannon writes, "Had he wanted to, Haqqani could have handed the United States the entire al-Qaeda network."

27. Cited in Michael Scheuer, "The Zawahiri-Zarqawi Letter: Al-Qaeda's Tactical and Theater-of-War Concerns", *Terrorism Focus*, Volume 2, Issue 21, 14 November 2005 at http://www.jamestown.org/programs/tm/single/?tx_ttnews%5Btt_news%5D=609&tx_ttnews%5BbackPid%5D=238&no_cache=1#.VbXSMfmqqko

28. Ibid.

29. See Syed Saleem Shahzad, "It's showdown time in Pakistan", *Asia Times Online*, 5 May 2006.

30. Ibid.

31. See report on HuMA at South Asia Terrorism Portal at http://www.satp.org/satporgtp/countries/Pakistan/terroristoutfits/HuMA.htm

32. In 2002, Kamran Atif a member of HuM-A tried to assassinate Gen Pervez Musharraf and he was arrested later in 2004 and sentenced to death in 2006 by the Anti-Terrorism court.

33. M. Ilyas Khan, "Profile of Nek Mohammad", *The Dawn*, 19 June 2004.

34. At the time of US attack the Uzbeks were located in Balkh in northern Afghanistan and they moved southward to escape into the tribal areas of Pakistan.

35. Farhat Taj goes to the extent of saying "The groups fighting in Pakistan, such as the TTP, were formed in the post-9/11 context in collusion with the intelligence establishment of Pakistan to ensure Pakistan's double role in the 'war on terror'." See her interview, "The Pashtuns want peace and plurality", Gateway House, 6 September 2013 at https://www.gatewayhouse.in/the-pashtuns-want-peace-and-plurality/

36. M. Ilyas Khan, "Who are these people?", *The Herald*, April 2004, p. 62.

37. "Tribal Justice", *The Herald*, April 2004, p. 72.

38. M. Illyas Khan, "Behind the Bluster", *The Herald*, April 2004, p. 67.

39. For details see, Rahimullah Yusufzai, "All Quiet on the North-Western Front", *Newsline*, May 2004.

40. Praveen Swami, "Such a long nightmare", *The Indian Express*, 19 December 2014 at http://indianexpress.com/article/opinion/columns/such-a-long-nightmare/#sthash.wLMVoipV.dpuf

41. Ismail Khan, "Payment to Wana militants: probe into missing millions initiated", *The Dawn*, 3 May 2005.

42. While disparate accounts of Pak-US deals appeared since late 2004 in Pakistani and international media, details of the secret deals emerged in an investigative piece in *The New York Times*, by Mark Mazetti on 6 April 2013. See Mark Mazzetti, "A Secret Deal on Drones, Sealed in Blood", *The New York Times*, 6 April 2013 at http://www.nytimes.com/2013/04/07/world/asia/origins-of-cias-not-so-secret-drone-war-in-pakistan.html?pagewanted=all&_r=0

43. See detailed reports about Hayat Ullah Khan at https://www.pbs.org/wgbh/pages/frontline/taliban/tribal/hayatullah.html

44. Dexter Filkins, "The Journalist And the Spies", *The New Yorker*, 19 September 2011.

45. For video clippings see the short film made by Martin Smith under the programme "Frontline" by Public Broadcasting Service (PBS), US, "Return of the Taliban", October 2006 at https://www.pbs.org/wgbh/frontline/film/taliban/

46. For details see *The News Line* (Karachi), January 1999.

3. Enter TTP: Formation and Growth

Post-Shakai Deals and Developments

After the failure of the Shakai deal, military action continued combined with mediation by political representatives from Maulana Fazlur Rehman's faction of JUI (JUI-F), which forced Nek Muhammad's successor, Haji Omar, a 55 year old fighter who hailed from Kalosha, and his colleagues to surrender in November-December 2004, as the government admitted to giving them US$ 540,000, ostensibly to repay their debts towards foreign militants.[1] No sooner than the Army thought it had tackled the Waziri militancy well, the Mehsud tribal belt erupted in late 2004. The military struck another deal at Sararogha in South Waziristan in February 2005 with Baitullah Meshud (1972-2009), who replaced Haji Omar as the leader of Pakistan Taliban, as the group tentatively called itself. Going by the terms of the deal, Baitullah agreed not to attack government functionaries and public property and not to harbour foreign militants. The government granted him and his men amnesty for their past actions, in return. Importantly, there was no prohibition on cross-border actions in the deal. Even then, the deal was violated by Baitullah and his men.

During this period, one-legged[2] Abdullah Mehsud (1977-2007), the Guantanamo-returned charismatic young militant briefly captured the imagination of the jihadis in the tribal areas. By some accounts, Baitullah regarded Abdullah as his mentor, even if he was five years younger to him in age. By other accounts, however, he was suspicious of Abdullah and regarded him as a double agent, because he did not trust Abdullah's account of his release from Guantanamo Bay. Known for his cruel disposition and association with both Taliban and Al-Qaeda, Abdullah was recognised as the *de facto* leader of the shadowy Pakistani Taliban group for quite some time. However, the local Taliban groups were reportedly unhappy with him for his involvement in the kidnapping and subsequent death of Chinese engineers working at a multi-million-dollar multi-purpose water project in the Gomal Zam area. Unwilling to antagonise the Pakistan army and the Chinese, they would, therefore, ask Abdullah to work closely with Afghan Taliban rather than complicate matters for them inside Pakistan. His influence gradually ebbed and after he committed suicide to evade capture by Pakistani security forces in Zhob while transiting from Helmand to South Waziristan on 24 July 2007, Baitullah emerged as the undisputed leader of the Taliban groups in Pakistan and held sway until he was killed by an American drone on 5 August 2009. Both Baitullah and Abdullah maintained close contact with Tahir Yuldashev, the fugitive leader of Islamic Movement of Uzbekistan, an affiliate of Al-Qaeda. Yuldashev was killed in another drone attack weeks after Baitullah's death in on 27 August 2009.

North Waziristan Operations

Just when the military claimed it had achieved peace in South, it faced increasing resistance from the militants in North Waziristan led by two clerics who were operating out of Miramshah—Abdul Khaliq and Sadiq Noor. The intensity of resistance was quite high and the tug of war went on through January and March 2006.

On 1 January 2006, the US drone allegedly attacked a cleric's house and in retaliation, the militants attacked a security check-post. Later, on 13 January 2006, a US drone attacked one suspected house upon information that Al-Qaeda leader, Al Zawahiri, was hiding there. On 1 March, Abdul Khaliq's madrassa in Dandy Saidgay in North Waziristan, was attacked by 12 army helicopters, exactly on the day the American President started his South Asian visit. The attack left 40 persons dead and many injured. This attack was followed by a suicide attack on the US embassy on 2 March 2006. On 9 March, madrassa of another important cleric, Sadiq Noor was attacked in his village at Khattay Killay.

The worst fears of the Pakistani government perhaps came true by the early 2006 as local Taliban presence in tribal areas surfaced in media reports. It was reported that local militants swearing allegiance to the Taliban had started imposing Taliban-style judicial system in parts of Waziristan and Bajaur by the end of 2005. Earlier assessment of a smoking-gun in the shape of isolated Islamist acts like imposition of ban on music or burning of electronic items in Malakand had suddenly morphed into a mushroom cloud.

Media reports in February-March 2006, carried interviews with Haji Omar[3] in South Waziristan who claimed that he was the head of 'Pakistani Taliban' in South Waziristan. In June 2006, he made his perspective immensely clear:

> I am not against Pakistan nor is Pakistan against me. If Pakistan goes against me, I will go against Pakistan. America is against us. America and its friends.... We have started jihad against them. In every country where they are being brutal, we will try to do jihad against them....They have become united to finish Muslims and God willing, we will unite to finish them. This process will continue.[4]

While the umbilical cord joining Pakistani Taliban with Taliban and Al-Qaeda might not be too easy to sever, there appeared to be a realisation dawning on the Pakistani militants that they should not antagonise the Pakistani state unnecessarily. Nevertheless, as Haji Omar's statement cited above would suggest, they would not hesitate to take on the Pakistan state if it acted against them. It also showed that the anti-US and anti-West feelings were visceral and it would take long before the tribal terrain shunned jihad and militancy.

By July 2006, the situation had worsened enough for Musharraf, who was, until then, not too much vocal about Taliban, to admit in Brussels:

The centre of gravity of terrorism has shifted from Al Qaeda to Taliban, this is a new element which has emerged, more dangerous element because it has roots in the people, Al Qaeda did not have roots in the people so Taliban are more organised, they have roots in the people and Talibanisation may I say is a separate thing altogether.[5]

Subsequently he even went to the extent of saying that he had "reports that some dissidents, some retired people who were in the forefront in ISI during the period of 1979 to 1989 may be assisting the links somewhere here and there" in an interview with NBC Television's "Meet the Press".[6]

Waziristan Accord on 5 September 2006

It was interesting to observe, on the face of regular artillery and gunship attack on local clerics, that the Taliban militants in North Waziristan, declared a unilateral conditional ceasefire in June 2006.[7] They laid down the conditions that Pakistan would have to withdraw its troops and stop targeting them. In return, they would not shelter any foreign militants.[8] This truce was extended in July for another month. While attacks continued on both the sides, in spite of the truce, on 5 September, the Pakistani government struck a deal known as the "Waziristan Accord" with the militants. Subsequent reports in the media suggested that Taliban leaders, Jalaluddin Haqqani, (1939 – 3 September 2018) and Mullah Dadullah, (1966 – 13 May 2007) had personally endorsed the June 2006 ceasefire offer by the Pakistani Taliban in North Waziristan[9] and later the 5 September deal was approved by Mullah Omar.[10] In accordance with the terms of the Accord, the government reportedly released many militants having links with Taliban.[11] The Taliban, however, went on killing suspected informers, castigating them as spies of the US.

There was massive criticism of the deal in the US media and security establishment. It was regarded as a brazen surrender of the Pakistani state. Some commentators wrote that Waziristan would "serve as a training base for Al-Qaeda operatives of all stripes".[12] Some of the well-known Pakistani observers like Rahimullah

Yusufzai argued that the deals had "empowered the militants, enhancing their status in the tribal society and prompting the common people to approach the pro-Taliban ulema and military commanders instead of the government to settle local disputes and solve their problems."[13] Some others called it a policy of "Hello-Al Qaeda, Good Bye America".[14] But Pakistani authorities claimed that the deal kept North Waziristan relatively quiet even when US intelligence reports said that the number of cross-border attacks increased from 40 in the two months before the pact to 140 in the two months afterwards.[15]

It took another heavy strike in Hamazola village near Razmak in North Waziristan, on 16 January 2007 for the September deal to die its natural death. The attack killed 11 militants of the Arab origin, in a missile attack at a cluster of compounds allegedly belonging to Baitullah Mehsud in Salamat village, Hamzola. Baitullah came out with a statement that echoed Haji Omar's statement quoted earlier: "As far as Jihad is concerned, we will continue to wage it. We will do what is in the interest of Islam ... Islam does not recognise any borders and for us Islam comes first, before Pakistan".[16] The suicide attacks increased after this attack. It was reported that Baituallah Mehsud and his aides imposed their writ in entire Waziristan by early 2007.

Bajaur Aflame

The whole region flared up again after attack on the Chengai hamlet in Damadola, Bajaur on 30 October 2006, which reportedly killed 80 Al-Qaeda militants. There were reports that the attack was conducted primarily by the fixed wing US drones even if the Pakistani government claimed the operations were carried out by Pakistani military.[17] Some analysts argued that the attack by US might have been aimed at scotching the move[18] by Pakistani government to enter into yet another deal with Bajaur militants. The militants avenged this with a suicide attack on Pakistani Army training base at Dargai, in the then NWFP killing 42 army cadets. This had a ripple effect in the tribal areas. Other suicide attacks on security forces continued. However, the government could finally pressurise the local Taliban in Bajaur to sign a five-point undertaking (to be distinguished from a deal). It was signed by 800 local tribal elders with indirect approval by local Taliban leader Maulana Faqir Mohammad, on 26 March 2007.[19]

Later, one saw Pakistani Taliban threatening to fan out into the adjoining settled areas of Bannu, Tank, Kohat, Dera Ismail Khan and Peshawar. The militants were seen to be adopting suicide tactics which was interpreted as a quantum turn in their approach to match and deter military attacks. As the situation worsened, the militants targeted pro-government tribal elders on regular basis and the figure went up to 150 for the year.[20] In all these deals, the JUI-F played a significant role in drawing the militants into the discussions; however, their involvement could not ensure the success of the deals.

The Local versus Foreign Militants

In the midst of rising criticism of the policy of appeasement of tribal militants,[21] the situation turned for the better for the military regime in Pakistan when the central Asian militants took on the local militants in March 2007 in Waziristan. As per media reports, the local Taliban retaliated with all their might and the Pakistani security forces struck a chord of unity with Mullah Nazir, the Taliban commander for Waziristan, who reportedly undertook a vow to remove all Uzbek militants from the area. The government joined the pro-Taliban militants in a bid to oust the foreign militants.[22] The whole episode came as a respite and a bonanza for the government, which projected it as a proof of its policy succeeding in the area. This also induced a false sense of confidence and complacency in Musharraf, which was visible in the piquant way in which he addressed an international gathering of Land Forces Symposium in Islamabad. In his unique style of resorting to media diplomacy, he took on his detractors head on and said that if the blame-game continued (that Pakistan was not doing enough), then he was ready to pull out of the coalition against terror.[23]

The Case of Lal Masjid

The Lal Masjid or Red Mosque, one of the oldest mosques in the capital city of Islamabad was built out of government funds (Ministry of Finance) by Capital Development Authority (CDA), Islamabad, in the early 1960s. Maulana Muhammad Abdullah Ghazi (1935-1998) was appointed its first Imam or prayer leader in 1966. Hailing from a village named Basti-Abdullah near Rajanpur, in south-western Punjab, Ghazi belonged to the Mazari tribe of Balochistan. His father, Ghazi Muhammad, was regarded as a rebel and imprisoned by the British. He received education in a madrassa and later sent to the famous Deobandi Jamiat Uloom-ul Islamia madrassa in Banoori (also written as Banuri) Town in Karachi (estd. 1954), where he became a favourite student of Maulana Muhammad Yusuf Banuri (1908-1977).

Muhammad Abdullah Ghazi founded many seminaries including *Jamia Fareediya* for boys and also a madrassa for girls, *Jamia Hafsa*, which was the first of its kind in Pakistan. He was appointed as Chairman of Ruet-e-Hilal committee in 1977. He was opposed to most of the Pakistani rulers and played a critical role in inciting the people against Zulfikar Ali Bhutto in the capital city in 1977, finally leading to Bhutto's fall.

He was treated with respect by Zia-ul-Haq and played a significant role in mobilising recruits from Pakistan to fight the Soviet forces in Afghanistan alongside the mujahideen groups. In 1981, Zia allocated funds generously for restructuring of the mosque. After Soviet withdrawal, when the Taliban rose to power, Maulana Abdullah Ghazi developed good relations with Taliban and Al-Qaeda, which can be gleaned from the fact that he led a group of scholars, including his younger son, Abdul Rashid Ghazi, in October 1998, immediately after August 1998 Operation Infinite Reach (OIR) by the US, to meet Mullah Omar, Osama Bin Laden and Ayman Al Zawahiri among others. Under suspicious circumstances, he was assassinated within the precincts of the Red Mosque in 17 October 1998, a week after his return from Afghanistan. His elder son Abdul Aziz, who was with him during the assassination, managed to survive the attack.

Rashid Ghazi, his younger son, had infamously dared the Americans by way of responding to OIR that "The USA's troops will enter Afghanistan in tanks and planes yet they will leave Afghanistan only in body bags like their predecessor [the Soviet Union]".[24] His life embodied the spirit of radical Islam that engulfed Pakistan in the 1980s and 1990s. Born in January 1964, he was raised for the early part of his childhood in Basti-Abdullah, his parental home. Shifting to Islamabad after his father was appointed Imam of the Lal Mosque, he took to secular education in a Federal Government School, disregarding his father's advice to join religious education in a madrassa, and excelled in studies. However, in the 1980s, he joined the Afghan Jihad and after Soviet pull-out he rejoined his studies and completed his Masters in International Relations from Qaid-e-Azam University, Islamabad, in early 1990s. He even served briefly at the Ministry of Education in Islamabad, and later at the United Nations Educational, Scientific and Cultural Organisation (UNESCO). He edited *"Diyami"*, the monthly magazine of the Ministry of Education, while serving there. Despite his training in secular education, he remained very conservative at heart, like many Jihadis of his time. An interesting anecdote from his life attests to the fact of his having been attracted by the concept of global jihad. While touring Afghanistan with his father in 1998, he begged for a separate conversation with Bin Laden which was granted to him. It lasted for over an hour and at the end of it, he drank left-over water from the glass of Bin Laden and upon being asked by the latter as to why he did it, he reportedly said that by drinking Bin Laden's left-over he wished to be a warrior in the path of Allah like him!

His father's assassination left him and his elder brother Maulana Abdul Aziz devastated. Against the wishes of his brother, Abdul Aziz, who had received much of his education in madrassas and especially at his father's alma mater at Banuri Town, he lodged an FIR (first information report) with the police and sensed state collusion in his father's assassination, when a person involved in the case according to eye-witnesses was released without any convincing reason days after his arrest. He was reportedly asked by powerful people in the establishment not to pursue the matter failing which he was threatened to meet the same fate as his father. From this point onwards, in his life, Rashid Ghazi developed a grouse against the system/establishment. By this time, his elder brother, Abdul Aziz had succeeded his father as the Khateeb or Imam of the mosque and Rashid Ghazi helped him in running the madrassas. He would begin teaching history, English and philosophy, what he was good at, because of his secular education. He was given the post of Naib-Khatib (Vice Prayer Leader) and Vice Chancellor of *Jamia Fareediya*. It was from this time onwards that he criticised the state's policies and his voice grew shriller in the aftermath of 9/11, when Musharraf administration, under threat of being bombed-to-stone-age, did a policy somersault on Afghanistan. He became an ardent critic of Pakistan joining the war on terror being steered by the US. One of his quotes summarises his position against the Pakistan army:

"We have neither killed anyone nor have we committed any crime for so many of our children to be murdered here each day as a punishment. We believe that if even a few people stand up to a large army, they can confront it if they are on the Truth; and we are on the Truth—that is why we have been able to fight them for so long."[25]

During these days, Red Mosque acted as a nerve centre for radical Islamist activities. By early 2007, in fact, the Maulana siblings had started taking a militant position on the issue of bringing Islamic rule to Pakistan. The students of the seminaries attached to Lal Masjid (*Jamia Fareediya* for boys and *Jamia Hafsa* for girls) took control of a public library in February 2007 in protest against the government's move to demolish some mosques constructed illegally on government lands in Islamabad. Emboldened by the approach of the Musharraf government to deal with the issue through negotiations, the students went out of the mosque into the city and closed down music shops, burnt down music cassettes and CDs and shut down beauty parlours. They even attacked the Pakistani Rangers guarding the office of Ministry of Environment and burnt down part of its premises. The Maulana brothers even issued a fatwa saying they would impose Sharia in Pakistan soon. When the state wanted to intervene, they took some policemen hostage. The government was seen to be ignoring such intense provocations and stooping to their demands for the release of the policemen.

There were allegations that Musharraf government, under heavy criticism over the case of suspension of the then Chief Justice of Pakistan, allowed the Lal Masjid issue to fester as a diversionary tactic. However, the situation came to a head with the abduction of some Chinese lady-workers from a beauty parlour in Islamabad in early July 2007 and the Pakistani state had to intervene through a direct military operation, codenamed 'Operation Silence' to flush out militants from the mosque. The operation led to the death of Abdul Ghazi Rashid. The elder brother, Abdul Aziz, was rounded up while reportedly trying to escape wearing a burqa, and kept under custody. The version provided by the Red Mosque was different, however. According to it, Abdul Aziz was called 'by a senior Government official with whom he had been in touch for a long time' to negotiate peace between him and the government. Since this man could have entered into the mosque to meet him, he asked Aziz to come down to Aabpara police station, close to the mosque and asked him to wear a burqa to avoid identification. When Aziz came out of the mosque, he was arrested immediately and this was portrayed on national television as if he was trying to escape. Aziz lost his only son, Hassan Ghazi, during the operation. He was released on 16 April 2009 at the order of the Supreme Court, which held that he was on trial for falsely accused charges of murder, incitement and kidnapping. Today, he remains the Khateeb of the Red Mosque and the chancellor of both *Jamia Hafsa* and *Jamia Fareediya*.

The reaction to the army's 'Operation Silence' of July 2007 was on expected lines. There were several cases of bomb blasts and suicide attacks throughout Pakistan. But most of them occurred in the Pashtun dominated north western Pakistan. Pakistani sources point out to a sudden spurt in conservative assertion in the tribal areas following the Red Mosque operation. In one particular case, Abdul Wali Raghib, also known as Omar Khalid Khorasani in the Mohmand Agency led a group of enthusiastic militant Islamists and occupied a famous local mosque in a village called Ghaziabad and renamed it as Lal Masjid (Red Mosque). He was later recognised as chief of TTP, Mohmand Agency, once TTP was formed in December 2007. In Waziristan, the militants responded by attacking army check posts and soldiers. A suicide bomber attacked a Pakistan Army convoy killing 25 soldiers and wounding 54 on 14 July 2007. Two suicide bombers attacked another Army convoy killing 16 soldiers, 5 civilians and wounding another 47 people on 15 July 2007. In yet another incident, on the same day, a suicide bomber attacked a police station killing 28 police officers.

The Pakistani state, as a follow-up action, attacked militant hideouts primarily in Waziristan and Bajaur, but also elsewhere along the Pakistan-Afghanistan border. In one such case in Zhob, in north-Balochistan, Abdullah Mehsud, one of the dreaded Taliban sympathisers and companion of Baitullah Mehsud, unable to escape the security raid, committed suicide in late July 2007. While the army operations, well-coordinated by American intelligence and tactical help, are still on, even after Zarb-e-Azb (Sharp and Cutting Strike)[26] launched in 2014, the Pakistani State has failed to diagnose the problem well because of which the TTP continues to raise its head even after humongous kinetic action by the army in the tribal belt. There is hardly any realisation that it has failed to tackle the whirlwind primarily because it has unwittingly nourished Taliban-like elements through its policy of active encouragement of radical forces as an instrument of its foreign policy vis-à-vis Afghanistan and Kashmir.

That the Lal Masjid operation continued to provoke the Islamists, years after its execution, can be gleaned from the fact that many terror acts were connected to the incident in the following years. In one such incidents, on 3 March 2014, an Additional Sessions Judge (ASJ) in the Islamabad district court, Rafaqat Ahmad Awan, was taken out by two suicide bombers when the latter was hearing a case in his courtroom. The judge was targeted, it was suspected, because he had rejected a petition in April 2013 for registration of an FIR against former president General (retd.) Pervez Musharraf for killing students during the Lal Masjid operation, saying: "The petition has been filed to gain cheap popularity".[27] The attacks was claimed by a group called Ahrar-ul Hind (Liberators of India) and the TTP disowned it. The attack took place against the backdrop of talks between the TTP and the government by this group which was regarded as a split-away faction of TTP, which opposed dialogue with the government. The attack claimed 11 lives. Clearly, splinter groups affiliated with the TTP pulled in several ways, even of the TTP-central rooted for dialogue. However, dialogue with TTP would lead nowhere, as would be seen later, and the TTP would continue to invoke the spirit of Lal Masjid on the anniversary of the attack. The latest being on 10 July 2020, when the TTP went to the extent of saying: "The tragedy of Lal Masjid and Jamia Hafsa would even make historic tyrants like Genghis Khan, Hulagu Khan and Hitler, feel ashamed of such an act."[28]

Musharraf's Approach: More Carrot Less Stick for Taliban

It is generally observed that the military regime headed by Musharraf adopted a *more-carrot-less-stick approach* towards the militants in the FATA.[29] Musharraf was soft on Taliban because he was aware of his limitations as the head of an establishment which had raised the Taliban and had deep association with it, till his abrupt somersault in the aftermath of 9/11. Musharraf was also extremely aware of the *disinclination among the Pashtun component within the army to take on fellow Pashtuns* in the tribal areas. The Frontier Corps (FC)—a paramilitary force stationed in the area, led by Pakistan army officers—which was primarily in charge of ground operations there, was overwhelmingly Pashtun in composition.

As per reports, since 2004, there were many desertions from the FC. One Major General from the Orakzai tribe preferred premature retirement to joining the army operations against Pashtuns. Some other Pashtun colonels were also posted out of the terrain for expressing their reservations in the army operations. As per the estimates provided by Hassan Abbas,[30] the Pashtuns constitute about 20-25 per cent of the Pakistan armed forces and at the level of officer they have a fairly good representation of about 15-22 per cent. Hence, it was difficult for Musharraf to disregard this reality. He could not have afforded to repeat his Balochistan policy in the tribal areas for fear of division within the army and a serious backlash at the political level by the Islamist parties. In fact, the bulk of the leadership of the Islamist groups came from the Pashtun community and the religious parties tended to have a dent in the Pashtun-dominated areas of Pakistan, spread across NWFP, the erstwhile FATA and northern Balochistan.

If one follows Musharraf's public utterances against terror, he was always *more critical of Al-Qaeda* than *Taliban*. He seemed to make a distinction between the Al-Qaeda and the Taliban and between the 'foreign militants' and the domestic ones. His autobiography released in October 2006 devoted more space to Al-Qaeda than to the Taliban. And his discussions on Taliban lacked the punch and the bite that he reserved for Al-Qaeda. Perhaps, he sought to convince his interlocutors in the West that he could not be harsh on his own people in the tribal areas who felt it natural to come to the rescue of their co-ethnic Pashtun people across the border. He argued very convincingly that he had managed to shatter Al-Qaeda networks in the region, severing its lateral and vertical linkages, but towards the close of the year 2006, the US asked Musharraf to do more to contain both Al-Qaeda and Taliban. However, by capturing many Al-Qaeda dregs so far and reportedly turning them over to US security agencies for a well-bargained price, Musharraf administration succeeded in convincing the US that there could never have been a better alternative to him and his strategy in Pakistan.[31]

Duplicity in Approach

Musharraf's reluctance to carry out large-scale attacks on tribal militants was borne out by the fact that most of the high-impact and heavy-casualty attacks on either madrassas or private houses in the tribal areas were coordinated with US forces or carried out by the latter alone.[32] This was followed, in some cases, by condemnation of US action by Musharraf's government as irresponsible, and as an assault on the sovereignty of Pakistan.[33] Musharraf was coy about taking on the Afghan Taliban in spite of the increasing proofs of their deep linkages with the Pakistani Taliban, which was posing a critical challenge to Pakistan army and the state. While it is true that Pakistan Taliban mostly tried to dig its heels deeper in the tribal terrain in Pakistan, its growing assertion and capacity in the tribal belt served as a force-multiplier for the resurgent Taliban forces active in Afghanistan. Pakistani Taliban did indeed provide the latter with shelter and active moral support. The policy followed by Musharraf's successor as the army chief, General Ashfaq Parvez Kayani was not much different. The latter tried his best to prove to the Americans his sincerity in executing the operations against an assertive Taliban especially in the tribal belt, while in reality he was seen to be hesitating, like his predecessor, to take military action beyond a point. If the army chose to take action later under the leadership of Kayani's successor almost a decade hence, it was more because of active provocation by the Pakistani Taliban than because of any conviction from within that such action was absolutely necessary. More of that would be dealt with later in the book.

The democratic government led by Asif Ali Zardari that assumed office since 2008 after almost nice years of military dictatorship, could not much alter the overall direction of the governmental policy towards the militancy primarily in the tribal belt, but also elsewhere in the country, gathering further momentum since 2008. In fact, following the attack on Red Mosque and army operations in the tribal areas, the resolve of the militants to take on the might of the Pakistani state seemed to grow exponentially. The TTP militants went on a mad spree from the end of 2007 throughout the year 2008 as can be gauged from the following attacks—twin attacks on Benazir Bhutto (October and December 2007), the attack on a meeting of tribal elders on 2 March 2008, the sectarian attack on Shias of Kurram in August 2008, the Mariott bombing of September 2008, and attacks on security forces throughout the year. Most of these attacks were traced to the tribal areas and claimed by the TTP.

There are other accounts by the analysts in the West that the Pakistani government's *relationship with Afghan Taliban may persist for long* given the sympathy in the establishment towards them. There are reports that the strategic somersault by Musharraf after 9/11 did not go down well with the rank and file of the Pakistan army[34] and lower ranks continued to retain their links with the Taliban, not unknown to the top leadership, who allowed it to remain as it is for possible use in future, in case there was a change in the ground situation. At the top level, therefore, there was a tendency to overlook this inertial relationship at the lower levels, in anticipation of Taliban's role in any future set-up in Afghanistan.[35] Conversations with observers on the ground in Pakistan revealed that the Pakistan army deeply believed that the US would not be there for the long haul and as and when they would leave the scene, the return of the Taliban was inevitable. Therefore, it was considered prudent for the army to maintain linkages with para-Taliban groups and affiliates. Concomitantly, there was a dominant view outside Pakistan that Taliban continued to remain in the shadow of the Pakistani intelligence and posed critical problems for reconstruction efforts in Afghanistan. Since mid-2006, therefore, the US adopted a proactive policy over the issue of militancy in the tribal areas, primarily orchestrated by the shadowy group called Pakistani Taliban. This could be gauged from the upscaling of drone attacks from 2007 onward. There were 386 drone strikes between June 2004, when Nek Muhammad was killed and June 2015, out of which 375 strikes took place between 2008 and 2015.[36] The two Waziristans accounted for 96 per cent of the strikes—73 per cent of these attacks targeted North Waziristan while 23 per cent attacks targeted South Waziristan.

That Pakistan continued to hobnob with Afghan Taliban all this while and tried to use its leadership to calm down the tribal militants is a fact which is quite well-known. Pakistan army even tried to divide the groups and soften up some of the militant leaders, which explained the defection of leaders like Mullah Nazir (1975-2013) and Hafiz Gul Bahadur (1961-) to the pro-government camp. Both of them, distrustful of the Mehsuds under Baitullah's leadership, even formed a Waziri alliance called the *Muqami Tehrik-e-Taliban* (Local Talban Movement) in July 2008. Pakistan army offered a lot of concessions in return for their position against the groups harbouring foreign militants (read mostly Uzbeks). Both these groups later turned against the Pakistani state provoking attacks from the army. Gul Bahadur was known to maintain close links with the Haqqani group of Taliban and his group was the target of various US drone attacks despite the fact that he had struck a deal with the Pakistan army not to attack its interest. In one major drone attack in the Dattakhel area on 17 March 2011, Gul Bahadur lost one of his trusted commanders, Sherbet Khan Wazir, following which he realised that even if he compromised with the Pakistan army, he would not be safe from US attacks. Indeed, the then army chief of Pakistan, Gen Kayani condemned the attack in no uncertain terms saying it was "in complete violation of human rights" and that such aggression was "unjustified and intolerable under any circumstances", which could not have convinced Gul Bahadur to trust Pakistan Army with his security. It is believed that following this, he was cautious about his relations with the Pakistan Army and subsequent to the 2014 operations,[37] he fled to Afghanistan, only to return in 2018-19 reportedly to base himself in a place called "Gurwek—a historic village of North Waziristan because of its role in Pashtuns' resistance against British forces in 1930s—near Afghan border".[38] Mullah Nazir was killed in a drone attack on 2 January 2013.

The Pakistani vacillation on how to effectively deal with militants in the tribal belt can be understood in terms of the political compulsions of different regimes in power. The military regime of Musharraf had its own compulsions while the democratic forces have their own too. The army responsible for the overall policy towards these militants has its own constraints too. Steve Coll,[39] known for his incisive analysis of the Afghan situation and the development of Taliban and Al-Qaeda would argue that the state of Pakistan does not have a clear-cut policy vis-à-vis the tribal belt. He would argue that the authorities have found it useful to just "to renew the approach to managing the frontier that dated back to the British period, which was essentially to operate through cooption, bribery and the construction of infrastructure, to find political intermediaries in villages and towns on the frontier who would be willing to work with the Pakistan army in order to reap the benefits of the Pakistan army's patronage."[40] There are others who would argue that even before a moderate approach was duly tried by the government, Pakistan army was pushed down a confrontationist path unnecessarily by the US.[41]

The governments in Islamabad, both civilian and military, have also not demonstrated enough grit to have a military solution and have returned to crack unworkable deals in situations which have reflected badly on their ability to uphold the agreements and demonstrate the strength and willingness to counter the militants.

TTP: Movement of the Islamic Students of Pakistan

The Tehrik-e-Taliban Pakistan (TTP) was formed as an umbrella group on 14 December 2007 to bring together more than 30 disparate pro-Taliban jihadi groups operating in the tribal areas of Pakistan comprising FATA, PATA and adjacent regions of Khyber Pakhtunkhwa (KP). The new organisation formed under the leadership of now deceased Baitullah Mehsud (1972-2009) sought to co-ordinate the activities of different groups and pool their resources to put up a common font against Pakistan state's efforts to control them through coercive tactics. Most individual groups constituting TTP are recognised by their leaders in different pockets of the tribal agencies and frontier regions and were loosely identified as Pakistani Taliban by outside observers. Apart from resident groups from tribal agencies, many outside groups and individuals from Central Asia, the Middle East, Xinjiang region of China, North Africa, European and Asian countries as well as other provinces of Pakistan also joined TTP as constituents making it a powerful jihadi conglomerate. According to some investigative accounts from Pakistan, the Punjabi group within the TTP—consisting of runaway leaders and foot-soldiers of sectarian Lashkar-e-Jhangvi (LeJ) and various India-focused jihadi groups like Lashkar-e-Taiba (LeT), Jaish-e-Muhammad (J-e-M), Harkat-ul-Mujahideen (HuM), factions of Harkat-ul-Jihad-al-Islami (HUJI) and some neo-Taliban groups—has been able to hold the outfit together by focusing on the media and publications section and maintaining linkages with like-minded groups in whole of Pakistan. Some observers would even assert that many of these non-tribal elements are affiliated to Al-Qaeda and manage to influence TTP's ideological outlook. The TTP publication, *Nawa-i-Afghan Jihad* which had a savvy online run from January 2009 till March 2020 was supposedly run by the Punjabi clique with overt sympathies for Al Qaeda, within TTP. This monthly magazine was published in Urdu with a deliberate attempt to communicate primarily with the urdu-speaking audience in Pakistan and showcase the viewpoint as well as achievements of the TTP mujahideen. The Umar Media which has been aggressively putting forward TTP's viewpoint communicates both in Urdu and English language.

Another affiliate of TTP, TNSM, based in the PATA is much older than most of the groups within TTP and aims at bringing Sharia to Pakistan. It is known for its rigid and inflexible position on Islam. Most of these, however, subscribe to an extreme form of Deobandi philosophy bordering on Wahabism. They are divided on tribal lines but display a strange sense of unity in the face of external threat or attack. During the attack on Lal Masjid and *Jamia Hafsa* in Islamabad in July 2007, these groups came together to extend their unstinted support to the Maulana brothers—Abdul Rashid Ghazi (who was killed in the operation) and Abdul Aziz, who was later nominated by TTP[42] as one of the interlocutors from its side when the Nawaz Sharif government proposed a dialogue in 2014. Thanks to the connection TTP has maintained through its Punjabi cadres it has managed to develop a Pan-Pakistan appeal, if not influence. The appeal may be limited, but it is there unmistakably.

The TTP was formed at the initiative of forces aligned with Al-Qaeda and the Haqqani group operating out of the tribal agencies, more specifically, North Waziristan.[43] In the face of increasing operations by Pakistani security forces under pressure from the US, there was an effort to gather all the tribal militant groups under one umbrella and consolidate their position in the area. After the death of Nek Muhammad, Baitullah Mehsud, who had signed the Shakai agreement with his face wrapped in a muffler, had made an impression among the militants as a diehard Islamist and after the death of Abdullah Mehsud he had emerged as a militant who could assume leadership of a coalition of militant groups. Some Pakistani sources say that the Abdullah Mehsud faction, which was then led by Qari Zainuddin Mehsud, was opposed to Baitullah's nomination; however, there was a larger consensus among 30 odd groups to have Baitullah as the *amir* of the new outfit, TTP, and Hafiz Gul Bahadur, a Waziri, mostly operating in North Waziristan agency was chosen as his deputy or *naib amir*. Qari Zainuddin, cousin of Abdullah Mehsud, continued to oppose Baitullah, along with Tank-based former member of the Frontier Corps, Turkestan Bhittani, for conducting suicide attacks inside Pakistan, which led many to believe that Qari was acting at the behest of the military. There was also a personal angle to Qari's opposition to Baitullah because the latter was involved in the killing of many of Qari's family members including his father. He was finally assassinated by his own personal body guard in June 2009 months before Baitullah's death. Baituallah operated in South Waziristan until his death on 23 August 2009 from wounds sustained in a US unmanned aerial vehicle (UAV) missile strike on 5 August 2009.

The group's *shura* (council) selected Hakimullah Mehsud (1979-2013), operating mainly in Orakzai, Kurram and Khyber agencies as Baitullah's successor on 22 August, a day before Baitullah died. Hakimullah, whose original name was Zulfiqar, served as a bodyguard of Baitullah and rose to prominence by planning and executing audacious attacks on Pakistan security forces. Hailing from Kotkai region in South Waziristan, he received his early education in a local madrassa in Hangu and then went on to join militancy in the wake of US attack on Taliban in 2001-2002. He became close to Baitullah and established himself as a dare-devil fighter, much like Nek Muhammad and achieved notoriety with his handling of AK 47 and maneuvering of Toyota pick-up trucks with amazing skill. He organised the capture of around 300 Pakistani soldiers in 2007 and was regarded as the mastermind behind attacks on NATO supply trucks. He was made commander of TTP in Khyber, Orakzai and Kurram.

Hakimullah's selection was also not received well among some of the top militant leaders. Faqir Muhammad, TTP chief of Bajaur, had already declared himself chief of TTP when he heard of Baitullah's demise. Waliur Rahman (1970-2013), a Mehsud from South Waziristan, also reportedly staked his claim for leadership which led to a fight between him and Hakimullah. Finally, Hakimullah was chosen as the amir and Waliur Rehman became his principal deputy. Under Hakimullah, TTP orchestrated some of the most ruthless attacks inside Pakistan while Waliur Rahman concentrated more on Afghanistan. According to reports, In 2010, Hakimullah appeared in a farewell video alongside a Jordanian militant, in which the latter claimed responsibility for a suicide attack in Afghanistan in which seven CIA agents were killed.[44] He maintained covert linkages with Al-Qaeda and other extremist militant groups spread across Pakistan which included Lashkar-e-Taiba, Harkat-ul-Ansar and even Jaish-e-Muhammad. However, Rahman played a key role in generating funds through ransom, kidnapping and smugglings through his faction's operatives in Karachi. Despite the fact that Waliur Rahman was regarded as a moderate within Pakistan and was open to the idea of dialogue with Pakistani authorities, he was a dreaded militant whose contribution to strengthening of TTP's position was immense.[45]

Hakimullah was killed in a drone strike in North Waziristan on 1 November 2013. By then, his deputy, Waliur Rehman, regarded as the main strategist of TTP, had already been killed in a drone attack in May 2013, on suspicion of his involvement in the suicide bomb attack that killed seven CIA employees at Forward Operating Base Chapman in Khost, Afghanistan, in December 2009. Khalid Mehsud alias Khan Saeed Sajna (1973-8 February 2018), who succeeded Waliur Rahman to head the TTP faction in South Waziristan agency, was initially reported as the front runner for assuming the leadership of TTP.[46] A local shura, in fact, named him as the successor. However, the central shura of TTP finally chose Maulana Qazi Fazlullah, son-in-law of Sufi Muhammad heading TTP faction in Swat and also amir of the TNSM, by lot (qurayndaazi) to succeed Hakimullah on 7 November 2013. The Mehsuds of the area who traditionally dominated TTP were reportedly unhappy with the selection process and Mehsud forces more or less functioned as independent militant outfits pledging their loyalty to Mullah Omar without actively supporting Fazlullah's leadership of TTP. Later in February 2017, the TTP announced that Khan Saeed Sajna also known as Khalid Mehsud had rejoined TTP and appointed deputy chief of the outfit.

At one point of time in his college days, Khan Saeed was a follower of Tablighi Jamaat and also worked for Jamiat ul Ulema-e-Islam-Fazlur (JUI-F). Hailing from Sara Rogha in Ladha subdivision, South Waziristan, he served as Fazlullah's deputy and concentrated his attention on Waziristan, until his death in a drone strike on 8 February 2018 in Kharh Tangi area (Barmal district) in Paktia province of Afghanistan, bordering Pakistan, in an area where the TTP and Haqqani faction of Taliban hold sway. He was supposed to have collaborated in the planning for attack on Mehran naval base in May 2011 and masterminded the Banu jailbreak in 2012, leading to release of over 400 inmates, many of them belonging to TTP.

Another group representing TTP of Mohmand agency led by Omar Khalid Khorasani which split away in February 2014 over the issue of Fazlullah's decision to have dialogue with the government called itself Ahrar-ul-Hind (more details about the split is provided below). Initially thought of as a ploy by TTP to carry out attack under the veil of deniability, the group later merged with other dissident factions of TTP to form TTP Jamiat-ul-Ahrar (JuA) in August 2014. According to media reports, Maulan Qasim Khurasani was the Ameer of JuA and its shura included Omar Khalid Khorasani from Mohmand, Qari Shakil Haqqani from Charsadda, Maulana Yasin from Swat, Qari Ismail from Khyber Agency, Maulana Adbullah from Bajaur , Mufti Misbah from Peshawar, Maulana Haider and Mansoor Nazim from Orakzai. The group reportedly rejoined TTP in March 2015 but conducted its operations independently. This group conducted some deadly attacks inside Pakistan, some of them against Christians, including the infamous suicide attack in a Lahore park on Easter Sunday on 27 March 2016, which led to the death of over 70 people, the suicide blast close to the Pakistan-India border at Wagah in November 2014 which killed at least 55 people and left more than 150 wounded at the end of a daily flag-lowering ceremony, and the suicide attack in a hospital in Quetta that killed at least 70 people, most of them lawyers mourning their dead in August 2016. It is interesting to note that even if Fazlullah's heinous attack on Army Public School Peshawar on 16 December 2014 was not received well by some of the splinter groups, there was a quiet competition among them to carry out high-profile violent attacks inside Pakistan to establish their jihadi credibility in their rank and file.

There were other splinter groups like Jundullah, and some other factions who announced their allegiance to ISIS raising its head in Iraq and Syria. However, despite these challenges, the Fazlullah-led TTP-central (if one can call it so) continued to owe allegiance to Mullah Omar and work with Al-Qaeda as could be gleaned from TTP literature during this period.

With the changing political currents in the region leading to US-Pakistan understanding on the need to prepare the region for reconciliation with the Taliban, from early 2018, there was greater coordination between the agencies of the two countries and top TTP commanders were eliminated through drone strikes. That the US was prepared to oblige and placate Pakistan was clear from the way the drone strikes targeted militants Pakistan was worried about. Mullah Fazlullah's luck finally ran out on 14 June 2018, when he was killed in Kunar, Afghanistan by a drone-strike, on his vehicle.[47] Attacks on other TTP commanders (Khalid Haqqani, former deputy leader of TTP, Qari Saif Younis in Kabul and Shahryar Mehsud, leader of the Hakimullah Mehsud group in February 2020 in Kunar) followed.

Fazlullah's death and Return of the Mehsuds

With Mullah Fazlullah's death the locus of power within TTP shifted back to the Mehsuds. For a brief period though, Fazlullah's trusted lieutenant and deputy, Omar Rehman (also known as Ustad Fateh) from Swat served as interim amir for few days. Finally, on 23 June, the TTP Shura elected Mufti Noor Wali Mehsud (1978-), a native of Sararogha subdivision in South Waziristan, educated in various madrassas in Faisalabad, Gujranwala and Karachi, as amir of TTP and Mufti Hazratullah as deputy amir. Noor Wali (also known as Abu Mansoor Asim) had also participated in Taliban military efforts in the late 1990s, especially in Mazar-e-Sharif in 1997-98, before he graduated in his studies in 1999. He briefly taught for two years at Imdad-ul-Uloom in the Gorgoray area in South Waziristan. He is widely respected as quite knowledgeable in religious/theological affairs and as a prolific writer. He is the author of *Inquilab-e-Mehsud South Waziristan, Firangi Raaj se Amriki Samraj Tak* (*The Revolution of the Mehsuds of South Waziristan: From British Rule till American Imperialism*), which runs into 689 pages detailing the travails of the Mehsuds in the making of the movement for Islam under TTP. In the book he revealed TTP's role in Benazir Bhutto's assassination on 27 December 2007, and the *modus operandi* of the TTP to gather funds for its operations. The book says the plot to assassinate Benazir was hatched by Maulvi Imran, Ahmad (Noor Wali's assistant), Qari Ismail and Mullah Ehshan and two assassins named as Bilal (also known as Saeed) and Ikramullah, were assigned to carry out the attack, and it was Bilal who first fired at Benazir from his pistol and the bullet hit her neck, following which he detonated his suicide jacket and blew himself up, while Ikramullah successfully fled the scene and is still alive.

The book also claimed that two suicide bombers Mohsin Mehsud (also known as Noor Hussain) and Rehmatullah Mehsud, trained by Maulvi Asmatullah of TTP, had carried out attacks on her procession at Karsaz area of Karachi when she returned from exile on 18 October 2007 leaving behind 180 dead (Noor Wali gives the figure of 200) and 500 injured.[48] He also says that few days later, TTP had planned to attack Benazir again in Larkana, but it was leaked to the security forces and therefore the plan did not succeed. Noor Wali showers his praise on one of the suicide bombers, Noor Hussain, because his marriage had been fixed and Baitullah had permitted him to drop out of the plan, but in spite of it he chose to go on this mission saying that he was rather looking forward to achieve martyrdom and marry the fairies in heaven (*Lekin woh saaf inkaar kiya ke main duniya mein saadi ke bajai Jannat ki hooron se saadi karne jaa raha hoon*). Noor Wali compares him with Hanzallah, who had married immediately before the Battle of Uhud and had just left the bed of his wife to take bath when he heard about the battle and rushed out sword in hand and fought on, till he attained martyrdom. Such invocation of Islamic history is quite natural for Islamists to attract cadres into the fold of Jihad.

Noor Wali is considered a workaholic, a shrewd strategist, a meticulous planner and an effective negotiator. While working with

Baitullah, he reportedly convinced him about the need for disparate jihadi groups to come together, even if it was in the form of a loose political alliance, and that is how a shadowy outfit called Ittehad-ul-Mujahideen (United Mujahideen) had taken shape in March 2009, including Mullah Nazir and Hafiz Gul Bahadur, both Waziris, who were opposed to Baitullah. He also roped in Al-Qaeda leader Hafiz Sultan into the discussions. He claims in his book that the *shura* of this group comprised of Ustad Ihsan, Dr Abu Khalid, Ustad Farooq and Mansur alias Turyalia (from Al-Qaeda), Maulvi Mohammad Azeem, Hafiz Gul Bahadur, Mullah Nazir, Qari Zia-ur-Rehman (from TTP) and Ilyas Kashmiri (from Brigade 313).[49] It is another thing that the group collapsed following Baitullah's death when some of the members like Hafiz Gul Bahadur and Mullah Nazir, partly out of their own conviction and partly because of persuasions from Pakistan army, expressed their reservations to host and support foreign militants (Uzbeks, Chechens, Uyghurs, etc. who are termed as *Ghair mulki muhajir mujahideen* by TTP writers) who had entered from Afghanistan and drew the attention and wrath of coalition forces, complicating the security situation in the tribal belt.

Noor Wali remains committed to his concept of 'defensive jihad' and advocacy of unity among mujahideen. In his book he mentions that TTP suffered huge setbacks because of internecine power struggle among its constituents and he would devote his time and energy to bring factions together and establish linkages with global and regional militant Islamist groups to strengthen TTP and bring Sharia rule to Pakistan. Although his writing suggests his inclination towards a Deobandi/Wahabi version of Islam, he displays marked sympathy for Pashtunwali as well. In his book he has several chapters devoted to defence of tribal (*qabalyili*) customs for example one of the chapters (45th) raises the question: "*Kaunsa nizam nakam aur farsudaa hai? Qabayili yah Jumhoori?*" (Which rule is ineffective and outdated? Tribal or Democratic?); another (48th) says "*Qabayili muashara deen ki baghi nahin hai*" (Tribal society is not against religion). There are comparative analyses of performance of tribal and democratic systems on issues like freedom and liberty (*azadi*), welfare (*falah-o-bahbood*), equality (*mushawat*), family rule (*khandani nizam*), crime and punishment (*jurm-o-saza*), etc. There are certain emphatic assertions about Pashtun values and lifestyle, such as: *"Har qabayil Pashtun hai, magar har Pashtun qabayil nahin hai"* (All tribal people are Pashtun but all Pashtuns are not tribals); *"Qabayil ko azadi se koi bhi mahroom nahin kar saktaa hai"* (Nobody can deprive the Pashtuns of their freedom). He does not hide his animus towards the 'Punjabi' ethnic community and the 'Punjabi' dominated army of Pakistan, but expresses his willingness to work with the Punjabi cadres within TTP. In early 2020, there were reports of splinter groups of TTP coming together and showing their desire to work within TTP, which could be ascribed to Noor Wali's determination to work towards unity among these groups. By August 2020, the TTP spokesperson announced that JuA and Hizb-ul-Ahrar (a split away group from JuA) had joined TTP along with some other groups, i.e., Lashkar-e Jhangvi (Saifullah Kurd faction, led by Maulvi Khush Muhammad Sindhi), Punjabi Taliban (led by the Amjad Farooqi), and the Sayyid Ahmad Shaheed faction. A Pakistani observer following Noor Wali closely writes that he is faced with the most difficult challenge of reviving a group which is "entering the elimination phase of its life cycle", however, "notwithstanding TTP's degradation, the terrorist threat to Pakistan is far from over" and as "TTP slides down the precipice, the threat is morphing and metastasizing"[50] with newer groups like Islamic State-Khorasan (IS-K) asserting in the horizon.

Ideological Orientation

For the Pashtuns of the tribal areas of Pakistan, Islam has always been considered a political tool rather than an ideological creed. Tribalism oftentimes prevailed over Islamic principles while dealing with worldly issues, and therefore the radical elements coming from the Arab land found it difficult to persuade the tribes to dispense with their tribal mores. Fired by their sense of defiance to any authority that wishes to control them, the tribal population has time and again turned to Islam as a means to an end. In a way, Islam has retained its appeal over the centuries and, therefore, the Pashtuns are regarded as slaves of mullahs who always contended with tribal elders who according to Pashtun tradition wielded temporal authority to maintain order in tribal societies. However, the mullah with his claim to spiritual authority always posed a challenge to the tribal elders and often incited the tribal population to revolt against the existing order.

Be that as it may, such centuries-old tribal tradition underwent a significant reordering during the years of Afghan Jihad, when Islam was actively promoted by petro-dollars and Pak-US intelligence over tribal values. There is a view that the Pakistani authorities found in the process of aggressive Islamicisation initiated by the US a chance to blunt the edge of tribal ethnic national consciousness among the Pashtuns which always threatened to pull the population of the frontier areas into the orbit of Pashtun nationalism promoted by Afghanistan. The madrassas established along the Durand Line promoted an ultra-Deobandi Islamic world-view akin to Saudi Wahabism, under pressure from the funders from the Gulf and soon the jihadi elements drawn into the Afghan vortex used the tribal areas as their second home and influenced the madrassas and the students with their rigid views about jihad, *takfir* (the practice of excommunicating a Muslim from the community) and *Khuruj* (to go out and revolt against a Muslim ruler for not following tenets of Islam) which brought about radical change in the Islamic outlook that the tribal people had until the 1980s.

The Muslim world has been in tumult since the year 1979. The year saw the victory of Shia Islamists succeed in Iran, the seize of Mecca by Juhayman's Ikhwan (in November 1979) and the start of Afghan Jihad which continued for a decade (1979-89), supported by the US and the West. The pouring in of like-minded youth from Muslim countries of the world, especially from the Arab countries, with their orthodox Wahabi/Salafi views and their zeal for waging jihad to establish Sharia in the world changed the complexion of Islamic discourse in the region. The formation of Islamic groups like Al-Qaeda (1989) and Taliban (1994) and collusion between them indicated that there was a 'demotic cocktail'[51] of Deobandi and Wahabi ideology in the Pak-Af region which greatly altered the socio-cultural context in the region among the Muslims and gave rise to a combative ideological matrix where diversity within

Islam was regarded as heretical and imposition of Sharia of the Salafi/Wahabi kind became the ruling principle for which jihad was though absolutely necessary, a religious duty, an obligation to Allah, reinforced by Quranic interpretations, which peddled the theory that to rise in revolt against heresy was the command of the Allah.

It is a fact that the tribal areas bordering Pakistan and Afghanistan were left to its people to largely evolve their own socio-political order, while the central government was only concerned with maintaining order to the extent that it did not hurt its strategic interests. This was true of the principalities like Swat, Dir and Bajaur where Islamic system was tolerated for a long time. In the tribal areas, a queer mix of tribal and Islamic system prevailed. Such insularity granted to the people of the region whetted the appetite of the local mullahs to experiment with their own Taliban-like systems in the region in the aftermath of the Afghan jihad, which glorified the idea of armed uprising backed by Islamic principles. The success of the jihadi endeavor also duly encouraged the local mujahideen who had participated in the Afghan jihad to take up arms in favour of Taliban when it rose to power in 1994 and Taliban's success further intensified the trend in the region in favour of greater Islamisation.

TTP's Views

Wedded to Jihad

It is true that the idea of waging an Islamic jihad against *kafirs* and *munafiqin* (a Muslim hypocrite who outwardly practices Islam while engages in activities contrary to the spirit of Islamic perhaps even unknowingly) is not new. To rise in revolt against a Muslim ruler who is not practicing true Islam is also not new. Such jihadi revolts had taken place in the region in the past. As has been mentioned earlier, Syed Ahmad Barelvi, Shah Ismail, Mad Mullah, Faqir of Ippi had waged relentless jihad against non-Muslim rulers in the 19th and 20th centuries. What is new, however, is the fresh lease of life given to the idea of Takfir and Khuruj.

The TTP is seen to be devoting lot of space and spending lot of energy to brand Pakistani rulers un-Islamic in the literature it produces to reach out to fellow Muslims in the country, and it is advocating the position that it is incumbent upon all Muslims to rise in revolt against the rulers of Pakistan, especially the Pakistani army. In its mouthpiece *Nawai Afghan Jihad* which was being brought out in Urdu from January 2009 till March 2020, when it was discontinued and replaced with *Nawai-Ghazwa-e-Hind* (from April 2020),, there is constant refrain that the TTP had no alternative but to engage itself in a defensive jihad against the Pakistani security forces. For example, Adnan Rashid—a native Pakistani and former technician in Pakistan Airforce, convicted and sentenced to death for his role in assassination attempt on Musharraf in December 2003, released by the TTP on 15 April 2012 from Bannu jail,[52] and now functioning as the head of the TTP wing tasked with rescuing TTP militants from Pakistani prisons—narrated his experiences while serving in Pakistan Air Force (PAF) in a series of articles.[53] He argues very forcefully that Pakistan army is a *kafir* army because it has *kafir* officers in it and, whoever dies in the army (whether he is a Christian or Shia) is called a *shaheed* or martyr which is unacceptable to him. He gives the example of some Shias who died in action during the Kargil war and were called *Shuhda*.[54]

About Jihad in Kashmir he says that he was asked to fight in Kashmir against the Indian Forces but he did not accept it because he realised being in the military that even if Kashmir was liberated from Indian control it would become part of a country which did not function according to Islamic principles. Therefore, he implied that it was necessary for undertaking jihad against the Pakistan military.[55] He also mentions that Pakistan army wrongly invoked Islam to wage jihad against India for its own interests rather than for its love of Islam. On every Friday, he says "the Ulema employed in the services of the Pakistan military receives a written sermon from the ministry of religious affairs through fax, which he has to relay to the soldiers. He cannot say anything of his own. When relations with India suffered and war seemed inevitable, the Ulema were instructed to provoke the soldiers for jihad against India by invoking relevant passages from *Hadees* and Quran.[56] However, this did not mean that people in Pakistan military were not amenable to call for true jihad. Due to our *dawah* (invite people to faith) activities, the security personnel in jail were impressed by our action and many of them joined our mission. All of them swore by Quran to extend their help to us whenever it was needed. When our friend Islamuddin Siddqui[57] was martyred those security personnel collected money for his family and sent it to his home".[58] There were many who were always ready to help the mujahideen, he would say, and TTP should exploit such sentiments, he would imply.

The TTP publications are replete with accounts by Al-Qaeda, Taliban and Jihadi leaders from other theatres of the world. In all these, there is an excessive emphasis on a rigid interpretation of jihad-fi-sabilillah and the need for Muslims to wage armed jihad and not to rest until the goal is achieved. Like Jihadi literature elsewhere, there is a lot of hatred for the US, Israel and India and often these countries are bracketed together as almost an axis of evil against whom jihad was perfectly legitimate. There is regular mention of sufferings of the Rohingyas of Myanmar, the Uyghurs of Xinjiang, the Palestinians and the Muslims of India. The Muslim ummah is urged to undertake jihad for ameliorating their condition. However, the *takfiri* mention of Pakistan army as an embodiment of evil and as being worse than all these *kafir* countries in the running theme in much of literature dealing with Pakistan.

Pakistan Army, Stooge of the Americans must be Countered

Dwelling on the Jihadi attack on Karachi dockyard to capture Pakistani naval vessels and target US and Indian navy, *Nawa-i-Afghan Jihad* in its November 2014 issue wrote "For carrying out operation, we had several Taliban mujahideen working on two Pakistani frigates—PNS *Zulfiqar* and PNS *Aslat*" and there were insiders from the navy working with TTP/Al-Qaeda militants. It was also mentioned that "the whole story that the attack on Karachi dockyard was engineered from outside is incorrect and completely wrong so as to cover up the death of Pakistani naval officials.... Could it not be concluded then that sentiments of rebellion has arisen within the ranks of officers of Pakistani military and they are inclined to carry out jihadi attacks upon US, Bharat and its allies and eliminate them?"[59]

The same issue carried an article "Pakistani regime is an agent of the Satan", by Adam Yahya Gadahn, the Egyptian American Al-Qaeda spokesperson which called Pakistan "the lieutenant of the Satan (read the US)" and that "Pakistani military and security agencies have been, for the past 65 years, dancing to the tune of Uncle Sam and the Bull Dog [Britain]", who have "control over all our 55 Muslim nations" with the help of Saudi Arabia, their "most wicked and Satanic partner". He goes on to exhort Pakistani people to rise in revolt:

> How many of us are ready to resort to extreme steps and dare to come forward to remind our puppet rulers that they are on the wrong path, which cannot be tolerated anymore? How many of us have come out in protests on roads with the resolve that we would not return to our homes until the puppet regime in Pakistan is replaced with Shariat laws! ... [Pakistan] has become an "ulcer" for the Muslim world! *That is why I invite all my Pakistani brethren to revolt against the present rulers in Islamabad and Rawalpindi and thus perform your pious duty to serve your religion.* We have to dislodge the present rulers and target US/Western interests, their officers, embassies, and this should continue till all the foreigners retreat to their own countries.... If this was not the right/opportune moment for removing them, then could there be a better time? Or should we wait until Pakistan is torn into further pieces and Uncle Sam takes over our atomic assets, or China and India plan attacks on Pakistan with the help of their own local assets inside Pakistan? Have we not learnt our lessons from losing Bangladesh?[60]

Wage Jihad against Pakistan Army

In December 2014 issue of *Nawa-i-Afghan Jihad,* the deputy amir of Al-Qaeda in the Indian Subcontinent (AQIS), Ustad Ahmed Farooq (who was killed in the tribal region in April 2015) quotes Prophet

Muhammad to substantiate his exhortation to the people of Pakistan for joining Jihad:

> The Prophet went on to say that one section of his community would continue its fight even if some people, by the will of Allah, might turn against them. This group will finally receive Allah's blessings and continue to fight till the final Day of Judgment. (*Qayamat tak*)

He goes on to provoke people by narrating the brutal action of the Pakistan army—

> During raids they kidnapped our women-folk and infants (milk-fed babies). In this operation they dumped our sisters and wives into dungeons (police secret cells) where there was no ray of light. Our ladies were molested and they are raped.... Prima facie, they have made an excellent show of maintaining diplomatic rapport with CIA, to please their US bosses and win their favours at the cost of national dignity ...

> Waziristan is being penalized because it is an eye-sore for America, Israel and Bharat and the whole world of infidels.... Do our people pay taxes for such Army actions, which are fully dedicated to Kafirs and are murdering unarmed, gullible Muslims?[61]

Criticising the anti-terror laws of Pakistan he says that the Pakistan is even worse than the US in its treatment of prisoners:

> Anybody who sings praises of Kalma (anywhere in the world) can be specifically targeted by this Ordinance. PPO has tagged all lovers of Islam as "Enemy Aliens". They could be arrested even before a crime is proved against them. It is lamentable that these courts and jails are much worse than the rules followed in Guatanamo Bay.... The army chief of Pakistan, instead of fighting Western powers, Bharat and other enemies on our borders, has instead directed its resources against our Muslim brethren.[62]

In the same issue, Ayman Al Zawahiri calls upon the people of Pakistan to turn their country into a citadel for mujahideen of the world.

> ... the Americans have carried out attacks in Pakistan only as a supplement to the US war in Afghanistan. But we should try our best to have one safe and secure and well-guarded place for the Mujahideen in Pakistan. This should be our sole objective so that Pakistan would function as a "citadel" for Mujahideen and implementation of Shariah laws. Our sole aim is that we should have an Islamic regime in Pakistan.

The main aim of TTP and jihadis to establish Shariah-based system of government in Pakistan is a lasting refrain with most writers. In the March (2015) issue of *Nawa-i-Afghan Jihad* also this rhetoric is very obvious:

> ... there is a religious and moral obligation upon every one of us to stop Pakistani *fauj* (military) and government from hatching malicious intrigues and plans to disturb our jihad! On the one hand, the purpose of Pakistani jihadi groups is to oust an infidel government and establish a Shariat regime, while on the other hand, there has been full-fledged popular support for Sharia regime in Afghanistan, and its stability and security![63]

Clarifying the TTP position on what they meant by Islamic state, Fazlullah said in a video message that if Muslims lived peacefully in either a Muslim or non-Muslim majority country, where only their religious freedoms were guaranteed, they were not being true to Islam. They would have to work towards imposing Sharia rule in their countries through jihad. This shows the resolve of the TTP leadership to impose Sharia rule in Pakistan by all means. He would say:

> I want to tell my countrymen that our people have made great sacrifices for this nation. Hundreds of thousand people have sacrificed their lives just because the essence of Pakistan is "La ila ha Illallah". They wanted la ila ha illallah to be our system, otherwise

it would have been better to live with the Hindus. We did not fight for this country so that we will pray, fast, go for Haj and open Madrassas. I want to inform you that when we were under British rule nobody was stopped from praying, fasting and going to Haj. Namaz is allowed in America and Europe. If a country becomes Islamic just by allowing its citizens to offer prayers and go to Haj then India is also an Islamic country; so is Europe and America. Unless and until Islamic principles are collectively implemented a country cannot be called 'Islamic'.[64]

Peshawar attack Justified

TTP leaders do not hide their antipathy and revulsion for Pakistan army in their articles and even justified the suicide attack on Peshawar army school as a tit-for-tat act which should not have surprised not shocked the military of Pakistan when it was engaging itself in much worse barbaric acts.

> It is time to ponder that there was no halt to oppression inflicted on us for 13 long years. All these years, the bodies of our small infants and school-going children were smothered by indiscriminate shooting from helicopter gun-ships. Their mothers used to collect their body parts strewn around the compound of their homes with unbearable pain in their hearts. These unfortunate mothers, while burying their sweethearts made genuine complaints to Allah as to why they were suffering like this and what crime was committed by these little angels that their lives were cut short by Pakistani tyrants. They were also school children like those studying in the military school at Peshawar. They were not terrorists. No candle-light vigil was observed for them. Needless to say, these killings continued for 13 long years. Why so?[65]

Very brazenly, one of the commentators even drew his own lessons from Muhammad's acts and justified the killings in Peshawar:

> ... there was some special medical course being conducted in the School by military officers and actually they were our target ...

we only killed those children of army officers, who had developed moustaches. *From the point of view of Shariah, this is akin to the killings of Banū Qurayẓah, which is quite legitimate.* (italicized by author) ... [66]

On China

In a sister publication *Ihaya-e-Khilafat*, published by TTP splinter group TTP-Jamat-ul-Ahrar, former spokesperson of TTP, Ehsanullah Ehsan, criticised China for its position on Muslims in Xinjiang in its November 2014 issue and said that China was "emerging as the greatest enemy of Islam". He warned China to revise its policies towards Muslims or suffer the fate of Russia, US and Britain:

> ... we warn (*tanbiya karte hain*) the Chinese government to shed its anti-Islamic policies; otherwise, days are not far off when they would have to face the wrath of the Mujahideen. Remember that we are like an unsheathed sword (*shamser-e-beniyam*) for the tyrant. The disintegration of Russia is not hidden from you. The economic distress of America, Britain and Pakistan is also not unknown to you. If you don't change your attitude now then your business and economic infrastructure will be attacked [by our fighters] and all your vanity will evaporate (*tumahra gumaan tak na hoga*).[67]

This line is sustained in the TTP publications. For example, in the March 2019 issue of *Nawai Jihad Afghanistan*, the same concerns were expressed again. This time the commentator, Usama Saeed, takes the issue forward and says:

> In the name of fighting extremism, the Chinese government has filled its labour camps with lakhs of Uighur Muslims. They call it 'training camps'. The Muslims interred there say that they are being compelled to abandon their faith and become atheists.... [About] 1.5 million Muslims are living in these camps, where ... Islamic teachings are interpreted in light of communist philosophy and Chinese tradition.... They are not allowed to pray and served pork. They are told that pork and alcohol are permitted because

they are produced in hygienic environment. They are asked to show their love and affection for President Xi rather than Prophet Mohammad ... Human rights Watch called it one form of ethnic cleansing....[68]

He would condemn the Pakistani government for adopting the Chinese model unthinkingly while countries like Turkey were protesting Chinese policy of Sinicizing the Muslims in 'Eastern Turkestan', the name they would prefer to Xinjiang. This is interesting because the article in the journal came up against the backdrop of Imran Khan's interview to *Financial Times* (London) on 26 March 2019 where he said that he did not know much about the Uyghurs of Xinjiang. This was not the first time Imran would do that. He had done it earlier in January in another interview to TRT World of Turkey.[69]

On India

India, always referred to as Bharat, draws special indignation from the writers in TTP publication, as can be seen from above. There is a tendency to equate India with the US and Israel and a desire to shift the venue of jihad from Pakistan to India once Sharia is established in Pakistan. Asim Umar, amir of Al-Qaeda in the Indian Subcontinent (AQIS) warns India for example in a special message:

> This caravan of Jihadis will not stop at Pakistan alone. It will obliterate the blood-stained border (of Pakistan on the east), enter Hindustan and reach Delhi. Let it be known to you, our ranks are full of such devoted jihadis that they will also not stop at Delhi, and move ahead to carry the wave of Islam to Dhaka and Burma.[70]

TTP-Al-Qaeda Position on ISIS

The TTP-Al-Qaeda linkage becomes quite clear from the TTP publication as can be discerned from above. Various Al-Qaeda leaders used the TTP publication to reach out to Pakistanis. In the face of ISIS penetration into Pakistan and reports of an ISIS delegation touring Pakistan for recruitment into its rank, Zawahiri appealed to the people of Pakistan through the TTP publication *Nawa-i-Afghan Jihad*, not to take ISIS seriously and in an interesting twist to the well-known Al-Qaeda revulsion for Shias, Zawahiri condemns sectarian violence and urges people to refrain from it:

> … As I understand, some of you, who want to join the jihad in Sham (Iraq and Syria), do so because you think that by participating in such jihad you can reinforce Allah's message and give a drubbing to the Kafirs. However, that may not be correct. Beware! Save yourselves from those leaders who want to use you for their selfish ends—to acquire power, to gain name and fame for themselves at your cost and to serve their *jaati* or sectional/sectarian interests. Remember, even if I were to ask you to persecute our fellow Muslim brothers, you are under no obligation to obey me. If I ask you to kill your own brothers in the name of Islam do not pay any heed to my words. Rather, you must disregard my instructions, because if you commit such acts, I shall not be able to come to your rescue on the final Day of Judgment (*Qayamat ke din*).[71]

In the same issue, a feature on "Al-Qaeda conquests in Karachi" toes a line very close to ISIS. It says that Al-Qaeda has managed to kill two Shia naval officials and targeted pseudo-intellectuals bringing disrepute to Islam. A warning has been advanced to people not to subscribe to false interpretation on Islam. Ridiculing terms like moderate and modern Islam, the article says that there is only one version of Islam and emphasises that "only those interpretations would be acceptable to us, which were attempted by our *salaf*, or the first three generations of Muslims. It is a very precious asset for us which will remain so till the doom's day (*Qayamat*)".[72] Celebrating intolerance and disharmony among people like the ISIS, the article states:

> It should be remembered that the real, hidden purpose of the war on terror is to impose an incorrect version of Islam on the Muslims of the world. They are making all kinds of efforts to persuade gullible Muslims to live in harmony (*hum-ahangi se*) with falsehood (*kufria*) or infidelity. This is an open insult to Islam and Allah.[73]

Avoid Jihad Fatigue, Fight on

In few instances, the commentators express their frustration at not being able to whip up enough passion for jihad which shows up in the depleting ranks of jihadi outfits. One commentator writes for example:

> Out of crores of Muslims, if only one crore, nay one lakh Muslims decide to embark on this path, this number would be quite sufficient for jihad, but it appears that the whole Muslim ummah has turned its attention away from jihad and everyone says that all paths to jihad are closed. But we should not look for lame excuses to avoid jihad. If we tread the path of jihad and win Allah, the Merciful, will favour us with his rewards.[74]

Even then, there is a determination to fight on. Expressing their resolve to fight back even if the mujahideen suffered reverses due to Operation Zarb-e-Azb, chief of TTP Mehsud, Khalid Saeed writes:

> We should be contented with our limited means and suffer the miseries thrust upon us with patience, during this phase of Hijrat. Allah the Great would surely shower happiness upon us at the end. Actually, we had agreed to resume dialogue with these tyrants of falsehood so that we could save our qabayali people from the excesses committed by these tyrants.... It has been wrongly propagated through media that we are now tired and exhausted by their excesses and that we are repenting.[75]

Mullah Fazlullah in his recent video posted in Umar Media website strikes a defiant tone and vows to fight on. He says:

> Our Jihad will continue. Either we will achieve Islamic rule or attain martyrdom; there is no other choice. We should be aware of the fact that life and death is in the hands of Allah and it is up to Allah whether we will be killed by missile or by disease or in a car accident. We cannot change whatever the destiny has in store for us. We should accept the will of Allah with open hearts and

must show our satisfaction over whatever is provided to us by our destiny. There is one special door in heaven for those who strictly believe in destiny. Trust in Allah and victory would be ours.

As these select passages depict, the TTP, deeply aligned to Al-Qaeda and Taliban, has adopted their rhetoric and its Islamic world-view is getting radicalised. Its views on India, US, Israel remain same in kind but there has been substantial increase in the degree of hatred for these countries. While there is a view in Pakistan that the Pashtun tribals are unlikely to shed their ethnic character which will dilute their position on Islam, in the face of impending failure of the American project in Afghanistan and the smell of yet another victory pervading the air in Afghanistan primarily because of lack of patience and the fatigued approach of the international community towards Afghanistan. The reconciliation attempts by the West, supposedly being midwifed by multiple actors worldwide but primarily by Pakistan intelligence, may not succeed in preserving the system of liberal democratic order in Afghanistan. The apparent success of the Afghan Taliban, despite the fact that the Taliban is a divided house, is likely to boost the morale of the TTP further to take on the military and teach it a lesson.

What are TTP's Objectives? From Local to Global

From the literature that the TTP churns out and the statements made by its leaders from time to time, it becomes clear that the TTP aims at uniting all militant groups operating in the tribal terrain of Pakistan under one platform and guard against divisive policies of the Pakistan government or international agencies. It intends to stand shoulder to shoulder with the Afghan Taliban and help them in their efforts to dislodge the puppet regime in Afghanistan and resume their rule in Kabul. The most important agenda that they have within Pakistan is to work towards imposing Sharia in Pakistan and then take it forward to the global stage.

The TTP, like its counterpart in Afghanistan, (Taliban) to which it owes its allegiance, is primarily a local phenomenon. However, because of its covert alliance with Al-Qaeda, which has been provided shelter in the tribal areas by TTP affiliated groups, the TTP has shown global ambitions too. Baitullah Mehsud waxed eloquent about TTP's international obligations in his famous Al-Jazeera interview[76] on 25 January 2008 and later he reportedly set up a terrorist cell uncovered in Barcelona that same year. He also threatened the US after massive attack in Lahore in March 2009, to carry out a similar attack in the US. Under his successor Hakimullah's leadership and especially under the guidance of Hakimullah's cousin Qari Hussein Mehsud—who ran the so called 'suicide factory' of the organisation in Spinkai and was known for his ruthless manners and cruel habits—the TTP went global by associating its name with the attempted Times Square Bombing by Faisal Shahzad on 1 May 2010, to avenge the death of Baitullah Mehsud.

TTP-Al-Qaeda Nexus

The TTP's association with Al-Qaeda, is becoming clearer with the OBL files slowly being translated and released for consumption by strategic analysts worldwide. A letter written by Atiyah Abd al-Rahman, popularly known as Atiyatullah al-Libi, in late 2005 to Abu Musab Al Zarqawi chastising him for not using violence judiciously and alienating Sunnis worldwide urged Zarqawi to come to Waziristan or send some emissary to interact with Al-Qaeda brothers and take directives from them on how to conduct the war. This clearly showed how Waziristan was important for Al-Qaeda operatives. Another letter written by Rahman, then general manager of Al-Qaeda, in July 2010 (few months before his death in a drone attack in tribal areas on 22 August 2010) to Osama Bin Laden reveals the links between TTP (Pakistani Taliban) and Al-Qaeda, as well as the efforts of Pakistani military establishment as well as political leadership to reach out to Al-Qaeda in quest of reconciliation. It is also revealing to note that Osama Bin Laden wanted the militants operating in the tribal areas to scale down their operations against Pakistani security forces just like he had advised Al-Qaeda in the Arabian Peninsula (AQAP) in Yemen so that he can focus on attacking the US. The letter says:

The Pakistani enemy has been corresponding with us and with Tahreek-i-Taliban (Hakimullah) for a very short time.... We discussed the matter internally, then we talked with Abu-Muhammad later once we were able to resume correspondence with him.... Our decision was this: We are prepared to leave you be. Our battle is primarily against the Americans. You became part of the battle when you sided with the Americans.... If you were to leave us and our affairs alone, we would leave you alone. If not, we are men, and you will be surprised by what you see; God is with us.... We let slip (through Siraj Haqqani, with the help of the brothers in Mas'ud and others; through their communications) information indicating that al Qaeda and Tahreek-i-Taliban [the Pakistani Taliban] have big, earth shaking operations in Pakistan, but that their leaders had halted those operations in an attempt to calm things down and relieve the American pressure.... But if Pakistan does any harm to the Mujahidin in Waziristan, the operations will go forward, including enormous operations ready in the heart of the country.... We received a messenger from them bringing us a letter from the Intelligence leaders including Shuja' Shah, and others.[77]

The correspondence from Pakistani ISI chief Shuja Pasha to Al Qaeda was sent through Fazlur Rahman Khalil, the leader of HuM, in the first instance and later he went to see Al-Qaeda leadership in the tribal areas accompanied by former ISI Chief Hamid Gul. This showed that Pakistani intelligence knew how to get in touch with the Al-Qaeda leadership at will through jihadi leaders like Khalil who were nurtured carefully for use at critical moments. The letter also makes it amply clear that there was an overall impression among the TTP-Al-Qaeda militants that Pakistani army was busy serving American interests and they would have no problems with it and would not hurt its interests if it allowed them freedom of operation within Pakistani territory. If one were to pit Rahman's position against what TTP spokesperson Azam Tariq had to say in June 2010, there is remarkable convergence between the two arguments. Tariq said:

We are not against Pakistan, but we don't like its pro-American policies; we will target their security forces, the secular leaders and other sensitive installations until the government does not change its anti-Islamic policies.[78]

However, the TTP's world-view had changed vastly by its contact with foreign militants and therefore from 2008 onwards most statements issued by senior TTP commanders indicated that the short-term aim of the group was to establish Islamic emirates in Pakistan and Afghanistan whereas its long-term aim was to work towards its goal of establishing a global Islamic emriates.

The militants associated with the TTP have also viewed attack on India as a religious duty (*Ghazwa-e-Hind*) before embarking on the final battle against the false prophet (*Al Masih ad Dajjal*). This world-view is shared by Al-Qaeda operating in the terrain as well. The Mumbai attack which took place on 26 November 2008 and its linkages with Al-Qaeda revealed by both David Coleman Headley's confessions, and investigative analysis by Saleem Shahzad, based on his frequent travel to the tribal areas, demonstrated that Al-Qaeda leadership did retain its linkages with the ISI intelligence network and moulded its agenda at will.[79] Most of the pronouncements by Jawahiri against Musharraf pointed to his going soft on India and its indirect involvement in Mumbai attack underlined its continuing efforts to bring India within its operational purview. It was natural therefore that the TTP which hosted the Al-Qaeda in the tribal areas and was greatly influenced by its ideology would develop an anti-India outlook. In fact, the TTP's anti-India stance is well-known and the TTP leaders are known for hurling their choicest abuses at India at the drop of a hat. They would call India their *Jagir* (legitimate possession) and hold that they would have to first fight a decisive battle with India before fighting the final battle in Syria and India's defeat s written in their religious textbooks. In December 2008, in the immediate aftermath of Mumbai attacks when speculations were rife that India might launch an attack on Pakistan, Baitullah Mehsud sank his cudgels with the Pakistan Army and offered either to fight under its command or alongside it as a separate force. The report in *The News* stated that Baitullah spoke from an undisclosed location and said:

> We know very well that the visible and invisible enemies of the country have been planning to weaken this lone Islamic nuclear power. But the "mujahideen" will foil all such nefarious designs of our enemies ... hundreds of would-be bombers were Monday given suicide jackets and explosives-laden vehicles for protection of the border in case of any aggression by the Indian forces. Our mujahideen would be in the vanguard if fighting broke out. Our fighters will fall on the enemy like thunder.[80]

However, despite such emotive responses in an emergency situation, there was a perceptible shift in TTP rhetoric on India since 2009. There was a greater resolve to overrun Islamabad ahead of attack on India in normal circumstances. Hakimullah made it clear on many occasions that the primary aim of TTP was to bring Islam to Pakistan first and then help out Muslims in Kashmir and other parts of India. In October 2009, few months after assuming leadership, Hakimullah Mehsud, stated clearly: "We want an Islamic state. If we get that [in Pakistan], then we will go to the borders and help fight the Indians [in Kashmir]." In December 2012, addressing the media with Hakimullah, his deputy Waliur Rahman held both India and Pakistan responsible for non-settlement of the Kashmir issue. He said:

> India and Pakistan are running their businesses in the name of Kashmir. Pakistan has played havoc with Kashmiris in the name of freedom. We condemn this policy in the same way as we abhor the brutality of Indian government. The war that we fight in Kashmir is under the banner of *Ghazwa-e-Hind* (battle of Hindustan). Our jihad is not just limited to tribal areas, but it covers the whole of Pakistan, Kashmir and India.... The registered jihad that Pakistan had started in Kashmir can't liberate it—and even if does, it cannot change its system. Only the Taliban can establish Islamic system in Kashmir.[81]

The TTP's intent to fight the US and Western forces also indicates its ideological parity with both Afghan Taliban and Al-Qaeda. In his first interview to media in January 2008, mentioned earlier, Baitullah was very definitive about TTP's aim to destroy the West apart from waging a jihad to brining Islamic Sharia to Pakistan. He said reportedly: Our main aim is to finish Britain and United States and to crush the pride of the non-Muslims. We pray to God to give us the ability to destroy the White House, New York and London".[82] In May 2010, Hakimullah appeared in a video, dispelling rumours of his death doing the rounds for nearly four months since the drone attack in January 2010 to kill him and said that "the time is very near when our fidayeen will attack the American states in their major cities", adding that "Our fidayeen have penetrated the terrorist America, we will give extremely painful blows to the fanatic America".[83] The video was released hours after TTP claimed responsibility for the 1 May failed bombing of Times Square in New York City. On 7 October 2010, Qari Hussain, cousin of Hakimullah and chief organiser of TTP's suicide death squad was killed in a drone attack.

From their willingness to engage Pakistan and the demands they placed on the state since late 2011, the TTP appeared to be on a path of reconciliation. This is well in line the communications that have come to light recently between Osama Bin Laden and Al-Qaeda manager cited earlier. There was an effort on the part of the Pak intelligence agencies to reach out to Al-Qaeda and hold talks with TTP. The correspondence makes it clear that the TTP was persuaded by Al-Qaeda to buy peace in return for promise of non-attack by Pakistani forces and an assurance that they could focus their attention on Afghanistan against American forces. Interestingly, then TTP leader Hakimullah was willing to negotiate in behalf of Al-Qaeda and urged its leadership not to be present during the talks because of the apparent risks involved. This situation continued for a long time, even if there was little respite from attacks by TTP all this while. However, with the failure of talks with the Pakistani state, and subsequent indiscriminate army operations (Operations Zarb-e-Azb and Radd-ul-Fassad)in the tribal areas, the TTP's reconciliatory approach seemed to be replaced by a determination to relaunch their movement with a vengeance in the post-Fazlullah phase.

Recent Phase: Show of Resilience, Resurgence?

After Zarb-e-Azb and appearance of Islamic State of Iraq and al-Sham (ISIS) the TTP constituents were faced with ideological pulls from ISIS. Some groups gravitated towards the uncompromising sectarian position of ISIS and there were splits. However, TTP-central stuck to its pro-Al-Qaeda and pro-Taliban line and refused to accept ISIS leader Abu Bakr al-Baghdadi's claim to be the *Amir-ul-momineen* or leader of all Muslims of the world. The TTP's rejection followed similar rejection by the Afghan Taliban in 2015. The TTP said in a statement. "Baghdadi is not a Islamic Khalifa because his selection is not according to Islamic rules", adding that the IS leader had little control in Muslim countries like Egypt, Libya, Yemen and Afghanistan. This was in line with Afghan Taliban's letter (in June 2015) to al-Baghdadi asking him to stop recruiting from Afghanistan, and asserting that there was room for only "one flag, one leadership" in their fight to re-establish strict Islamist rule.[84]

Going by TTP's linkages with disparate groups professing hardcore Islamist outlook, the TTP's has, nevertheless, has chosen to work with local Daesh/ISIS sympathisers and operatives supporting its agenda of bringing Islamic Sharia-based rule to Pakistan. It has demonstrated its unwavering resolve to fight Pakistani security forces and their supporters inside Pakistan. Two UN reports focusing on activities of ISIS, Al-Qaeda and associated individuals and entities in 2020[85] pointed to "resilience of radical ecosystems strengthened by online propaganda and ineffective disengagement programmes" in the face of "economic and political toll of the pandemic, its aggravation of underlying drivers of violent extremism and its expected impact on counter-terrorism efforts are likely to increase the long-term threat everywhere".[86] The Twenty-sixth report of the UN Analytical Support and Sanctions Monitoring Team dated 16 July 2020 held that "the total number of Pakistani foreign terrorist fighters in Afghanistan, posing a threat to both countries, is estimated at between 6,000 and 6,500, most of them with TTP" and approximately 500 Eastern Turkestan Islamic Movement (ETIM) fighters operate in Badakhshan, primarily in Raghistan and Warduj Districts, and this outfit collaborates in Afghanistan with the Islamic Jihad Group, Lashkar-e-Islam and TTP. The 27th report focusing on the later half of 2020, said that TTP oversaw a "reunification of splinter groups that took place in Afghanistan and was moderated by Al-Qaeda". It mentioned that five entities pledged alliance to TTP in July and August, "including the Shehryar Mehsud group, Jamaat-ul-Ahrar, Hizb-ul-Ahrar, the Amjad Farooqi group [led by Shani and Muneeb] and the Usman Saifullah group (formerly known as Lashkar-e-Jhangvi)", which "increased the strength of TTP and resulted in a sharp increase in attacks in the region". On 8 August 2020, Lashkar-e-Jhangvi's group belonging to Emir Usman Saifullah Kurd Shaheed, currently working under the leadership of Maulvi Khush Muhammad Sindhi, former Emir of Harkat-e-Jihad Islami, Sindh, joined TTP. On 18 August, Emir of Jamaat-ul-Ahrar Omar Khalid Khorasani and Emir of Hizb-ul-Ahrar Omar Khurasani pledged allegiance to TTP and announced the end of their former groups (Jamaat-ul-Ahrar and Hizb-ul-Ahrar). Syed Ahmad Shaheed Group also joined TTP in the same month. On 27 November, two other Jihadi groups led by Molvi Aalim Khan Ustad and Commander Ghazi Umar Azaam pledged their allegiance to the TTP amir, Mufti Noorwali, and formally joined the TTP. Videos were also released by Umar media to the effect signaling the confidence of the TTP to relay it to the world that they are alive and kicking, despite six years of crushing army action post-ZeA.

TTP came out with a spirited defence of its position saying that it did not have any linkage with ISIS and held that the "Khorasan branch of ISIS seems to be a plot of the regional intelligence agencies, in which Pakistan's notorious intelligence agency has played a central role" and the it has launched attacks on mosques, educational institutions and bazars on the instructions of the ISI, in coordination with *Operation Zarb-e-Azb* "to defame and malign the jihadist movement". Pakistan's covert support to ISIS is designed to pose critical challenge to the Taliban once the foreign forces leave because "A destabilized and weak Afghanistan is a historical policy of the Pakistani intelligence agencies, which they have sworn to continue at any cost."

In a bid to distance itself from the global Islamic agenda of ISIS (and to some extent of Al-Qaeda, which it left unmentioned), TTP said:

> We have repeatedly made it clear that *the centre and focus of our Jihadi activity is only Pakistan*. The oppressive and occupying forces of Pakistan have illegally occupied our homeland. We have been deprived of the right to live a free life in our lands according to our religion, creed and our traditional norms. The Islamic Shariah grants us the right to defend our lives and our religion, to fight for the liberation of our areas and homeland and to build our society in accordance with our religion, creed and traditions.[87]

The oblique reference here is to the tribal areas and characterisation of the Pakistan army as an occupying force. Interestingly, in the subsequent paragraphs, the TTP response to UN report betrays its overtly Pashtun nationalist sentiments:

> The Pashtuns, and especially the Pashtun tribes, did not gain[] independence on the basis of the conspiratorial partition of the Indian Subcontinent. Rather the Pashtuns as a nation have maintained their independence and sovereignty for centuries *through the blessed act of Jihad....* As far as the tribes are concerned, legally the independent tribes living along the Pak-Afghan border are neither part of Pakistan nor of Afghanistan, but the tribal areas represent the boundary between the two countries in the context of the unnatural Durand Line Treaty. Starting with the Russian-Afghan war and continuing on to the current conflict, the cunning Pakistani forces have illegally occupied the tribal areas and ... established [their] military bases there, and eventually ended the independent status of the tribes.... Freedom of Pakhtunkhwa and tribal areas is a religious and national duty in the eyes of every Pashtun and Afghan and whoever has sense of responsibility for

their religion and nation will never accept the occupation any area of their beloved homeland.

In his Eid-ul-Fitr message, TTP Chief Abu Mansoor Asim (Noor Wali) on 31 July 2020, gave out a hint of the TTP strategy. He told his follower mujahideen not to align with ISIS, who are regarded as having 'Khawariji mindset' (those who deviate from mainstream Islam), and rather than dissipating their energies in multiple areas, the mujahideen should focus on their "respective jihadi front and battlegrounds", because "[d]eclaring war with everyone everywhere at the same time is against the biography and Jihadi policy of the Prophet (peace and blessings of Allah be upon him) and his companions. It also puts the jihadi movements in unnecessary troubles." Referring to the Durand Line, which stokes Pakistan's worst fears he says that "the independent tribes on both sides of the Pak-Afghan border are neither part of Pakistan nor part of Afghanistan. In fact, based on the unjust and oppressive Durand Line Treaty our lands were declared as border region between British India (present day Pakistan) and Afghanistan" and he goes on to say that their land "did not gain independence due to the conspiratorial division of the Indian subcontinent, instead the Pashtuns have always maintained their independence due to their sacred Jihadi struggles throughout the history" and the "Pashtuns decided to join Pakistan (like many other Muslim ethnic groups in the region) based on the ideology of Pakistan, which has been violated by the rulers and armed forces of Pakistan, which is "a menace to the stability of the region" and it is an Islamic obligation for every Muslim, especially Pashtun and Afghan, to defeat such a force.

In its response to the 27th report of the UN Analytical Support and Sanctions Monitoring Team on 21 January 2021, the TTP reiterated its position vis-à-vis Pakistan army and said that TTP was "only against the illegitimate system and un-Islamic laws and policies of state of Pakistan and [their] fight [was] with Pakistani army and ISI is only for that matter" and went on to re-emphasize that TTP was focussed only on Pakistan and received no funding from any source other than from the people of Pakistan: "In all our fight only Pakistani land was involved and no other country has helped us nor we are having any need of them. This all has been going on with the unqualified financial support of Pakistani brothers and we reject all propaganda regarding it."

As TTP sticks to its agenda of fighting the Pakistan army, over the last six years, especially since ZeA operations, its focus is gradually shifting discernably from bringing Sharia-based Islamic rule to whole of Pakistan to fighting for freedom of Pashtuns in the borderlands of Pakistan and Afghanistan, especially under the leadership of Mufti Noorwali, the current amir of TTP.

Notes

1. "Pakistan pays tribe al-Qaeda debt", BBC News, 9 February 2005.
2. He had lost one of his legs to a landmine while fighting against the Northern Alliance forces in Afghanistan in 1996. In the battle of Kunduz in 2001, he had surrendered himself to Abdul Rashid Dostum, the Uzbek warlord in Afghanistan. He was later handed over to the US forces who took him to Guantanamo Bay and fitted a prosthetic limb for his lost leg. He pretended that he was a mere clerk of the Taliban and had nothing to do with Al-Qaeda. He was released after two years and one month and he headed for Waziristan. He played a critical role in putting together a militant force which later came to be known as Pakistani Taliban. He was reportedly responsible for the unsuccessful suicide attack on Aftab Ahmed Sherpao, then Interior Minister of Pakistan in April 2007, in which 31 people died.
3. For details see Aamer Ahmed Khan, "Meeting Taliban's Pakistan chief", BBC News, 20 April 2004.
4. The excerpts from his interview are at http://www.pbs.org/wgbh/pages/frontline/taliban/militants/omar.html.
5. General Pervez Musharraf's Address to European Union's Foreign Relation Committee- Brussels on 15 September 2006 at http://www.presidentofpakistan.gov.pk/, accessed on 3 March 2007.
6. This was recorded before Musharraf's trip to United States. It was aired on 1 October 2006, when he was in Washington. Quoted in *The Dawn*, 2 October 2006.
7. As per media analysis the militants had announced a one-month conditional ceasefire in the agency on June 25 to pave way for 'a permanent solution to the year-long bloody conflict'. See *The Dawn*, 13 July 2016.
8. For details see Ismail Khan, "Waziristan militants offer ceasefire", *The Dawn*, 26 June 2006.

9. Rahimullah Yusufzai, "We advised Pak Taliban not to fight army: Dadullah", *The News*, 17 September 2006. Mr Yusufzai writes later in another article that this was "understandable in view of Mulla Dadullah's argument that fighting between the militants and Pakistan Army served the interest of the US". Deal Piecemeal, Weekly, *The News*, 1 October 2006.

10. Massoud Ansari in Peshawar and Colin Freeman, "Omar role in truce reinforces fears that Pakistan 'caved in' to Taliban", *The Daily Telegraph*, 24 September 2006.

11. Isambard Wilkinson, "US outraged as Pakistan frees Taliban fighters", *Daily Telegraph*, UK, 15 September 2006 at http://www.telegraph.co.uk/news/main.jhtml?xml=/news/2006/09/15/wpak15.xml, accessed on 23 March 2016.

12. Daveed Gartenstein-Ross and Bill Roggio, "Pakistan Surrenders: The Taliban control the border with Afghanistan", *The Weekly Standard*, Volume 12, Issue 3, 2 October 2006, and also see Tony Blankley, "A battle lost", *Washington Times*, 23 September 2006.

13. Rahimullah Yusufzai, "Accord and Discord", *Newsline*, October 2006.

14. Syed Saleem Shahzad, "Pakistan: Hello al-Qaeda, goodbye America", *Asia Times Online*, 8 September 2006.

15. Declan Walsh wrote reporting from North Waziristan, "Rice puts Musharraf under pressure to rein in Taliban militants", *The Guardian*, 19 February 2007.

16. Ismail Khan, "Baitullah vows to avenge attack", *The Dawn*, 18 January 2007.

17. As about contradictory reports see Anwarullah Khan, "82 die as missiles rain on Bajaur: Pakistan owns up to strike; locals blame US drones", *The Dawn*, 31 October 2006 and Editorial, "The Bajaur Massacre", *The Dawn*, 1 November 2006.

18. There were reports in the media in US that intelligence assessment quoted by United Press International suggested that Pakistan is negotiating similar seals with Taliban militants in Khyber, Tank, Dera Ismail Khan and Bajaur.

19. Anwarullah Khan, "Tribesmen pledge not to shelter terrorists", *The Dawn*, 27 March 2007.

20. Zulfiqar Ghumman, "Taliban killed 150 pro-government maliks", *Daily Times*, 18 April 2006.

21. For a detailed discussion on the way Pakistani efforts at appeasement may have failed see "Pakistan's Tribal Areas: Appeasing The Militants", Asia Report No 125, 11 December 2006, International Crisis Group, Brussels.

22. Isambard Wilkinson, "Pakistan behind pro-Taliban tribesmen", *The Telegraph*, 13 April 2007 at http://www.telegraph.co.uk/news/main.jhtml?xml=/news/2007/04/13/wpak13.xml.

23. Ihtasham ul Haque, "President warns of quitting war against terror", *The Dawn*, 13 April 2007.

24. See *Lal Masjid: A Brief History*, 2018 at https://archive.org/details/LalMasjidABriefHistory.

25. Ibid.

26. Zarb-e-Azb means a sharp strike (Zarb) by the sword (Azb) that prophet Muhammad used in the battles of Badr and Uhud.

27. "11 dead in suicide attack on Islamabad district courts", *The News*, 4 March 2014 at https://www.thenews.com.pk/archive/print/636480-11-dead-in-suicide-attack-on-islamabad-district-courts.

28. Collected by the author from Telegram at https://t.me/umarmediaenglish_bot.

29. For a detailed discussion on FATA and how it serves as a seedbed for orthodox and extremist elements see Ashok K Behuria, "FATA: The New Epicentre of Terror", *Journal of Peace Studies*, New Delhi, April-June 2002.

30. See Hassan Abbas, "Musharraf Contends with the Pashtun Element in the Pakistani Army", *Terrorism Focus*, Volume 3, Issue 42, 31 October 2006.

31. For details see Pervez Musharraf, *In the Line of Fire: A Memoir*, Free Press: New York, 2006.

32. For example, the attack on Zamazola village in Bajaur agency on 13 January 2006, was not reportedly coordinated with Pakistani security forces, while in other cases the Pakistani security forces were involved. The Pakistani authorities had lodged official protest against the Bajaur attack subsequently.

33. The Bajaur attack was mentioned by then Pakistan Prime Minister, Sahukat Aziz, during his trip to the US later in January 2006.

34. Richard Armitage is categorical in his assertion: "I personally believe that Musharraf is genuine when he assists us in the tribal areas, but I don't think that affection for working with us extends up and down the rank and file of the Pakistani security community." (Transcript of his interaction with PBS at http://www.pbs.org/wgbh/pages/frontline/taliban/interviews/armitage.html)

35. Peter Tomsen in the above mentioned interview argues that "Pakistani military and in the ISI think that America does not have much staying power, and eventually it's going to leave the region once more, which will open the way for Pakistan to reassert this Islamist dynamic inside Afghanistan...."

36. Data provided by *Long War Journal* at www.longwarjournal.org/Pakistan-strikes

37. The army launched Operation Zarb-e-Azb (sharp strike, like the one by one of the nine swords of Prophet Muhammad called *Al Azb*) on 15

June 2014 (following terrorist attack on Jinnah International Airport in Karachi on 8 June 2014) to flush out foreign and local militants targeting the army. As per Pakistan Army releases: "We named Operation Zarb-e-Azb after the Sword of the Holy Prophet (Peace Be Upon Him) so that we'd be guided on every step by the Edicts of Allah Almighty and the examples of the Holy Prophet (Peace Be Upon Him). This sword can only be raised for the protection of the oppressed and the innocent and to eradicate evil and disorder from the land." Figures provided by Pakistan Army suggest that it was a successful tri-services operation and till September 2016, there were 19,000 operations conducted throughout the country. During 2002-2016, in the War on Terrorism, almost 18,000 innocent citizens and 5,000 officers and soldiers of the Armed Forces laid their lives while over 48,000 Pakistanis have suffered serious injuries. In the operation Zarb-e-Azb, according to some figures, the army lost over 700 troops while it killed more than 3,500 suspected militants in airstrikes, and clashes. The operation also displaced nearly a million tribesmen, of them, the army says, over 90 per cent have returned to their homes in recent years. (From the address by Gen Raheel Sharif, Chief of Army Staff of Pakistan, on 6 September 2016 at https://ispr.gov.pk/press-release-detail.php?id=3464.)

38. Aamir Latif, "What's brewing in northwest Pakistan?", *Anadolu Agency online*, 10 June 2019 at https://www.aa.com.tr/en/asia-pacific/whats-brewing-in-northwest-pakistan/1500402.

39. Better known for his book *Ghost Wars*, Penguin, NY, London, 2002.

40. In his interview with Martin Smith, of PBS on Frontline Show at http://www.pbs.org/wgbh/pages/frontline/taliban/interviews/coll.html.

41. See Assad Durranni's argument in ICG Asia report No 125, quoted op. cit.

42. Other members chosen by TTP as members of the committee that would represent it were Imran Khan, Maulana Samiul Haq, famously known as the 'father of the Taliban', Professor Ibrahim of the Jamaat-e-Islami (JI) and Mufti Kifayatullah.

43. For detailed discussion on Al-Qaeda's penetration into the tribal areas see Imtiaz Gul, *The Al Qaeda Connection*, Penguin, London, 2009 and Syed Aleem Shahzad's informed accounts in his book, Inside Al Qaeda and Taliban, Pluto Press, London, 2011.

44. See "Profile: Hakimullah Mehsud", *The Dawn*, 1 November 2021 at https://www.dawn.com/news/1053416.

45. See Daud Khattak, "A Profile of Khan Said: Waliur Rahman's Successor in the Pakistani Taliban", *CTC Sentinel*, Vol 6, Issue 6, 25 June 2013 at https://www.ctc.usma.edu/posts/a-profile-of-khan-said-waliur-rahmans-successor-in-the-pakistani-taliban.

46. Tahir Khan, "Khan Syed Mehsud alias Sajna replaces Hakimullah Mehsud as new TTP chief", *The Express Tribune*, 2 November 2013 at http://

tribune.com.pk/story/626173/khan-syed-mehsud-alias-sajna-replaces-hakimullah-mehsud-as-new-ttp-chief/.

47. *The Washington Post* carried a story on 15 June 2018, citing Pakistani and US sources: "Pakistani security analysts said the strike would help improve relations among Pakistan, Afghanistan and the United States. "This is a new beginning of cooperation," said retired Brig. Gen. Said Nazir. A retired air marshal, Shahid Latif, called the strike "a significant development" that addressed long-standing Pakistani appeals for help against the insurgents across the border. He said it would have "a positive impact on ties between the three nations." See William Branigin and Sayed Salahuddin, "Pakistani Taliban leader Mullah Fazlullah killed in U.S. airstrike in Afghanistan" at https://www.washingtonpost.com/world/asia_pacific/pakistan-taliban-leader-mullah-fazlullah-is-killed-in-a-us-airstrike-in-afghanistan/2018/06/15/9ea6cc56-70ab-11e8-b4d8-eaf78d4c544c_story.html.

48. Abu Mansoor Asim Mufti Noor Wali Mehsud, *Inquilab-e-Mehsud South Waziristan, Firangi Raaj se Amriki Samraj Tak* (*The Revolution of the Mehsuds of South Waziristan: From British Rule till American Imperialism*), Broadcasting Department, Al Sahab, South Waziristan, Mehsud Area, pp. 395-402.

49. Ibid., pp. 181-182.

50. Farhan Zahid, "Profile of New TTP Chief Mufti Noor Wali Mehsud: Challenges and Implications", Pakistan Institute of Peace Studies (PIPS), 2019 at https://www.pakpips.com/article/4952.

51. Demotic cocktail of Deobandi and Wahabi ideology Graham Usher, "The Pakistan Taliban", *Middle East Report*, 13 February 2007 at http://www.merip.org/mero/mero021307.html, accessed on 1 March 2007.

52. "Dangerous militants among 384 escape after Bannu jail attack", *The Dawn*, 16 April 2012 at http://www.dawn.com/news/710858/dangerous-militants-among-384-escape-after-bannu-jail-attack.

53. *Nawai Afghan Jihad,* March-August 2013.

54. Ibid., January 2013, p. 21.

55. Ibid., March 2013, pp. 13-14.

56. Ibid., April 2013, pp. 14-25.

57. Islamuddin Siddiqui was convicted for a failed assassination attempt on Gen Musharraf in December 2003 in Rawalpindi. Siddiqui was part of a group involved in the first attempt on 14 December 2003, in which a road bridge was blown up using powerful explosives, but they missed Gen Musharraf's car by seconds. He was hanged on 20 August 2005 in Multan. See related report at http://news.bbc.co.uk/2/hi/south_asia/4168284.stm.

58. *Nawa-i-Afghan Jihad*, August 2013, p. 19.

59. Ibid., November 2014.

60. Ibid., November 2014.

61. Ibid., December 2014.

62. Ibid.

63. Ustad Osama Mehmud, "Call for Support and Defence of Islamic Emirate of Afghanistan", *Nawa-i-Afghan Jihad*, March 2015.

64. "Special Speech of TTP Chief, Haq Fazlullah Khurasani, to Suicide Commandos" Umar Media, 23 June 2015 at https://umarmedia.wordpress.com/2015/06/23/.

65. Kashif ali al Khairi, "We remember all atrocities committed on us", *Nawa-i-Afghan Jihad*, p. 18.

66. Rab Nawaz Farooqi, "Do you have the strength to fight the American war inside Pakistan?", *Nawa-i-Afghan Jihad*, January 2015.

67. Ehsahn-ullah-Ehsahn, *Ihaya-e-Khilafat*, November 2014.

68. Usama Saeed, "Mashriqi Turkestan ke Mazloom Mussalmanon ki Halat-e-Zar", *Nawai-Afghan-i-Jihad*, March 2019, p. 100.

69. The interview is cited in "PM 'doesn't know much' about condition of Uighurs in China", *The Express Tribune*, 8 January 2019 at https://tribune.com.pk/story/1883992/1-pm-doesnt-know-much-condition-uighurs-china/.

70. Message of AQIS chief Asim Umar, *Nawa-i-Afghan Jihad*, p. 26.

71. "Message from Ayman Al Zawahiri not to join jihad spawned by IS", *Nawa-i-Afghan Jihad*, p. 28.

72. "Al-Qaeda's conquests in Karachi in 2014", *Nawa-i-Afghan Jihad*, January 2015.

73. Ibid.

74. Shaikh Yusuf al Ameer, "The Road to Jihad", *Nawa-i-Afghan Jihad*, March 2015.

75. *Nawa-i-Afghan Jihad*, December 2014.

76. Baitullah said in the interview: "Islam is one religion and there are no borders in Islam. We Muslims are one hand and will carry out jihad in Afghanistan and Pakistan. We will also carry out jihad in Palestine, Bosnia and Iraq. This is a religious duty."

77. Excerpted in Thomas Joscelyn, "Osama bin Laden's Files: The Pakistani government wanted to negotiate.", *The Long War Journal*, 9 March 2015 at http://www.longwarjournal.org/archives/2015/03/osama-bin-ladens-files-the-pakistani-government-wanted-to-negotiate.php.

78. Tahir Ali, "3,000 terrorists for India battle: Pak Taliban", Rediff news, 26 June 2010 at http://www.rediff.com/news/special/three-thousand-terrorists-for-india-battle-pak-taliban/20100726.htm.

79. Syed Sleem Shahzad, *Inside Al Qaeda and Taliban, Beyond Bin Laden and 9/11*, Pluto Press, 2011, pp. 67-71.

80. Mushtaq Yusufzai, "If Indians attack Taliban to fight alongside Army: Mahsud", *The News*, 23 December 2008 at http://www.thenews.com.pk/TodaysPrintDetail.aspx?ID=19147&Cat=13&dt=12/23/2008.

81. Rediff.com, "We will liberate Kashmiris from India and Pakistan", 29 December 2012 at http://www.rediff.com/news/slide-show/slide-show-1-taliban-we-will-liberate-kashmiris-from-india-and-pakistan/20121229.htm.

82. Cited in Amir Mir, *Talibanisation of Pakistan From 9/11 To 26/11 and Beyond*, Pentagon Security International, New Delhi, 2011, p. 285.

83. Carlotta Gall, "'Killed' Mehsud appears in video", *The New York Times*, 3 May 2010.

84. See "Pakistan Taliban reject Islamic State leader's claim to be 'caliph'", Reuters, 19 December 2015 at https://mobile.reuters.com/article/amp/idCAKBN0U20IT20151219?edition-redirect=in, see also "Taliban in Afghanistan tells Islamic State to stay out of country", *The Washington Post*, 16 June 2015 at https://www.washingtonpost.com/world/asia_pacific/taliban-warns-islamic-state-to-stay-out-of-afghanistan/2015/06/16/a88bafb8-1436-11e5-8457-4b431bf7ed4c_story.html.

85. "Twenty-sixth report of the Analytical Support and Sanctions Monitoring Team submitted pursuant to resolution 2368 (2017) concerning ISIL (Da'esh), Al-Qaida and associated individuals and entities", S/2020/71, dated 16 July 2020 at https://digitallibrary.un.org/record/3872989/files/S_2020_717-EN.pdf and "Twenty-seventh report of the Analytical Support and Sanctions Monitoring Team submitted pursuant to resolution 2368 (2017) concerning ISIL (Da'esh), Al-Qaida and associated individuals and entities", S/2021/68, dated 21 January 2021 at https://digitallibrary.un.org/record/3899838/files/S_2021_68-EN.pdf.

86. "Twenty-seventh report", p. 3.

87. "Culled out from Telegram", 30 July 2020 at https://t.me/umarmediaenglish_bot, also available at https://www.umarmediattp.co.

4. Monsters and the Master: TTP in Action in the Heartland and Response of the State

There is a growing consensus among analysts focusing on Pakistan that it has been a victim of growing violence during the last several decades primarily because of the temptation of the state, and especially its military, to use terrorism as an instrument of its security and foreign policy. Over the years, the military of Pakistan raised jihadi groups to enhance their strategic value and secure their strategic depth vis-à-vis India, which is perceived as a major threat to its existence. These groups have operated primarily in India and Afghanistan but have also developed global linkages, in view of the globalisation of radical Islamist militancy in the aftermath of the Afghan jihad (1979-89). Under pressure from the international community, when Pakistani military took action against some of these groups after 9/11, some of the monsters raised by the military turned against their creator/master. Splinter groups from all major jihadi outfits and the mujahideen from the tribal belt straddling the Af-Pak frontier, who had been encouraged to fight alongside the mujahideen (during 1979-89) and with the Taliban (since 19940 made common cause with one another and coalesced to form Pakistani Taliban, which has given Pakistan security forces sleepless nights. Pakistan has used overwhelming force to deal with this constituency of militants but failed to contain the menace altogether. The interaction between the master (Pakistan Army) and these monsters (TTP and its affiliates) is discussed in this chapter. TTP's formation and early years have been covered in the earlier chapter and the present chapter starts from the year 2010.

From the year 2010, the TTP was seen to be on a wholesale war-path with the security forces of Pakistan. The number and intensity of attacks increased during 2010-2012. A suicide bomber ramming his explosive-laden car on to a police station in Bannu in January 2011, a first-of its kind attack on a natural gas station in Faisalabad in March, two unsuccessful assassination attempts on Fazlur Rehman in March (Swabi) and April (Charsada). In the immediate aftermath of killing of Osama Bin Laden in Abottabad in the US operation on 2 May 2011, there was even a spike in terror attacks. On 13 May, two suicide bombers attacked a paramilitary academy, training young cadets in Charsada, killing more than 80 people and injuring at least 15. On 22 May, the militants intruded into PNS Mehran in Karachi, the headquarters of the Pakistan Navy's Naval Air wing and the most populous Pakistani military installation. In May TTP militants bombed a US consulate convoy in Peshawar, killing one Pakistani and wounding 10 others. On 3 June, Illyas Kashmiri, founder member of 313 Brigade and top Al Qaeda strategist, who was involved in planning Mumbai attack and also recce of a Dutch newspaper office, was killed in a drone strike.[1] This had some impact on the operational strength of TTP-Al Qaeda for some time.

During the year, there were also several cases of TTP attacking funeral gatherings of tribal elders or their relatives (on 2 March and 15 September 2011) allegedly working with the government against its interest. Such attacks led to major casualties. One police check-post in Lakki Marwat was attacked on 2 September. TTP made its presence felt in Karachi when a suicide bomber rammed an explosives-laden car into the house of SSP Chaudhry Aslam Khan in the posh Defence Housing Authority area of Karachi, Sindh, killing eight injuring several people. Aslam Khan escaped the attack but was later killed by TTP (Mohmand) militants on 8 January 2014, when a bomb blew up his vehicle on the Lyari expressway in Karachi. Aslam was targeted allegedly for his involvement in killing of Taliban prisoners in CID cells in Karachi, according to the TTP-

Mohmand spokesperson. On 2 October 2011, a police van carrying 32 recruits heading towards a training facility in Abbottabad was attacked by a remote-controlled bomb near Mansehra. There were familiar cases of security personnel ambushed in tribal areas and Awami National Party (ANP) activists gunned down and cases of Sufi shrines and mosque bombed in Khyber and Dera Ghazi Khan.

Early in January 2012, the TTP murdered 15 Frontier Constabulary soldiers in Orakzai Agency. These soldiers had been kidnapped and kept in TTP's custody for over a year. These bodies were recovered in North Waziristan; each body had 40 bullets in it and bore signs of torture. Another ten dead bodies of soldiers kidnapped in December 2011 were recovered few days later on 9 January 2012 from northern Orakzai. The killings were claimed by a TTP affiliate. Four suicide bombers, two of them foreigners, were sent by TTP to attack the district police station in Dera Ismail Khan on 19 January. Some sectarian attacks were also being conducted by TTP splinter groups in the tribal areas, especially in Shia-dominated Parachinar in Kurram agency (17 February) and also in Kohistan (28 February). On 12 July, TTP militants attacked a police academy in early morning hours in Lahore, killing nine police cadets, who belonged to Khyber Pakhtunkhwa (KP), and the TTP spokesman Ehsanullah claimed that these police cadet were specifically targeted in Lahore because of the KP police's record of treating Taliban detainees poorly. On 16 August, TTP attacked the Kamra Air Base of the Pakistan Air Force in Attock, Punjab. One security official was killed in the exchange while all eight attackers were shot dead by security forces. The TTP claimed that the attack was in revenge for the deaths of Baitullah Mehsud and Osama bin Laden. On 3 September, a suicide bomber killed himself and two others when he drove a car laden with explosives into a US consular vehicle in Peshawar. On 9 October, Malala Yousafzai was shot by a TTP militant in Swat. In a dramatic attack that year on 15 October, 300 militants attacked a police check-post set up on the main Peshawar-Kohat Road in the Matni area on the outskirts of Peshawar and killed a local Superintendent of Police (Rural) Khurshid Khan and six others, including police and Frontier Constabulary (FC) personnel.

The attackers ran away with Khurshid Khan's severed head which was later returned to his family after receiving a sum of PKR 3.5 million. According to TTP, the attack was in response to the raid launched by the security forces on its training camps in Peshawar. Soon afterwards on 7 November 2012, an assistant superintendent of police, Hilal Haider, was killed in Qissa Khawani bazaar by a suicide bomber who attacked him on foot. The TTP spokesperson claimed the attack and said that Hilal was targeted because he was "responsible for torturing Taliban suspects during interrogation". According to some estimates in media between December 2007 and October 2012, suicide attacks carried out by TTP militants accounted for 5400 deaths.

On 27 December 2012, a Punjabi Taliban leader Asmatullah Muawiya sent a letter to Pakistani newspaper *The News* expressing his group's willingness to engage in a ceasefire with the Pakistani government on the condition that the government would implement sharia and end its alliance with the United States. TTP spokesman Ehsanullah Ehsan also came out with a statement which said that the TTP was ready for a ceasefire as long as Pakistan authorities met TTP's demands, that an Islamic system should be put into place and in the conduct of their foreign policy they stopped agreeing to America's demands. In a video released the following day, Hakimullah Mehsud confirmed TTP's message signaling its willingness to engage in talks but stressed that disarming could not be a precondition for negotiations, saying: "We believe in dialogue but it should not be frivolous" and the government must not ask TTP to lay down arms. While making an offer for peace, he chided Pakistani authorities for being slaves of the US and held that as a slave they could not "make independent agreements." The TTP reiterated the offer in a video statement released in February 2013. TTP spokesman Ehsanullah Ehsan stated that the TTP would be willing to negotiate if three senior Pakistani political figures—the leader of PML-N, Nawaz Sharif; the leader of the JUI-F, Maulana Fazlur Rehman; and the leader of JI, Syed Munawar Hasan acted as guarantors for the talks. In addition, the government would have to release seven detained TTP militants, including former spokesmen Muslim Khan and Maulvi Omar.

During this period, from late December 2012 till May 2013, the TTP relaxed its attacks on security forces and focused mainly on wiping out ANP leaders in the wake of the May 2013 nation-wide elections. Islamic militants also targeted PPP leaders making it difficult for secular forces to conduct their electoral campaign. Hakimullah Mehsud claimed in a letter to local media on 30 April that the group would continue to attack the democratic system in Pakistan by hindering the upcoming election and its aim was to end the democratic system. Against the backdrop of the elections, even if firing across Line of Control from the beginning of January 2013 kept security forces of India and Pakistan quite busy and tense, there was no effort by the TTP to take advantage of it in any major way. During this time, the attacks on the security forces were rather scaled down and the offer of talks continued till May.

However, a day after the killing of Waliur Rahman, Hakimullah's deputy, on 30 May 2013 the TTP withdrew its offer of talks. Its spokesperson criticized the government for colluding with the US to kill TTP leaders in spite of their offer of talks and therefore doubted the intention of the government. Nevertheless, on 15 May, four days after the PML-N won the majority of seats in the general elections, the TTP spokesman Ehsanullah Ehsan renewed his offer of "ceasefire" if the newly-elected government was serious about holding talks. He further stated that the group may even be willing to stop attacks as a goodwill gesture if progress was made. While the offer was being considered, the TTP affiliates launched an attack on foreign tourists visiting Nanga Parbat in Gilgit-Baltistan and killed 10 of them. On 15 September, Major General Sanaullah Niazi, in charge of military operations in Swat, was killed along with two subordinates in a bomb attack in Upper Dir district near the Afghan border. TTP spokesman Shahidullah Shahid claimed responsibility for the attack on 15 September, just six days after he welcomed the recommendation by all political parties to start dialogue with TTP and said that government had shown seriousness for talks.

However, on 2 October 2013, Shahid announced that the drone strikes would have to stop as a precondition for peace talks with the government. He held that the "stoppage of drone strikes [was] essential, otherwise—if drones continue to strike—we [would] not accept the ceasefire." In an interview with BBC's Ahmed Wali Mujeeb on 10 October,[2] Hakimullah Mehsud also stated that he would personally guarantee the safety of the government negotiators, but all drone strikes would have to stop for peace talks to be credible. Hakimullah was categorical however that "We have targeted those who are with the infidels, America, and we will continue to target them". Soon afterwards, on 1 November 2013, Hakimullah Mehsud was injured in a drone strike, and died few days later leading to days of power struggle within TTP for choice of the next amir. Finally, under alleged pressure from Mullah Omar, a non-Mehsud, Mullah Fazlullah from Swat, son-in-law of Maulana Sufi Muhammad and famous as Radio Mullah, was chosen as the amir of TTP. A day after the killing of Hakimullah, the TTP spokesman had thundered:

> We warn the enemies of Allah—the Americans and their allies in Pakistan—that the blood of our amir Mullah Hakimullah Mehsud will not be wasted. We will take revenge for his blood at every cost. This is a promise from the mujahideen of Islam and an obligation which they will fulfil very soon. The war between you and us is a rivalry, and you will have to bear the consequences. This is the start of our crusade against the government, which is nothing more than an American puppet.[3]

There was internal dissidence about Fazlullah's selection and the Mehsuds were particularly incensed. There was pressure on Fazlullah to deliver, but without the Mehsuds who provided most of the suicide bombers, Fazlullah was not able to avenge the death of Hakimullah soon afterwards. The drone attack by the US in Hangu, killing many leaders associated with the Haqqani faction of Afghan Taliban, indicated the US resolve to go for the kill at all costs, disregarding the talk about 'talks' with the TTP in Pakistan. In this context, the TTP, perhaps in a bid to buy time, indicated in December 2013 that it was still willing to pursue talks with the government as proposed by Hakimullah shortly before his death.

Talks with Government (2014)

TTP representatives began preliminary talks with government representatives in Islamabad on 6 February 2014 and the talks aimed at charting a "roadmap" for peace negotiations. The three-man TTP team comprised Mr Shami-ul-Haq, known as the "Father of the Taliban"; the chief cleric of Islamabad's Red Mosque, Maulana Abdul Aziz; and the leader of Jamaat-e-Islami party, Ibrahim Khan. The negotiating team from the government's side consisted of Irfan Siddiqui, Rahimullah Yusufzai, former ambassador Rustam Shah Mohmand and a retired major from the ISI intelligence service, Amir Shah. The government's position was mentioned in the joint statement which listed five basic conditions that had been set out by the government side: (i) All talks will be held within the framework of the constitution; (ii) The scope of the talks should remain confined to areas affected by violence, not the whole country; (iii) All hostilities should cease during talks; (iv) The Taliban should clarify the role of a separate nine-member committee that they have established; and (v) The talks should not be protracted.[4]

Immediately after the talks, the TTP finalised a 15-point charter of demands on 9 February 2014. The demands pertained to end Pakistan's relations with the US, the introduction of sharia in the FATA and parts of Khyber Pakhtunkhwa, and the release of TTP and Taliban prisoners. When the talks were being debated in Pakistan, TTP faction in Mohmand led by Omar Khalid Khurasani executed 23 Pakistani Frontier Corps soldiers on 17 February 2014, which was a major shock to the peace process. This was an apparent bid to derail the process of talks. Khurasani held that the killing was to retaliate the killing of TTP cadres in custody of the Pakistan security forces.

Despite this provocation, the government team flew into Biland Khel area of Shawa Tehsil on the border of Orakzai and North Waziristan tribal agencies bordering Afghanistan in a helicopter on 26 March. There was a consensus on extending the ceasefire and the TTP agreed to release all non-combatants. A five-member

TTP Shura, including Qari Shakeel, Azam Tariq, Maulvi Zakir, Qari Bashir and another member, held talks with the government team. Commenting on the talks Pakistani newspaper *The Dawn* wrote: "The main challenges of negotiating a peace settlement are the many groups and factions behind the violence, with many operating outside the Taliban control, including both local and foreign al Qaeda-linked militant outfits".[5] Former ISI officer and one of negotiators, Major Muhammad Amir, excused himself from the process sensing an unbridgeable gulf between the two sides and held in May 2014 that no second face-to-face meeting with the Taliban was possible because "the Taliban infighting and the delay in release of non-combatant prisoners were the main factors behind the current impasse".[6]

According to credible media reports, the internal fighting within TTP delayed its response and haemorrhaged its capacity to negotiate. In March 2014, the clashes between two Mehsud groups led to the killing of about 90 militants. There was a conflict between Late Hakimullah Mehsud's faction, led by Sheheryar Mehsud, and Late Waliur Rahman's faction led by Khan Said Sajna.[7] Sajna had posed as the successor to Hakimullah but Shehryar group had opposed his candidature. Because of internal differences and infighting, the Taliban failed to come back for talks and release the non-combatants an, while on the government's side there was pressure from both civil society and the military to act against the TTP. Against this setting, the TTP refused to extend ceasefire from April 2014 and launched an attack on Jinnah International Airport in Karachi on 8 June. This tilted the balance in Pakistan in favour of launching an all-out operation to eliminate TTP. The attack, a typical Al-Qaeda one, kept the country exercised for the whole night and at least 30 people were killed in the attack launched 10 Militants who were killed in a combat that lasted for 5 hours. The TTP spokesperson Shaidullah Shahid claimed responsibility for the attack and went on to threaten the government: "It's just the beginning, we have taken revenge for one [read Hakimullah Mehsud], we have to take revenge for hundreds.... We carried out this attack on the Karachi airport and it is a message to the Pakistan government that we are still alive to react over the killings of innocent people in bomb attacks on their villages". He dismissed the Pakistani government's peace talks as a "tool of war".[8]

Zarb-e-Azb and TTP's Woes

This incident sealed the fate of the talks and the government launched Operation Zarb-e-Azb from 15 June 2014. Nawaz Sharif chose to remain silent while his defence minister, Khawaja Muhammad Asif appeared in Pakistan's *Dunya* Television and said, "Now we have to fight this do or die war.... We will fight it till the end." The first air-strikes reportedly targeted and killed Abu Abdul Rehman al-Maani, an Uzbek, who was allegedly the mastermind behind the airport siege.[9] Military operations against the group intensified in the FATA region while the TTP militants were apparently on the run. There was a clear dip in the rate of attacks launched by TTP for few months. Moreover, around this time, the TTP suffered internal division and splits. In August 2014, some factions split away to form TTP Jamaat-ul-Ahrar (JuA) led by Maulana Qasim Khurasani and Omer Khalid Khurasani (from Mohmand) as his deputy. This group was opposed to Fazlullah's alleged soft approach towards Pakistan government and promised to upscale attack against security forces. There was an upswing in sectarian attacks by this group after its formation. Other than the amir and naib-amir, other members of the group's political shura were Qari Shakil Haqqani from Charsada, Maulana Yasin from Swat, Qari Ismail from Khyber Agency, Maulana Adbullah from Bajaur Agency, Mufti Misbah from Peshawar, Maulana Haider and Mansoor Nazim from Orakzai Agency. Former TTP spokesperson Ehsanullah Ehsan, was nominated as the spokesman for the splinter group.[10]

As if this was not enough, TTP faced the threat of further division following the rise of Islamic State in Iraq and Syria (ISIS) which raised its head in the Middle East in early 2014. Attracted by its dramatic success, the lightning speed with which its occupied city after city in northern Iraq, and its resolve to usher in a global Islamic revolution many Islamist radical groups around the world veered towards it. Strangely, ISIS' well-advertised gruesome acts of brutality against

Shias and levelling of Shia places of worship must have appealed to many hardcore sectarian elements within TTP fold.[11] Jundullah joined the group quite early in February. In September 2014, there were rumours of ISIS sympathisers distributing leaflets written in Pashto and Dari titled *'Fateh'* in the tribal areas.[12] In October 2014, six top TTP militant leaders announced their allegiance to Abu Bakr Al Baghdadi as their Amir-ul-Momineen or Calipha.[13] They were the TTP spokesperson Shahidullah Shahid, TTP amir for Orakzai Agency Hafiz Saeed Khan, TTP's Kurram Agency chapter chief Daulat Khan, TTP in Khyber Agency chief Fateh Gul Zaman, TTP's Peshawar amir Mufti Hassan and TTP's Hangu chief Khalid Mansoor. There were reports of TTP Bajaur chief Abu Bakr also joining ISIS along with close militant aide Gul Bali and some others. Some other affiliates of TTP, well-known for their deep sectarian outlook like Lashkar-e-Jhangvi (LeJ) and Ahle Sunnat Wal Jamat (ASWJ) were also courted by ISIS during this period by ISIS to follow its agenda in late 2014 and certain LeJ leaders had even reportedly visited Saudi Arabia and met ISIS leaders along Saudi-Iraq border.[14] By November 2014, it was reported that ISIS had sent its delegates to visit tribal areas and Balochistan[15] to recruit militants from Pakistan. They even visited Khyber and met Mangal Bagh, head of Lashkar-e-Islam (LeI) who sympathised with ISIS philosophy but was too dependent on TTP to owe allegiance to ISIS.[16]

On 15 June 2015, the operation ZeA completed one year and the then Director General of Inter Services Public Relations (ISPR) Major General Asim Saleem Bajwa said security forces have killed 2,000 militants in North Waziristan so far. Bajwa added that 200 soldiers had been killed during the Operation Zarb-e-Azb and 800 others were injured. A year later, on 15 June 2016, on the second anniversary of Operation Zarb-e-Azb, DG, ISPR told the media that more than 3,500 militants were killed while around 490 soldiers lost their lives, 992 militant hideous were destroyed, 253 tonnes of explosives were confiscated, 7,500 bomb factories dismantled, 2,800 mines removed and 3,500 rockets and mortars recovered during the operation". He added that the "militants had enough explosives to continue bombing for 15 years with up to seven bombing every day".[17]

TTP shows Sign of Recovery

Despite such grave internal and external challenges, from September 2014 the TTP militants were able to launch attacks on security forces again. On 6 September, Pakistani Navy frigate PNS Zulfiquar was attacked and briefly captured by Al-Qaeda and rogue Pakistani Navy officers before being recaptured by Pakistani forces. This attack was given star projection by TTP magazine *Nawa-i-Afghan Jihad* in its October 2014 issue detailing the moves the militants took to carry out the attack. The attacker aimed at using the Zulfiquar's anti-ship missiles to attack the US Navy Fleet in the Arabian Sea. Ten militants including 4 rogue Pakistani navy officers were killed in the operation to recapture the ship. Four officers who were involved but did not participate in the attack were later apprehended. On 2 November 2014, Jamaat-ul-Ahrar (JuA), conducted a suicide attack on the Wagah Border, close to the Pakistani city of Lahore and the Indian city of Amritsar and killed more than 60 people and more than 110 were injured. The militants brought things to a head on 16 December 2014, when they attacked Army Public School in Peshawar and brutally killed 132 children resulting in the government ending a moratorium on capital punishment and going after militants in a more determined manner. On 25 December 2014, acting on a tip off my Military Intelligence (MI), a Special Services Group (SSG) of the Pakistan Navy chased down the alleged mastermind of Peshawar School attack, Saddam Jan (TTP chief of the Darra Adam Khel area) in Jamrud Tehsil of Khyber agency and killed him along with six of his accomplices.[18]

From December 2014, even if the government went on claiming success in its operations in the tribal areas, the militants continued to attack government forces in the FATA and adjacent tribal areas. The attacks on Shias and other minorities became more frequent since January 2015. On 30 January, Jundullah, a splinter group of the Taliban, which pledged support to the Islamic State group in 2014 claimed responsibility for an attack on a Shia mosque in Shikarpur in Sindh in southern Pakistan. On 13 February 2015, TTP militants stormed a Shi'ite mosque in Peshawar resulting in the death of at least 19 persons. On 15 March, TTP suicide bombers targeted two churches in the Christian neighbourhood of Youhana

Abad, Lahore, as worshippers were gathering for a Sunday mass. At least fourteen people were killed in the blasts and another 70 were reported injured. The Umar media of TTP reported attacks on security personnel on an everyday basis since the beginning of 2015 and announced formation of Taliban Special Group (TSG) who are being trained to carry out high-profile surgical attacks in future. The media website posts videos regularly showing training being imparted to the so-called TSG trainees.

In May 2015, the Umar Media of TTP released a video which said that, undeterred by Zarb-e-Azb and massive strike by Pakistan army on TTP facilities in the FATA region, the TTP had launched a Mujahideen Special Group (MSG) to carry out fidayeen (suicide) attacks and massive terrorist operations across Pakistan. In fact, the video came up a month after a month after the United Nations Security Council imposed sanctions on Mullah Fazlullah [on 7 April 2015. The spokesperson of TTP, Muhammad Khurasani said that the video titled "MSG Training," was filmed at the "Mehdi Alaih Rizwan Training Centre" somewhere in FATA. It showed dozens of TTP cadres going throw various stages of the commando training. It was around same time Omar Khalid Khurasani, chief of the Jamiat-ul-Ahraar (which had split away in 2014) and Mangal Bagh, the chief of Lashkar-e-Islam (LeI) announced that they would work with TTP. Similarly, Matiur Rehman aka Abdul Samad Sial, commander of Lashkar-e-Jhangvi and linked to Al-Qaeda, as well as factions led by militant commanders Qari Ehsanul Haq, and Ashfaq alias Shamil also joined hands with TTP.[19] The same month, on 8 May 2015, Khurasani claimed responsibility for bringing down an army chopper in Naltar area of Gilgit-Baltistan, Pakistan occupied Kashmir. The list of dead included Ambassador of Norway Leif H. Larsen, Ambassador of Philippines Domingo D. Lucenario Jr, wives of Indonesian and Malaysian envoys Mrs Heri Listyawati Burhan Muhammad and Mrs Datin Habibah Mahmud. Indonesian ambassador Burahan Muhammad succumbed to the injuries ten days later.[20] Although Pakistan army attributed it to technical fault, the TTP released a video showing four masked militants carrying SAM-7B missiles, with the help of which they downed the chopper.[21]

All this was happening in the background of the army launching Operation Khyber.

TTP's Operational Presence inside Pakistan

Federally Administered Tribal Areas (FATA)

When the TTP was founded, its constituent forces hailed from the seven agencies of FATA. Its shura had representatives from all these agencies. However, the fulcrum of TTP lied in South Waziristan. Mehsuds dominating the landscape controlled the affairs of TTP for all practical purposes, between 2004, when Nek Muhammad Waziri was killed and Fazluallah, a non-Mehsud took over as its amir. The other agencies where TTP militants have had a dominant presence are North Waziristan and Bajaur. The agencies of Mohmand, Orakzai, Khyber, and Kurram have many factions of TTP who contend for influence with non-TTP militant groups.

Khyber Pakhtunkhwa (KP)

Apart from tribal agencies of FATA, the TTP has presence in the adjacent PATA districts in the neighbouring province of Khyber Pakhtunkhwa. Representatives from the KPK districts of Bannu, Tank, Lakki Marwat, Dera Ismail Khan, Kohistan, Swat, Buner, and Malakand also find place in the TTP shura. The group has been particularly active in Swat district through one of its principal constituents—the Tehrik-e-Nifaz-e-Shariat-e-Mohammadi (TNSM), led by the present amir of TTP Maulana Qazi Fazlullah.

Rest of Pakistan

The TTP has demonstrated its will and intent backed by its capacity to carry out high profile attacks outside its original habitat in the tribal borderlands. The attack on Benazir's cavalcade in October 2007, even before it was launched formally, the Mariott Hotel attack in September 2008, many other attacks on military facilities in Lahore, Karachi, the Army General Headquarters in Rawalpindi and many other places in Punjab prove this point. For example, the attack on a police academy in Lahore on 30 March 2009, a two-day long assault on the (GHQ) of the Pakistani army in the garrison town of Rawalpindi on 10-11 October 2009.

Attacks against targets in Pakistan's Punjab heartland appeared to be an increasing priority following the death of Baitullah, as was shown with a series of urban bomb attacks in 2010, as well as a suicide attack in Lahore on 25 January 2011. The TTP claimed responsibility for a series of attacks in Punjab killing at least 17 security force personnel in two separate attacks near the city of Wazirabad in Gujranwala district and in the city of Lahore on 9 and 11 July, respectively. TTP spokesman Ehsanullah Ehsan proudly stated after these attacks that TTP fighters had "come out of the tribal areas", and that attacks would continue to take place throughout Pakistan, especially in Punjab. In Punjab, the TTP focused mainly on Lahore and Rawalpindi. Because of its relationship with LeJ activists who fled Punjab and operated out of tribal areas, the TTP expanded its presence to Jhang. LeJ cadres operate as local operatives of TTP in many cities and towns in Punjab.

However, the TTP suffered some reverses in Punjab following intensified army action in FATA since 15 June 2014 when operation Zarb-e-Azb started. Asmatullah Muawiya released a two-minute video message to the media in September 2014 where he said, "We have decided to give up militancy in Pakistan. I've taken the decision in the best interests of Islam and the nation. I also appeal to all other armed groups to stop violent activities in Pakistan" and went on to add that his group would "focus on Dawah (Islamic preaching) for the supremacy of Islam and protection of the system".[22]

Nevertheless, there were claims by TTP of carrying out attacks on other areas like the killing of a Deputy Superintendent of Police, Majeed Abbasi, a Shia, in Shah Latif Town of Karachi in Sindh, by the Swat Chapter of TTP. Khurasani claimed on 30 May 2015 that in Kamonki area of Gujranwala, Punjab, special training force STF of TTP targeted the PML-N Member of Provincial Assembly (MPA) Rana Shamshad and his son. He also said that three groups of Punjabi Taliban had decided to join the TTP, after which TTP had become stronger in Punjab and accelerated its activities there. In June 2015, when the army conducted its operations in Sahiwal,

North Waziristan, and the Tirah valley in Khyber Agency, the TTP threatened to attack Minar-e-Pakistan in Lahore and even threatened Karachi-Electric to stop load-shedding, or else face the consequence. There were reports of TTP militants of the Sajna groups being apprehended from Quetta, Balochistan as well as from Maripur area of Kiamari Town in provincial capital Karachi in July 2015. In August 2015, LeI, an affiliate of TTP, claimed responsibility for the suicide attack on then Home Minister of Punjab, Colonel (retd.) Shuja Khanzada in the village of Shadi Khan in Attock District of Punjab in retaliation for military operations against them in Khyber Agency (the claim was not verified). In October, TTP claimed in a video release that a military intelligence officer named Bashir Ahmad Khan was hanged by them because he was acting against their interest.

Balochistan

Reports of ISIS sending its delegates to meet TTP militants in Balochistan clearly indicated the dent of TTP in northern Balochistan especially in the Pashtun dominated districts north of Quetta. The surge in anti-Hazara/Shia attacks in the province is a grim reminder of penetration by TTP and its splinters/affiliates into Balochistan. These militants have also disrupted transport of fuel and other materials to the coalition forces in Afghanistan and targeted police and security officials in Quetta and Pashtun dominated areas. The attacks involving use of IEDs and suicides in the province were attributed to the TTP, as against the Baloch militants who are fighting a battle for independence for a long time.

Sindh

Various factions of TTP have their branches in Karachi thanks to the growing population of Pashtuns due to steady migration from the tribal areas following prolonged army operations since 2004. As the financial capital of the country, Karachi offers unique opportunities for these groups to base themselves there and discover ways of raising funds for their factions. Some reports suggest that wealthy Sheikhs from the Gulf countries use their links in Karachi to channel funds to TTP and other radical Islamic groups. As a close observer of the TTP in Karachi, Zia-Ur-Rehman would argue, that the TTP "may have been born in the tribal agencies, it might have even ruled Swat, but it is Karachi that has been crucial to the TTP's perpetuation of power across the country".

However, different factions of TTP—who have managed to pull on together in the tribal areas—have not had a peaceful relationship among them in Karachi. Fighting among TTP factions often led to worsening of security situation till the launching of army operation simultaneous to the Operation Zarb-e-Azb in Karachi. The Waliur Rahman and Hakimullah Mehsud groups often locked horns in Karachi on many occasions, both when these two militant leaders were alive and after their death. The former faction has been quite dominant and managed to expel the latter from Landhi, Sohrab Goth, Ittehad Town, and Manghopir areas. Other factions of the TTP active in Karachi are from Swat and Mohmand. Their networks are especially strong in Kunwari Colony, Pashtunabad, Pipri, Gulshen-e-Buner, SITE Town and some settlements in Sohrab Goth.[23] Even reports in April 2015 suggested that a new group of Afridi militants are active in Sohrab Goth, Ali Town, Keamari and Banaras areas of Karachi. Some reports said, "Truckers involved in transporting fuel to Nato forces at their bases in Afghanistan from Karachi are mostly members of the Afridi and Shinwari clans of Khyber Agency" and could be linked to Lashkar-e-Islam led by Mangal Bagh.[24]

Gilgit-Baltistan

The TTP's operational base expanded to even Gilgit-Baltistan when it claimed that it had kidnapped and subsequently killed 10 foreign tourists in the Nanga Parbat area in the Diamer district of Gilgit-Baltistan on 22 June 2013.

TTP's Operations outside Pakistan

Apart from working in Afghanistan as its extended operational ground, where it has worked in close cooperation with Afghan Taliban and attacked military facilities of the coalition forces, the TTP has used at least some Afghan border provinces like Kunar,

Nuristan and Nangarhar, as its strategic backyard. Swat TTP chief and now amir of both TTP and TNSM, Mullah Fazlullah or Mullah Radio as he was popularly called in Swat, has repeatedly sought shelter in Afghanistan every time Pakistan launched an operation against his outfit. Similarly, chief of TTP faction in Bajaur, Maulana Faqir Muhammad has used Afghan soil as a safe haven in the face of Pakistani attack.

The anti-West rhetoric used by the TTP has been noted earlier in the discussion. There is a deep conviction among the TTP leaders that Pakistan would not be as aggressive as it is vis-à-vis the local Taliban, were it not for the pressure from the US. Moreover, continued support by the US and its allies to the anti-Taliban forces in Afghanistan as well as repeated drone attacks in the tribal terrain have turned the TTP against the US and its Western allies as enemies. Therefore, it is not strange that the TTP did make an effort to internationalise its operation in the name of protecting Islam and avenging attacks on Muslim by governments in the West. The TTP connections were explored in the case of trial of 11 men, alleged by Spanish authorities to be planning suicide attacks on the city's subway system in Barcelona in November 2009. The then TTP spokesman, Maulvi Omar, acknowledged TTP's involvement in the Barcelona plot. All the accused were convicted and sentenced to long terms in prison. The case of Faisal Shahzad receiving training at the hands of TTP trainers to stage an attack in Times Square, New York on 1 May 2010 has been mentioned above. Faisal not only received training in Waziristan at TTP facilities but also received money from the outfit to stage the attack.

The TTP did not stop at that. One of its cells in the US was busted in Miami, Florida, in late 2011. Three Pakistani nationals were arrested in the city in March 2011 who pleaded guilty to charges of providing material support to the TTP. The defendants also admitted that they had taken money from TTP to smuggle a TTP militant into the US via Ecuador.

The TTP was linked to a series of shootings in France in 2012. A French national of Algerian descent, Mohammed Merah, received training at a TTP facility in North Waziristan and in a series of small-arms attacks around the French city of Toulouse, killed three soldiers, three Jewish children, and a local rabbi, before being killed by security forces on 22 March. On 15 March, spokesman of one of the TTP factions identifying himself as Ahmed Marwat, acknowledged that Merah had in fact trained with TTP in North Waziristan, but had carried out the attack alone. Many French nationals also reportedly trained with the TTP in North Waziristan in the use of explosives and small-arms in recent years.

TTP vs Pakistan Army: Operations and After

Starting with *Operation Al-Mizan* (Balancing scale) which was launched in 2002 and continued till 2006, Pakistan army went up on a learning curve as its efforts were resisted with surprising intensity by the militants/local Taliban in the tribal belt. By October 2007, the focus had shifted to the Swat Valley, with Mullah Fazlullah, famous as Mullah Radio, sweeping the former Malakand division (comprising the princely states of Chitral, Dir and Swat). The local Taliban sought to impose a strict version of Sharia law in the Swat valley which included campaign against polio-vaccination, preventing women's education, public execution of barbers, music-shop owners, and thieves. On 24 October 2007, Pakistan army launched *Operation Rah-e-Haq* (The path of truth) sent about 3,000 troops to Swat which swelled to about 5,000 in November with the onset of the second phase of the operation. The army sent in reinforcements to help out about 15,000 local police and para-military forces who found it difficult to rein in the Taliban of Swat. As has been described earlier Swati Taliban emerged out of the *Tehrik-Nifaz-e-Shariat-e-Muhammadi* (TNSM), founded in 1992 by Sufi Muhammad, father-in-law of Mullah Radio, who split away from Jamat-i-Islami to found the new outfit. He had defied the government orders and led a large number of volunteers to Afghanistan in 2001 to fight the US troops.

Deal with Swati Taliban and its Failure

In the initial phase, Swati Taliban surprised the army with few tactical moves sweeping few Tehshils in Swat and marched towards Shangla, occupying its district headquarters by early November. In the third phase, the army targeted Mullah Fazlullah's village Imam Dehri, wrested control of the peaks from the Taliban and launched a massive offensive forcing them to flee. The army freed the Tehsils occupied by the Taliban by December 2007. By July 2008, with the resurgent Swati Taliban upping their ante, the army took the help of the air-force to launch *Operation Rah-e-Haq-II* with use of massive artillery fire and air-power. While the army dominated the battle, the local Taliban continued to irritate the army with its surprise attacks and extension of control in adjacent areas, of Buner, Lower Dir and Kohistan, necessitating *Operation Rah-e-Haq III* in January 2009 to control the supply lines and push the Taliban out of the area.[25] The army was able to retake the main town in Swat in Mingora. However, at this juncture, in February 2009, the provincial government decided to strike a deal with the militants. The founder of TNSM and father-in-law of Fazlullah was brought in to negotiate a deal with his son-in-law.

Notably, Maulana Sufi Muhammad shot to limelight in 1994 when he staged a week-long sit-in protest with hundreds of his supporters at the Malakand Pass demanding enforcement of Shariah law there. His followers wore black turbans and were indoctrinated by him to work towards imposition of Sharia in Pakistan. In 1998, the Maulana had even declared people opposed to Sharia *wajib-ul-qatal* (worthy of being murdered). He was also known for his support of the Taliban and was credited with forcing the provincial and federal governments to concede local application of a separate Sharia-based judicial system in the Malakand Division. Long-held for his involvement in cross-border armed action in aid of Taliban in Afghanistan since 2002 and serving a sentence of seven years in prison, he was released by the provincial government of the left-wing nationalist Awami National Party (ANP) on 21 April 2008 to convince his son-in-law to pursue his movement peacefully. Sufi Muhammad was arrested in December 2001, upon his return from Afghanistan (after staging a rally in Timergara in Lower Dir district in 2001 and dubbing the then military ruler Gen Pervez Musharraf an agent of the US), and later convicted on 24 April 2002 and 'sentenced to seven years of imprisonment for defying government order and inciting people to illegally cross into Afghanistan'.[26] He advocated a pacifist line upon his release and tried to prevail upon Fazlullah, who also showed his interest in the deal in May 2008. The ANP-led NWFP government and the Taliban headed by Maulana Fazlullah signed a deal on 21 May 2008, which was signed by leaders of both the ANP and the PPP. However, this had not worked because Fazlullah felt empowered by this and enforced his strict version of Islam in and around Swat and videos of public flogging went viral, forcing the army to react to it. Bomb blasts, suicide attacks, throat-slitting and floggings by militants became routine.

In February 2009, the Maulana was called upon again to negotiate a deal with Fazlullah and this time under military pressure he also found in the deal a face-saver to enter into a ceasefire. His spokesperson Muslim Khan announced a ceasefire and draft Sharia Nazam-e-Adl Regulation (SNAR) was formulated "to provide for Nifaz-e-Nizam-e-Shariat through Courts in the Provincially Administered Tribal Areas (PATA) of the North-West Frontier Province, except the Tribal Area adjoining Manshera district and the former State of Amb". The draft was passed in the local assembly and sent to the president (Asif Ali Zardari) for approval. Zardari dilated, awaiting establishment of firm control of government forces over Swat and adjoining areas; however, a national assembly resolution approved of the regulation to establish Qazi courts and enforce Sharia law in Malakand division in April and on 13th of that month, Zardari signed it into law. It was regarded as a continuation of the Nifaz-e-Nizam-e-Sharia regulation of 1994 and Sharia Nizam-e-Adl regulation of 1999, both of which were conceded to TNSM in the past to ensure peace in the area. There was also an inertial case of Swat region having a dyarchy of legal systems under the ruler of Swat, which was abolished in 1969, which makes room for such parallel system of justice. It is also true that the local population do carry a sense of nostalgic attachment to the erstwhile local justice system that is deemed more responsive to their local needs, compared to the justice system in rest of Pakistan that is regarded as more expensive, time consuming and unjust.

Viewed from the vantage point of the political leadership of Pakistan, such concessions are regarded as pragmatic and in line with overall emphasis on Islam in the Pakistani statecraft. However, undeniably, this was a classic case of the capitulation of the state in the face of militant advocacy of Sharia law in Pakistan in a tribal corner of Pakistan, where the militants had rendered the state's justice system non-functional. The SNAR provided for a three-tier judicial system (*Ilaqa, Zilla* and at the apex level, *Dar-ul-Qaza* and *Dar-ul Dar-ul Qaza*). The system is controversially still in vogue today even after merger of the FATA and PATA regions into the province of Khyber Pakhtun Khwa following the passage of 25th Amendment Act of 2018, whereby all existing laws were meant to be inoperative. Keeping the legal complications in view, the provincial government passed Due to the same legal complication, the Khyber Pakhtunkhwa government enacted the KP Continuation of Laws in Erstwhile PATA Act in January 2019, followed by KP Continuation of Laws in Erstwhile FATA Act in April 2019 to maintain the legality of the existing laws in former FATA and PATA regions, until they would be expressly altered, repealed or amended by the competent authority. This has been challenged in the Supreme Court and the verdict is awaited.

Getting back to the local Taliban's assertion in Swat following the proclamation of the SNAR, the situation did not improve. Seeing the government responding meekly to his Shariah blackmail, Fazlullah started raising objections to the way the judges were appointed/ nominated by the government. Revealing his uncompromising attitude, Sufi Muhammad also stated that superior courts in Pakistan were un-Islamic and they could not hear appeals against decisions of the newly set up Qazi courts. He even went forward and said that parliamentary democracy itself was un-Islamic. The Swat Taliban even threatened to fan out of Swat and enforce Sharia in other parts of Pakistan. Faced with such an unenviable position, the state government urged the militants to lay down arms and vacate the territories under their control. The local TTP, on the contrary, asked the government forces to move out first. The situation became so tense within a month that on 18 May 2009, the federal government called an all-party conference, which reaffirmed its commitment to preserve, protect and defend the Constitution and sovereignty of the state and initiate military action in Swat. The local population were asked to leave the valley to enable all-out kinetic operations against the militants. In July 2009, Sufi Muhammad was arrested with his sons, Rizwanullah, Ziaullah and Hayatullah, from Sethi Town in Peshawar accused of delivering a fiery speech against democracy at Grassy Ground, Mingora, on 19 April 2009.[27] His sons were re-arrested in August 20009, immediately after they were released by Peshawar High Court.

In May 2009, the government launched *Operation Rah-e-Rast* (the straight path) to oust the Swati Taliban from the area and cleared Mingora town after a tough fight within days and spread out to adjacent areas. After fierce battles in the villages of Ghazi Gai and Shatkai, where the Pakistan army used helicopter gunships to destroy about two dozen homes housing Taliban militants leading to an unprecedented out-migration from Swat. Some media reports suggested that about 2.2 million people fled the area during the clashes. By September, the government claimed that majority of the migrants had returned following reinforcement of government's writ in the area.

Operations in FATA

While the operations were ongoing in Swat, there were assertions by Pakistani Taliban in the tribal belt around this time. In January 2007, the army launched *Operation Eagle Swoop* in Darra Adam Khel, when local militants seized government vehicles carrying ammunition and personnel. Lashkar-e-Islam (LeI) had started its assault on Barelvi Ansar-ul-Islam and held the Bara Tehsil to ransom. The army launched *Operation Rah-e-Mustaqeem* (Operation Righteous Path) on 28 June 2008 against LeI chief Mangal Bagh. Within weeks on 9 July Bara was brought under control and on the same day elsewhere the TTP attacked a paramilitary fort in Torawari area of Hangu injuring three Frontier Corps personnel forcing the army to launch *Operation Zarb-e-Kaleem* (Strike with the Staff of Moses). The army deployed about 1,500 troops backed by artillery, tanks and gunship helicopters for the operation along the border between Hangu and Kurram Agency. The army went ahead with its operation despite threat from Taliban to execute 29 police and paramilitary personnel from Swat held hostage by it. The army launched *Operation Sherdil* (Lion heart) on 7 August 2008 in aid of Frontier Corps in Bajaur, bordering Malakand and Lower Dir, responding to reports of Al-Qaeda using the area as its control-centre and TTP elements hiding there fleeing operations elsewhere. By October 2008, in a joint session of parliament, the military reportedly briefed the parliamentarians about the worsening situation in FATA and former NWFP and "there was an admission that the armed forces cannot curb the militants and extremists and it is important that the parliament also initiates a political dialogue to resolve the crisis".[28] The military also informed that during the military operation in Bajaur around 2,744 terrorists were killed, including 321 foreigners, while 1,400 were injured. Maj Gen Abid Mumtaz (retd.) wrote a memoir[29] detailing his experiences during the operation which shows that it was one of the toughest operations conducted by the army against the militants. By the end of the year the operation succeeded in establishing army control in the area. In Khyber agency, through which the major trade-route to Central Asia runs, the army launched *Operation Daraghalam* (Here I Come) on 28 December 2008, followed by *Operation Biya Daraghlam* (Here I Come Again) in September 2009, and *Operation Khwakh Ba De Shum* (I Will Teach You a Lesson) in November 2009 in the backdrop of increasing attacks on NATO supply convoys.[30] The army's operation continued in the Agency throughout 2010-2011 and beyond leading to thousands of people migrating to safer places inside Pakistan.

South Waziristan witnessed a spike in militancy by June 2009 and the army launched *Operation Rah-e-Nijat* on 19 June to take the war to Waziristan and target TTP chief Baitullah Mehsud. The operation continued till December 2009. In July a military helicopter crashed killing all 26 crew on board. On 5 August, American drone strikes targeted and successfully killed then TTP chief, Baitullah Mehsud. Following this, a major air and ground offensive began in October 2009 after a three-month-long blockade of the area to tire out the militants. Suspected militant hideouts were razed to ground with overwhelming air-action using fighter-jets and attack helicopters. In South Waziristan, places like Kotkai and Kaniguram, where Uzbek and other foreign militants operated according to military intelligence, the security forces overpowered the militants and gained control. By December, the army announced that it had established its control over entire South Waziristan. Some other operations that were conducted by the army included Operation Black Thunderstorm in Buner, Lower Dir and Shangla district (2009) and Operation Brekhna in Mohmand Agency (2009). However, despite these operations, through the death of Baitullah Mehsud and his successor, Hakimullah Mehsud, the militants regained their strength and carried out attacks as mentioned before in areas outside the tribal belt. Moreover, internally displaced persons (IDPs) from these areas appeared in Pakistani cities and town in Punjab and Sindh and carried the terror dynamics that characterised politics of the tribal region to rest of Pakistan.

Operation Zarb-e-Azb and After

As has been discussed earlier, country-wide attacks including many on military facilities like the attacks on PNS Mehran of May 2011, on the Minhas air base at Kamra, in Punjab in August 2012, on Malala Yousufzai in October 2012 and on Jinnah International Airport in Karachi led to a consensus to launch Operation Zarb-e-Azb, as discussed earlier.

There is no doubt that the operations launched by Pakistan since June 2014 led to displacement of TTP from the tribal terrain and weakened their capacity to strike. Many of the TTP cadres as well as their leaders escaped to Afghanistan across the Durand Line. Some Pakistani sources even say that they were informed by their moles in the Pakistan army about the impending action and left their areas of operations and fled across the border. Not a day passed in Pakistan without news of TTP cadres either eliminated successfully or captured by the security forces. There were also reports of some of the TTP cadres surrendering to the army. The military spokesperson heading the Inter Services Public Relations (ISPR) came out with regular updates claiming its achievements, which are all available in the social media (youtube.com). As per the February 2017 figures provided by the military, it lost about 770 officers and soldiers while 2225 were injured.

Following TTP's brutal attack on APS on 16 December 2014, the ruling elite of Pakistan overcame its precipitate inhibition to go the whole hog on its attempt to take on the radical Islamist forces parading as Pakistani Taliban in the ungoverned tribal terrain. Eight days later, on 24 December, a 20-point National Action Plan was drawn up by the Nawaz Sharif government aimed at eliminating terror and extremism from Pakistan. The moratorium on death penalty was lifted and in the subsequent days many convicted criminals were hanged. The government brought out legislation in January 2015 to establish Military courts for two years to deliver quick justice to the militants arrested under the charges of terrorism. Roughly about 11 military courts were set up around the country and a total of 274 individuals were convicted out of which 161 were sentenced to death. The number of the TTP convicts, including those belonging to LeI, Lashkar-e-Jhangvi (LeJ) and TTP-Swat was 98 out of 274 (while the affiliation of 115 convicts was not disclosed). 12 of these were executed and 113 were given jail terms, mostly life-sentences. The military courts drew wider-spread criticism from the civil society because of the murky and opaque procedures followed during trial. The international commission of jurists (ICJ) in a briefing paper published in 2016, strongly criticised the government and military authorities for having "failed to make public information about the time and place of their trials; the specific charges and evidence against the convicts; as well as the judgments of military courts including the essential findings, legal reasoning, and evidence on which the convictions were based."[31]

Pakistan also started registering mobile phone sim cards countywide; madrassas were asked to register and reveal their sources of funding (with limited success). National Counter-Terrorism Authority (NACTA) which was conceived and organised during 2009 as the highest body to coordinate sharing of intelligence gathered by

26 spy agencies to curb terrorism in the country, was revived and the Prime Minister of Pakistan formed an Apex Committee to regularly monitor the success of NAP. The entire operation involving kinetic and non-kinetic measures against terrorists, stricter law-enforcement and socio-economic measures to address the consequences of the operations in the shape of internal displacement and loss of public property was known to the outside world as Zarb-e-Azb. It was claimed by Pakistan as the largest anti-terrorism campaign against terrorism anywhere, involving over 180,000 security forces.

Operation Khyber

While Operation Zarb-e-Azb was going on in North and South Waziristan agencies, the Pakistan army responded to militant activities by Lashkar-e-Islam (LeI) in Khyber agency with equal vehemence by launching operations Khyber I, II, III and IV from October 2014 till 21 August 2017.

LeI, established in 2004 by Mufti Munir Shakir and now led by Mangal Bagh had a chequered history. Known for his rigid Deobandi-Wahabi outlook and its continued confrontation with a Barelvi group called Ansar-ul-Islam in Khyber agency, the LeI chief Mangal Bagh was alternately wooed and shunned by the security forces depending upon their requirement. Mangal Bagh used to work with the military at times to reinforce his position while the army used to flirt with him to keep the supply line open for NATO forces, which inevitably passed through the agency. On several occasions, however, the army had to use force to repulse LeI's advance and its sectarian attack against other groups in the region. LeI shared TTP's perspective but chose to operate alone strengthening its position in the Tirah valley. However, during the operation Zarb-e-Azb, the military found out that many Al-Qaeda and TTP militants were holed up in Tirah valley supposedly under the protection of LeI. Therefore, on 16 October 2014, the army launched its Khyber-I operation to flush out militants from the Tirah valley. Forced to make common cause with TTP, Mangal Bagh asked the latter to send its fighters to help it meet the Pakistan army onslaught.

Operation Khyber entered its second phase in March-April 2015 and reportedly the security forces made huge progress in dismantling the militant infrastructure put in place by TTP and its allies in Tirah valley[32]—a kidney shaped areas, spread over 1,500 sq km straddling Tora Bora, which served as a natural shelter for Al-Qaeda fleeing Afghanistan during 2001-2002—where major training centres of TTP were located—especially in Sipaha and Akka Khel areas of Bara tehsil. Pakistan military officials called it the last major and most intense battle in their operations in the tribal areas.[33] Khyber-III launched in August 2016, targeted border areas beyond the Tirah valley primarily to destroy militant facilities close to the Pak-Af border and stop cross-border movement of militants with ease. Khyber-IV started in July 2017 to aid Pakistan army's operation Radd-ul-Fsssad (RuF) and targeted Rajgal and Shawal valleys to clear out Jamaat-ul-Ahrar militants. Within six weeks, these valleys were under the control of the Pakistan army. According to Pakistan army figures, in Khyber-IV, 52 terrorists were killed and 32 injured while four of them surrendered. Rajgal Valley, spread over an area of 250 sq km, one of the most difficult areas for military operation, acted as a major entry point for Daesh elements, and Khyber operations drew to a close with the military taking control over the area, according to the DG, ISPR.[34]

Operation Radd-ul-Fassad

Operation *Zarb-e-Azb* was followed by Operation *Radd-ul-Fassad* (Elimination of Discord), which was launched on 22 February 2017. As per the statement of the ISPR, the operation aimed at indiscriminately eliminating the "residual/latent threat of terrorism, consolidating the gains made in other military operations, and further ensuring the security of Pakistan's borders". The efforts would entail, it stated, "conduct of Broad Spectrum Security/Counter-Terrorism (CT) operations by Rangers in Punjab, continuation of ongoing operations across the country, and focus on more effective border security management. Countrywide de-weaponisation and explosive control are additional cardinals of the effort. Pursuance of National Action Plan will be the hallmark of this operation".[35]

The fact that the operation followed a meeting between Army Chief Qamar Javed Bajwa, the corps commanders of Punjab, the director general of Pakistan Rangers Punjab, and the heads of intelligence agencies, in Lahore, which suggested that the army, satisfied with its operations in the tribal areas was now turning its attention towards Punjab, where on 13 February 2017, a suicide bomber struck a protest meeting at Lahore's Charing Cross interchange, right outside the gates of Punjab's Provincial Assembly, killing 13 and injuring 85. In fact, there were a sudden spurt in terror violence all over the country in February 2017. On 15 February, a vehicle carrying judges in Peshawar's Hayatabad Phase-5 area, was ambushed by a TTP suicide bomber in his motorcycle resulting in the death of the driver and causing injury to four other occupants. The same day, in an attack claimed by JuA, a suicide bomber struck in Mohmand, killing three Khasadar force personnel and five civilians. On 16 February, the shrine of Sufi saint Syed Usman Marwandi (13th century AD), a saint poet and contemporary of Rumi, also famously known as Lal Shahbaz Qalandar in Sehwan, Sindh, was struck by a suicide bomber, leaving more than 88 dead and many injured. This was claimed by Islamic State.

In April 2017, spokesperson of JuA, Ehshanullah Ehshan alias Liaqat Ali, who was earlier in TTP but had later joined Khalid Khorasani when he split away to form JuA, surrendered after striking a deal with Pakistani security forces. He came out with tame stories about involvement of external forces in internal terror activities in Pakistan. This was the second most important achievement for Pakistani forces after the US handover of another high-value TTP leader Latif Mehsud in December 2014. Ehshan was kept under house-arrest in the upscale Hayatabad suburb of Peshawar, where he lived in relative comfort, and even fathered a child until his escape in January 2020.

After the launch of Radd-ul-Fassad (RuF), reports of security forces engaging and eliminating terrorists poured in month after month. However, terrorists struck in Mastung, Balochistan, on 12 May 2017, attacking the convoy of Senate Deputy Chairman Maulana Abdul Ghafoor Haideri of Jamiat-ul-Ulema-i-Islam

(Fazlur), on the Quetta-Karachi National Highway, killing at least 28 people and injuring 40 others. Haideri suffered injuries and survived. While ISIS claimed responsibility for the attack, observers in Pakistan attributed it to TTP split away factions working with ISIS. On 14 July 2017, four armed men riding two motorcycles ambushed the official vehicle of Superintendent of Police Mubarak Shah while he was leaving for his office in Quaidabad from his residence in Killi Deba. JuA claimed responsibility for the attack. Days earlier, the district police officer of Qila Abdullah was killed with his two security guards in a suicide attack in Chaman. TTP claimed responsibility for a suicide blast near the Arfa Karim IT Tower on the Ferozepur Road of Lahore, in Punjab on 24 July. At least 26 persons, including nine policemen, were killed and 56 injured in the incident. In an operation in Karachi, the security forces killed four terrorists who were affiliated to Al-Qaeda in Indian Subcontinent (AQIS), demonstrating the spread of anti-state militants linked to TTP throughout Pakistan.

The Counter Terrorism Department (CTD), Punjab Police claimed to have eliminated militants affiliated to TTP in August during a raid at University Road of Gujrat Town and in an encounter near Sagian bridge in Lahore. Suspected TTP suicide attacker targeted an army truck in August killing 15, mostly military personnel, ramming his motorcycle, rigged with explosives, into a military truck at Old Pishin bus stop, in Quetta, Balochistan. Mullah Fazlullah's cousin, Khursheed, was killed in a shootout in Sadaf society area in Karachi in September, 2017. Apart from targeting security forces, the TTP affiliated terrorists targeted Barelvi places of worship and people belonging to the Shia sect, especially the Hazaras. Dargah Pir Rakhel Shah in Fatehpur, a small town in the Jhal Magsi district of Balochistan was targeted by a suicide bomber on 5 October 2017 killing 20 and injuring 30 (this shrine was also attacked in March 2005). Four days later, Hazara Shias were targeted by unidentified assailants who opened fire at their vehicle on Kasi road in Gawalmandi area of Quetta killing at least five and seriously injuring one. Later in the month, on 23 October, Abdul Hashmi alias Shehryar, leader of a shadowy group called Ansarul

Sharia Pakistan (ASP)[36] was eliminated in a joint raid by Pakistan Rangers and CTD, in Raees Goth area of Baldia Town in Karachi. Four alleged TTP militants were killed in an encounter with CTD, Punjab on the Sargodha Road in late November. In December, alleged TTP operatives were killed in a CTD operation in Fasialabad (3 December) and suspected ISIS militants were killed in Karachi (30 December).

The trend continued in the beginning of the year 2018. Attacks on Frontier Corps personnel continued especially in the tribal areas. Pakistani security forces also carried out operations in the Af-Pak border areas of Chaman and claimed to have killed many TTP terrorists. In January 2018, a suicide blast by a TTP militant near GPO Chowk on Zarghoon Road of Quetta, seven people, including five policemen, were killed and 16 others, including eight Policemen, injured. During the counter terror operations, Sindh Senior Superintendent of Police (SSP) in the Malir District of Karachi, Rao Anwar, notorious for encounter killing claimed to have killed four TTP militants in Karachi on 13 January 2018. He also escaped a suicide attack by a TTP militant narrowly while four of his associates were killed. Rao Anwar's ill-acquired reputation[37] as an 'encounter specialist' (conducted 444 encounters between 2011-2018 as SSP, Malir) suffered a huge set-back when it turned out that he had in fact killed, in a clear case of fake encounter, an aspiring Pashtun model from Waziristan named Naseemullah Mehsud, better known as Naqeeb, with three of his friends, Sabir, Nazar Jan and Ishaq. This cold-blooded killing stirred the conscience of the whole nation and civil society groups held nation-wide strikes, so much so that the then Chief Justice of Pakistan, Justice Saqib Nisar to take *suo moto* notice of the case on 18 February and the case continues to drag on with two key prosecution witnesses turning hostile, and there is a possibility of him waking free someday soon, despite the fact that there is enough evidence of his flagrant abuse of power, his arrogant and criminal mindset and imposition of sanctions against him for human rights violations by US and UK. One prominent daily newspaper wrote editorially on 2 November 2020: "The trial of retired SSP Malir Rao Anwar in the Naqeebullah Mehsud murder case is emblematic of a dysfunctional state where those with the right connections can seemingly commit heinous acts with impunity."[38]

In February 2018, a suicide attack on an army camp killed 11 and injured 13 soldiers in Kabal area of Swat. On 14 March, right when Tablighi Jamaat was organising its *Ijtima* (congregation), a police check-post on the Raiwind Road, set up specially to provide security to the people attending the *Ijtima*, was attacked allegedly by a TTP suicide bomber who drove a motorcycle into the check-post and blasted himself killing five policemen and three civilians, injuring 20 others. That Lashkar-e-Jhangvi (LeJ) was using Balochistan as its launching-pad for orchestrating attack on Shia Hazaras became increasingly clear during 2014-2018. The Balochistan chief of LeJ was killed in an armed engagement on 16 May 2018. On 13 June 2018, Mullah Fazlullah was killed in "a joint air operation [with the US] in the border area of Marawera district of Kunar province", declared Mohammad Radmanish, spokesman for Afghan defence ministry. Afghan President called up Pakistan Army Chief to intimate the news of joint US-Afghan air mission.[39] His son Abdullah was killed in March and one of his assistants, Qari Abdullah Dawar was killed in July, in separate drone strikes.

TTP influence in the Hinterland

Some arrests in June from Karachi revealed that the roots of TTP ran deeper than imagined. On 11 June, three suspects, named Shahsawar, Mujeeb Rehman and Khalid Pervez, were arrested by the CTD in Sultanabad and Jubilee areas of Karachi. Khalid was an IT expert and holder of an MBA degree from a reputed institute, while Shahsawar was a faculty at a government university in Dera Ismail Khan.[40] They had links with ISIS, LeJ and maintained their links with militant leaders in Afghanistan. On 27 June, CTD, Sindh police arrested four suspects, including a government doctor (an orthopedic surgeon) Abdur Rehman, for their involvement in helping and treating militants linked with TTP. In September, Hafiz Imran Khan, Zahid Khan and Asmatullah were arrested from Orangi Town for providing financial assistance to militants and collecting donations besides treating injured militants.

With Pakistan slipping into election mode during this period, TTP was seen targeting politicians regarded as secular and liberal in Balochistan and Khyber Pakhtunkhwa. The deadliest attack since APS school attacks targetted a Balochistan Awami Party (BAP) rally on 13 July killing the election candidate Sirja Raisani and more than 149 people and injured over 200 others, in Dringarh village of Mastung District, which was claimed by TTP's Ghazi Force Lal Masjid in a whatsapp message. On 19 July, the police said that the suicide bomber had been identified as Hafeez Nawaz, a member of LeI, originally from Abottabad but living in Thatta in Sindh for decades, but had migrated to Afghanistan with some of his family members to Afghanistan recently.[41] A week later, the security forces claimed that they had killed Mufti Hidayatullah, who allegedly masterminded this attack.[42]

Almost month later, on 11 August, the CTD, Karachi arrested the father (Muhammad Nawaz) and brother (Haq Nawaz) of Hafeez Nawaz, one of the suicide bombers from in Banaras area of Karachi, while they were planning to escape into Afghanistan. Media reports based on the initial confessions of these two arrested revealed that Hafeez had other accomplices and had joined TTP-Daud Mehsud group after leaving TTP-Fazlullah group.[43] He was trained in Panjgur (Balochistan) and Afghanistan by Jaishul Adl group. Based on further information, the police conducted raids in Manghopir and old Subzi Mandi areas of Karachi and arrested two suspects—Sheeraz, alias Saifullah and Wali Ahmed, alias Abu Ubaid, who were Hafeez's accomplices. The investigations pointed to a complex web of random anti-State activities being conducted by a wide array of radical Islamist groups dispersed across Pakistan and Eastern and Southern Afghanistan which cumulatively posed a continual security challenge for the Pakistani state, despite its vigilance and its inclination to at least 'do more' at home.

On 17 July, search operations were carried out in Attock, Sialkot, Lahore, Mianwali and Faisalabad. 24 suspects were reportedly nabbed from Lahore.[44] A PTI candidate, Ikramullah Gandapur, was targeted on 22 July in Dera Ismaili Khan. On 25 July, 31 persons, including five policemen and two minors, were killed and 30 injured in a suicide attack targeting the convoy of Deputy Inspector General (DIG) of Police, Abdul Razzaq Cheema near a school area in the Bhosa Mandi area on the Eastern Bypass of Quetta. Razaaq remained unhurt in the attack, while Station House Officer (SHO) Bhosa Mandi succumbed to his injuries. Karachi police said soon afterwards that activists of banned outfits were adopting 'new methods of reconnaissance, transportation of arms and explosives, and carrying out terror acts' working 'as drivers, cleaners, guards, cobblers and even garbage collectors in order to conduct reconnaissance and transport arms and explosives'.[45] On 5 September, Punjab police arrested three terrorist belonging to ISIS from Basti Shorkot in Multan, who had reportedly planned to carry out attacks on the occasion of defence day of Pakistan a day later.

On 13 November, TTP-Khurasani faction claimed that it had kidnapped and later killed Tahir Khan Dawar, a Superintendent of Police (SP) from Peshawar, Khyber Pakhtunkhwa), days after he was abducted and taken away to Afghanistan, by unidentified militants. His body was found body was found by local people in Dur Baba District of Nangarhar province in Afghanistan. The pictures of his body, with a handwritten note in Pashto from "Wilayat Khorasan (province of Khorasan)" were in circulation on social media stating that he was killed "to convey a message to people like him as he was involved in the arrest and murder of a number of militants".[46]

On 23 November, a suicide bomber blew himself up in a crowded market adjacent to a Shia Imambargha killing about 33, including 22 Shias in Kalaya town in Lower Orakzai.[47] On 28 November 2018, the Pakistan Interior ministry announced that it was time for Pakistan to roll out the second the phase of National Action Plan (NAP) and restructure the National Counter Terrorism Authority (NACTA), with inclusion of a cyber security cell, upgrading of the safe city projects and curbing of currency smuggling from airports and borders, to effectively tackle internal threats to security.[48] All in all in 2018, according to reports, average militant attacks per month decreased from 35 in 2017 to 19 in 2018. To put into perspective, this number was 134 in 2014, which dropped to 59 in 2015 and 42 in 2016.[49] Another report suggested that out of a total of 262 attacks in 2018, 171 were carried out by TTP and its affiliates.[50]

On 28 December, the Army organised the visit of a delegation of journalists to the Pak-Afghan border and announced that fencing of the first 482-km-long patch of the 1,403 km long Pak-Afghan border in the KP (out of a total length of 2601 km to be fenced) had been completed ahead of schedule and affirmed that it had resulted in a visible decline in smuggling and terrorism. It was also reported earlier on 15 December that 233 forts (out of a proposed total of 843) had been constructed along the border equipped with water, solar electricity and protection mines and safe tracks were being constructed to connect these forts. The fencing consists of a pair of nine-foot wire fences, with a six-foot gap in between, topped with barbed wire. It would run along a very difficult terrain and the total expense for raising the fence would amount to about US$ 550 million.[51] Showing its anxiety about Pakistan's border with Afghanistan, the government, possibly at the behest of the army, on 3 January 2019, Pakistan withdrew, the long-standing facility of on-arrival visas for Afghan nationals, citing security risks amid a spike in terror attacks. Earlier, Afghan nationals were granted a 30-day visa on arrival at the entry points but they would henceforth be required to apply for visa from Pakistani missions in Afghanistan in a set-back to people-to-people ties between the two states.

Emergence of Pakistan Tahaffuz Movement (PTM)

Another important development in the meanwhile in Pakistan politics was the birth of a pacifist civil society movement led by Pashtun youth from the tribal areas following the extra-judicial killing of Naqeebulla (also Naseemullah) Mehsud in January 2018, mentioned above. Initially known as Mehsud Tahaffuz Movement (MTM), founded by some Mehsud students in Gomal University in Dera Ismail Khan in May 2014. It aimed at peace-building and reconstruction following army action in the tribal belt. Its work focused on removal of landmines and addressing genuine concerns of displaced Pashtuns seeking rehabilitation. In the aftermath of gruesome killing of Naqeebullah and his friends painting them as terrorists, MTM transformed itself into Pashtun Tahaffuz Movement (PTM) since January 2018. Led by a human rights activist, Manzoor Pashteen from South Waziristan, PTM soon assumed centre-stage in ventilating Tribal frustration and anger against the army and the administration. One of its popular slogans is *"Yah jo dahshatgardi hai, iss ke pichhe wardi hai"* (It is the uniform, or the military, which is behind every act of terror in Pakistan). The other defining slogan that betrays the sense of alienation that the Pashtuns have developed in Pakistan is *Da sanga azadi da* (what kind of freedom is this)? In an impassioned commentary in a leading Pakistani daily, a former Pashtun bureaucrat echoed the sentiments of the Pashtuns of the FATA region:

> Many believe this is the dawn of a Pakhtun renaissance, as the youth seek to redefine their political status and create a new social contract with the state. Fata's people in particular have stopped looking up to the recognised leaders, the maliks and mullahs, and have come up with an alternate leadership among the youth.[52]

PTM started a justice movement and a long march on 26 January 2018 from Dera Ismail Khan with 20 activists and passing through Lakki Marwat, Bannu, Domel, Karak, Kohat, and Darra Adam Khel, Peshawar, Charsadda, Mardan, Swabi, and Tarnol, it reached Islamabad on 1 February 2018, and demanded that racial profiling of Pashtuns should be ended, set up a judicial enquiry into Naqeebullah's murder, bring Pashtun missing persons before the judiciary, stop using firepower against civilians in the tribal belt and imposing collective punishment on villages and communities, stop the practice of enforced disappearances (about 32,000 have gone missing over a decade)[53] and remove all landmines from the tribal areas. In the July 2018 elections, some of the PTM leaders contested the elections as independent candidates (because PTM leader Manzoor Pashteen was opposed to PTM functioning as a political party) and two of them, Ali Wazir and Mohsin Dawar won MNA seats from the tribal areas. Ali Wazir contested from South Waziristan and polled an impressive 23, 550 votes while his two competitors from PTI and the religious MMA polled 8,250 and 7,515 votes respectively. Mohsin Dawar (16,496 votes) won by a smaller margin, defeating his nearest rival, an MMA candidate (15,352 votes). Ali Wazir was targeted allegedly by a local Taliban group loyal to Afghan Taliban in June 2018, but survived. PTM leaders claimed that Pakistan military had organised this attack. Ali Wazir had lost his father, brother, two uncles, and two cousins to an ambush near their home by Taliban in July 2005. The latest member of his extended family to fall to the assassin's bullet was Arif Wazir on 2 May 2020.

In November 2018, after Pashtun police officer's (Tahir Dawar's) body was found in Nangarhar, Afghanistan, after abduction from Peshawar, it demanded enquiry into the matter. PTM has been staging demonstration all over the tribal areas. On 2 February 2019, Arman Loni, another PTM activist and professor of Pashto literature from University of Balochistan succumbed to the injury caused to his neck by the bayonet of a policeman while staging a sit-in protest to protest forced eviction from the area following the incident of exchange of fire between the police and TTP terrorists in Loralai on 29 January 2019 (resulting in the death of eight policemen three militants and a civilian). In the protests against Loni's murder, 20 PTM activists were apprehended by the police, which included Gulalai Ismail (who later escaped to the US in September 2019 for fear of reprisal) and Abdullah Nangyal (is a Pakistani politician and PTM activist).

On 27 May 2019, a peaceful protest by PTM activist near Kharqamar check post, Boyya, North Waziristan against the police beating up a local woman, was fired upon by the security personnel killing three PTM supporters and injuring 15 persons. The military version was different; it said that Ali Wazir and Dawar provoked protesters who attacked the military check post forcing the cops to fire.[54] PTM activists have been unfairly booked under law, made to lose their jobs and those more unfortunate, have been picked up from their homes never to return. Ali Wazir's mother, it is reported, leaves in a doorless room fearing that any knock on the door could bring her more tragic news.[55] Pakistan's ham-handed dealing with the peaceful Pashtun movement has engendered a popular anti-establishment impulse in the tribal Pashtun terrain, which feeds into the local antipathy against the military post-military operations, especially since 2014. Pakistani State on the contrary castigates PTM as an outfit pursuing an anti-state agenda through their "engineered protests"[56] at the behest of foreign powers as part of their "hybrid war"[57] against Pakistan. The Boya area close to Kharqamar witnessed several attacks on Pakistani security forces in the aftermath of the PTM protests and arrest of PTM activists. On 7 June, an IED blast in Kharqamar took the lives of four officers and a soldier of the Quick Response Force while on routine patrol in the Doga Macha Madakhel area of Dattakhel tehsil in the evening.[58]

Against this backdrop, the possibility of PTM's interface with the TTP worries Islamabad a lot. While it has, in effect, turned sections of local Taliban amenable to its influence and loyal to the diktats of the Afghan Taliban against the PTM, the probability of those TTP factions opposed to the army and the Pakistani state making common cause with PTM remains. While the PTM is likely to remain steadfast in its pacifist agenda, any such coupling with TTP is likely to make the task of the military easier, which can they go full blast against the movement and tear it asunder. As it is, there are rumoured machinations by the army to divide the PTM leadership over the issue of participation in politics. While Pashteen wants PTM to remain an apolitical movement, Mohsin Dawar and Ali Wazir are pulling towards active political participation. PTM is, thus, an interesting case of a movement emerging as an unintended consequence of the violent engagement between security forces and local Islamist radicals in the tribal belt.

Regular Attacks on Security Forces (2019-2021)

Throughout 2019, the same trend of Pakistani security forces liquidating and arresting suspected terrorists continued. The TTP attacks on security forces, tribal elders, levies and Khasadars (in April 2019, these two groups were merged into provincial police force) and minority sects continued too with decreased frequency and intensity. By this time, it had become quite clear that the LeJ on the run in Punjab had started operating in and out of Balochistan as many LeJ operatives were killed in operations in the province.

On 28 February, security forces claimed to have killed Islamic State chief of Sindh-Balochistan chapter, Molvi Abdullah Brohi and his deputy Hafeez Brohi, in an encounter in Sibi District of Balochistan. Hazara Shias were targeted by an ISIS suicide bomber, this time a vegetable market in Hazarganj area of Quetta on 12 April 2019 resulting in the death of 16, eight of them Hazara Shias, and causing injuries to 32 persons. Hazaras protested in a sit-in in Quetta and demanded that the PM should come and see them. On 1 May 2019, there were reports of 6-7 terrorists attacking army troops engaged in the fencing work. Three soldiers were killed and Pakistan lodged a strong protest with Afghan embassy and held that "Afghan Security Forces and the authorities need to have more effective control in [the] border region to support Pakistan's efforts as well as deny use of Afghan soil against Pakistan".[59] On 8 May, a suicide bomber attacked a police van outside the gate of the Data Darbar Shrine in Lahore killing 13 including five policemen. The attack was claimed by Hizbul Ahrar, a splinter group of Jamat-ul-Ahrar (JuA), which is an affiliate of TTP, while police suspected all the three offshoots of TTP, the other two being JuA and Ghazi Force, operating in Punjab.[60]

On 20 May, the police apprehended the facilitator of the suicide bomber, Mohsin Khan, belonging to Shabqadar area in Charsada. The suicide bomber was identified as Sadiqullah Mohmand, who had entered Pakistan through Torkham border from Afghanistan on 6 May. He was received by Tayyabullah alias Raaki, a resident of Mohmand, who brought him to Lahore and made him stay with Mohsin, whom he had radicalised earlier during their stay in Saudi Arabia a few years back. Tayyab accompanied Sadiqulah to the spot and, disappeared once the bombing was over.[61] The incident showed how easily the TTP terrorists could move across the border from Afghanistan and carry out the attack in an area closely guarded by the security forces, Since the deadly blast inside shrine of Sufi saint Hazrat Syed Ali bin Usman Hajweri (1009-1072), popularly known as Data Ganj Bakhsh, on 1 July 2010, which had killed 50 and injured 200,[62] the authorities had tightened security near the shrine.

On 20 June, CTD, Punjab, arrested three TTP militants from Khanewal town of Punjab and recovered six hand grenades and hate literature from them. On 23 June, two TTP terrorists attacked a police station in Dera Ismail Khan and one of them, named Zia, was killed by security forces while the other was arrested.[63] In retaliation, TTP carried out two back-to-back attacks killing nine people including six security personnel in Dera Ismail Khan on 21 July. The TTP gunmen came on four motorcycles and opened fire on policemen at the Kotla Saidan check-post in a residential area killing two policemen and immediately afterwards, when they were carried to the local hospital a female suicide bomber struck at the entrance of the hospital killing four more policemen and three civilians.[64]

Two days later, at United States Institute of Peace (USIP), on 23 July, Imran Khan admitted that there are still about 30,000 to 40,000 terrorists operating inside Pakistan belonging to about 40 different militant groups, which is why it was becoming difficult to deal with them, even with the resolve of his government (because previous governments, Khan would say, did not have the political will to do it) to root out terror.[65] In the same month, NATO trucks were attacked in Jamrud Tehsil of KP and militants fired upon a border patrolling convoy near Gurbaz area of North Waziristan. Similar attacks took place on September 2019 in Abba Khel area of Spin Wam tehsil (revenue unit) in North Waziristan. After a long while, TTP brought out a pamphlet forbidding use of DJs or playing of loud music, polio vaccination and movement of women alone outside their homes. It warned people that the TTP had "one informer ... in every three people and it was a misconception on the part of the people to think we will not get information about non-compliance of our order. Follow the order or be ready to face worst consequences".[66] On 26 December, CTD, Punjab and ISI, in a joint operation busted a media cell of the Al-Qaeda in the Indian Subcontinent (AQIS) and arrested five members of the cell in Gujranwala, Punjab and recovered a large quantity of media equipment, funds for terror financing, suicide jackets, explosives and deadly arms. Such incidents brought to light the depth of TTP and its allies/affiliates like Al-Qaeda, JuA penetrating Punjab, the largest and most consequential province in terms of power and influence in entire Pakistan.

The year 2020 began with the news of former spokesperson of TTP & JuA, Ehsanullah Ehsan giving a slip to the security forces and fleeing from the safe house in which he was detained in downtown Peshawar in 11 January. He announced the news of his escape in an audio clip on 6 February. In his video message later he indicated that Pakistan authorities did not honour their commitment as per the deal with him, which had led him to surrender in April 2017, compelling him to look for opportunity to escape. His tweet, interviews and some comments in online media portals provided insights into the *modus operandi* of the Pakistani security agencies. In a commentary written by him in the weekly *Sunday Guardian* he wrote about the desperation with which the then ISI Chief, Suja Pasha, was trying to reach out to the deputy amir of TTP in 2011, calling TTP 'a necessity for Pakistan'. In a letter delivered to the deputy amir of TTP, Wali-ur-Rehman, through Naseeruddin, one of the sons of Jalaluddin Haqqani, Pasha would even offer TTP safe passage to strike NATO forces in Afghanistan, and to work towards removing all misunderstandings between the army and the TTP, so that both could work together to drive out the great enemy (read the US) from Afghanistan. Pasha had even expressed his desire to meet Wali physically, if he so desired, and had written in the letter that Wali, like his forefathers should fight for independence of Kashmir and "join the Pakistan army in the 'Ghazwa e Hind' war against India, because the war against India is a true and just jihad against the real infidels and polytheists."[67] He persuaded TTP to fight for the interests of Pakistan like LeT and JeM, if it wanted to be helped by the Pakistan Army like these groups. In another article that he wrote in November 2020, Ehsan wrote that "Pakistan's state policy in the war on terror has always been based on hypocrisy, lies and deception". He said that while Pakistan was trying to convince the world that TTP was backed by external forces (India in particular), Gen Bajwa, the army chief and Director General of the ISI, Faiz Ahmad were employing Sirajuddian Haqqani, son of Jalaluddin Haqqani and head of the Haqqani group in Afghanistan, to negotiate with Mufti

Noor Wali Mehsud, the amir of TTP. They are doing it, he wrote because they apprehend that there is a "possibility of the emergence of a strong alliance of anti-Pakistan armed groups" and "Pakistan is terrified of the fact that if these armed groups regroup and reorganise, there could be large-scale unrest again in Pakistan and in the event of such a situation, the Army may have to carry out operations that are likely to affect the local population."[68] Calling Pakistan army as "a bunch of real estate contractors" he said that people of Pakistan no longer looked at it as their protectors but "as an organ which has usurped their rights". He held that TTP had understood the futility of talking to Pakistan because in the past it was defrauded by Pakistan army when the latter arrested its leaders after inviting them for talks in Swat in 2009. One of the clerics, Shiekh Muhammad Rahim, head of the TTP Shura, Swat, after signing the agreement with Pakistan Army landed up in prison and became a mental patient, he wrote. He suspected that Pakistan army through its offer of talks wanted to placate TTP and use it against PTM and resettle TTP in the tribal areas basically because, it "wants the two major anti-government forces to fight each other in the Pashtun areas" and revealed that this project had already begun and Hakimullah Mehsud's brother, Ejaj Mehsud had been roped in to fight and kill PTM leaders and the first victim of Ejaj Mehsud's group was Arif Wazir, Ali Wazir's cousin, who was killed at the behest of the Pakistan Army. All this only reinforce Pakistan's nervousness about TTP and its operations. Going by the assertion of the TTP and its country-wide presence, it appears that even of the army might have weakened the TTP with its operations, the TTP may be 'down but not out' as far as its determination to take on the Pakistan army is concerned.

Throughout the year the Pakistan Army as well as TTP came out with their respective claims of conducting operations against each other. On 1 June 2020, Inter-Services Intelligence (ISI) and CTD, Punjab arrested two TTP members, Kaleemullah and Farid Khan, in a joint raid in Rawalpindi for allegedly beheading a Polish engineer Piotr Stanczak (who had been abducted from Attock in September 2008) in 2009 in South Waziristan.[69] On 18 July, the TTP claimed that a military unit of the Pakistan Army stationed at Ladah college, consisting of around 400 soldiers and known for conducting night raids, was raided by TTP mujahideen. In September 2020, the army conducted its Shaktoi operation in South Waziristan, which was not covered by the media, but TTP said in its telegram message that the army was wreaking havoc in the area for days together. It brought out the case of a local woman called Malala Mohmand, of Mohmand agency, who reportedly killed one of the soldiers who tried to 'protect her honour and dignity'. Days later, on 14 September, the TTP militants shot dead Malik Tahir Iqbal, Vice President of Pakistan Tehreek-e-Insaf (PTI) Khyber Pakhtunkhwa during a targeted operation at Kotitra and held that he was targeted because of his anti-Islamic activities and links with the anti-Sharia Pakistani army. Day by day, such claims and counter-claims continued, year after year.

What do the Data Reveal?

According to figures collated by both South Asia Terrorism Portal (SATP) in India (Table 1) and Pakistan Institute for Peace Studies (PIPS) in Pakistan[70] (Table 2), the operations (ZeA and RuF) did lead to a significant drop in terror incidents and civilian fatalities.

Table 1: Terrorist Incidents and Casualties (SATP)

Year	Incidents of Killing	Civilians	Security Forces	Terrorists/ Insurgents/ Extremists	Not Specified	Total
2000*	65	137	8	20	1	166
2001	110	190	31	26	48	295
2002	103	148	20	65	24	257
2003	55	137	23	29	8	197
2004	168	347	208	302	68	925
2005	167	482	79	124	18	703
2006	317	541	301	568	56	1466
2007	531	1311	548	1271	464	3594
2008	1149	1796	647	3724	516	6683

2009	1665	2154	1012	7884	267	11317
2010	1246	1537	512	4945	348	7342
2011	1573	2371	674	2752	253	6050
2012	2347	2743	734	2444	267	6188
2013	2034	2713	665	1541	375	5294
2014	1569	1478	508	3268	263	5517
2015	950	866	339	2407	73	3685
2016	526	541	291	897	68	1797
2017	294	439	216	533	81	1269
2018	162	363	158	161	10	692
2019	136	142	137	86	0	365
2020	193	169	178	159	0	506
2021	37	31	29	30	0	90
Total**	15397	20636	7318	33236	3208	64398

Source: "Terrorism in Pakistan—Yearly Fatalities", South Asia Terrorism Portal[71]

Notes: *Data since 6 March 2000.

** Data till 18 February 2021, sourced from news reports and are provisional.

Table 2: Terrorist Attacks and Casualties in Pakistan*

Year	No of Attacks	Killed	Injured
2005	254	216	571
2006	675	907	1543
2007	1503	3448	5353
2008	2577	7997	9670
2009	1137	1439	3616
2010	2113	2913	5824
2011	1966	2391	4389
2012	1577	2050	3822
2013	1717	2451	5438
2014	1206	1723	3143
2015	625	1069	1443
2016	441	908	1627

2017	370	815	1736
2018	262	595	1030
2019	229	357	729
2020	146	220	547

Note: * Data collated from Pakistan Annual Security Reports from 2008-2020 published by PIPS at https://www.pakpips.com/publications#1512730923805-d52fde57-07fa

The data provided above confirm the broad trend in terrorist occurrences and resultant fatalities in Pakistan, which point to overall success of the operations launched by Pakistani security forces.

In comparison, TTP released its first annual report, counter-claiming that it had kept its operations alive and carried out 73 target killings, 12 ambush attacks, 10 raids, 19 IED blasts, five suicide attacks, 17 missile attacks and shot down two helicopters, and claims it killed some 686 people in 2015. Year after year, TTP produced annual reports of the attacks it carried out in Pakistan against security forces and others they counted as enemies of Islam. For the year 2020, the data provided by TTP suggested that during the year TTP carried out 177 attacks.[72]

TTP's Evolving Strategy

The TTP, post-Fazlullah, is advocating a different strategy. It has reduced its emphasis on organising high profile attacks and dissociating itself from ISIS-like elements and hoping to keep ISIS-sympathisers within its ranks in check. The emphasis now under Noor Wali's leadership is to strike unity and launch planned attacks mostly sniper and IED attacks on security forces. Under Noor Wali, the TTP spokesperson has, in recent months, the TTP has started condemning attacks on educational institutions and public facilities. Perhaps, the top leadership has realised the adverse impact of the APS attack and is attempting a course-correction in its strategy. What remains common during the pre- and post-Fazlullah phase is its deep aversion for the Pakistan army and the democratic system in Pakistan. Another important shift is back-pedaling on its earlier agenda of bringing Sharia to entire Pakistan. It is now seeking to inflame tribal Pashtun passion around popular disaffection against Pakistan Army's excessive action in the tribal areas as well as the political leadership's apathy and complacency about addressing local concerns.

All in all, the situation obtaining in the tribal areas point to a return of jihadi assertion in the absence of the state's policies to build on its gains from the operations. Moreover, the over-reaction of the army to TTP's slow penetration into the hinterland signal a return to Islamist politics in the mainland Pakistan which is likely to provide the oxygen for TTP's return in other areas. In the following chapter, an attempt has been made to understand the root causes of TTP's rise in Pakistan and why it is likely to remain a constant worry for the security forces of Pakistan in future.

Notes

1. Syed Saleem Shahzad, "Drones ever-closer to Pakistan's militants", *Asia Times Online*, 27 October 2010 at http://www.atimes.com/atimes/South_Asia/LJ27Df02.html.

2. "Pakistan Taliban head Hakimullah Mehsud 'open to talks'", 10 October 2013 at http://www.bbc.com/news/world-asia-24463839.

3. Amir Mir, "Mullah Fazlullah to operate", *The News*, 6 December 2013 at http://www.thenews.com.pk/Todays-News-2-218567-Mullah-Fazlullah-to-operate.

4. "Pakistan enters peace talks with Taliban", BBC.com, 6 February 2013 at http://www.bbc.com/news/world-asia-26065385.

5. "First round of direct talks between govt, TTP concludes", *The Dawn*, 26 March 2014 at http://www.dawn.com/news/1095687.

6. Qamar Zaman, "Taliban peace dialogue: Govt negotiator sees little hope for success", *The Express Tribune*, 18 May 2014 at http://tribune.com.pk/story/709872/taliban-peace-dialogue-govt-negotiator-sees-little-hope-for-success/.

7. "Taliban infighting impedes Pakistan peace talks", *The Dawn*, 19 May 2014 at http://www.dawn.com/news/1107309.

8. "TTP claims attack on Karachi airport", *The Dawn*, 9 June 2014 at http://www.dawn.com/news/1111397.

9. Rebecca Santana and Asif Shahzad, "Pakistan Launches Offensive Against Militants Near Afghan Border", Associated Press, 15 June 2014 at http://www.webcitation.org/6QhxuqpnN.

10. Zahir Shah Sherazi, "TTP commanders form new splinter group 'Jamatul Ahrar'", *The Dawn*, 26 August 2014 at http://www.dawn.com/news/1127905.

11. Looking at the damage the rise of ISIS could cause in Pakistan Ulema Council of Pakistan termed killing of innocent people by ISIS against the teachings of Islam, and appealed to the youth not to join such extremist organisations, which promote violence. See "IS is anti-Islamic: Ulema Council", *The Dawn*, 2 October 2014 at http://www.dawn.com/news/1135717.

12. "IS literature circulated in parts of KP", *The Dawn*, 4 September 2014 at http://www.dawn.com/news/1129775/is-literature-circulated-in-parts-of-kp.

13. Sailab Mahsud, "Six TTP leaders pledge allegiance to IS chief", *The Dawn*, 15 October 2014 at http://www.dawn.com/news/1138042/six-ttp-leaders-pledge-allegiance-to-is-chief.

14. "Taliban splinter group in Pakistan vows allegiance to ISIS", *Al Akhbar* English version online, 18 November 2014 at http://english.al-akhbar.com/node/22530.

15. "IS visits militants in Balochistan: Jundullah spokesman", *The Dawn*, 12 November 2014 at http://www.dawn.com/news/1143997.

16. Ali Akbar, "From TTP to IS: Pakistan's terror landscape evolves", *The Dawn,* 16 March 2015 at http://www.dawn.com/news/1169542, also see Naimat Khan, "IS versus Taliban", *The Friday Times*, 10 July 2015 at http://www.thefridaytimes.com/tft/is-versus-taliban/.

17. The video of the press briefing given by then DG ISPR on 15 June 2016 at https://www.youtube.com/watch?v=fivgmmCQrrs.

18. Ashfaq Yusufzai, "Mastermind of Peshawar school attack killed", *The Daily Telegraph*, 26 December 2014 at http://www.telegraph.co.uk/news/worldnews/asia/pakistan/11313678/Mastermind-of-Peshawar-school-attack-killed.html.

19. According to media reports, Matiur Rehman masterminded two failed assassination attempts against General Pervez Musharraf (in Rawalpindi in December 2003) and Shaukat Aziz (in Fateh Jang in July 2004). The Americans had sought his arrest as a key member of Al-Qaeda's external operations council who had attempted to target American interests in Pakistan and abroad. The UN Security Council tagged him as a most—wanted Al-Qaeda linked terrorist on 22 August 2011 for financing and planning some major terrorist activities, including the failed plot to destroy mid-air as many as 10 US-bound British jetliners in August 2006. Amir Mir, "TTP launches special group for terrorist operations", *The News*, 9 May 2015 at https://www.thenews.com.pk/print/39531-ttp-launches-special-group-for-terrorist-operations.

20. See "Army copter crashes in Naltar; 7 die", *The Dawn*, 9 May 2015 at https://www.dawn.com/news/1180922, and "Indonesian envoy dies after Pakistan helicopter crash", *The Dawn*, 19 May 2015 at https://www.dawn.com/news/1182921/newspaper/newspaper/column.

21. "Pakistan Taliban says it shot down helicopter", *Al Jazeera*, 10 May 2015 at https://www.aljazeera.com/news/2015/5/10/pakistan-taliban-says-it-shot-down-helicopter.

22. Tahir Khan, "Watershed event: Punjabi Taliban renounce violence", *The Express Tribune*, 14 September 2014 at http://tribune.com.pk/story/762038/watershed-event-punjabi-taliban-renounce-violence/.

23. Zia Ur Rehman, "Taliban factions fight over Karachi turf", *The Friday Times*, Vol. XXV, Issue 25, October 2013 at http://www.thefridaytimes.com/tft/taliban-factions-fight-over-karachi-turf, also see Zia Ur Rehman, Taliban bringing their war to streets of Karachi, *The Friday Times*, Vol. XXIV, No. 26, 10-16 August 2012 at http://www.thefridaytimes.com/beta3/tft/article.php?issue=20120810&page=2.

24. Zia Ur Rehman, "New militant group seen rising in Pashtun areas", *The News*, 5 April 2015 at http://www.thenews.com.pk/Todays-News-4-310819-New-militant-group-seen-rising-in-Pashtun-areas.

25. See Mustaq Yusuzai, "Enemy at the Gates", Special Report, *The News on Sunday*, 26 April 2009 at https://jang.com.pk/thenews/apr2009-weekly/nos-26-04-2009/spr.htm#3.

26. See report by Jamestown Foundation, "Imtiaz Ali, "Militant or Peace Broker? A Profile of the Swat Valley's Maulana Sufi Muhammad", Terrorism Monitor Volume 7 Issue 7, 26 March 2009 at https://jamestown.org/program/militant-or-peace-broker-a-profile-of-the-swat-valleys-maulana-sufi-muhammad/.

27. Akhtar Amin, "PHC issues release order of Sufi Mohammad", *The News*, 9 January 2018 at https://www.thenews.com.pk/print/266125-phc-issues-release-order-of-sufi-mohammad. Maulana Sufi remained in prison charged with sedition and waging war against Pakistan till January 2018, when he was released on humanitarian grounds after his son submitted bail bonds worth PKR 700,000 (about US$ 6,300) to authorities in Mingora, the capital of Swat district. The court ordered him to report to his local police station once in a month as well as whenever he would plan to leave his town. He also promised not to take part in political activities and gave an undertaking to the court not to involve himself in any type of activities that are against the writ of the government promote the Taliban movement. He died on 11 July 2019 at the ripe age of 86.

28. Dr Masooda Bano, "Dissenting Note", *The News*, 10 October 2008 at https://web.archive.org/web/20090617210532/; http://thenews.jang.com.pk/daily_detail.asp?id=140151.

29. Major Gen. Abid Mumtaz, *Operation Sherdil: Battle for Bajaur*, ISPR Publications, Islamabad, 2019 at https://www.hilal.gov.pk/uploads/ebook/pdf/182be0c5cdcd5072bb1864cdee4d3d6e.pdf.

30. Imtiaz Ali, "NATO's Khyber Lifeline", Terrorism Monitor Volume 7

Issue 1, Jamestown Foundation, 9 January 2009 at https://jamestown. org/program/natos-khyber-lifeline/; Mehlaqa Samdani, "Governance and Militancy in Pakistan's Khyber Agency", December 2011, CSIS at https://csis-website-prod.s3.amazonaws.com/s3fs-public/legacy_files/files/ publication/111213_Samdani_KyberAgency.pdf.

31. "The sun has set on Pakistan's military courts—here's why it should never rise again", *The Dawn*, 6 March 2017 at https://www.dawn.com/ news/1306792.

32. See reports by Ismail Khan, "Intense Khyber operation enters last phase", *The Dawn*, 26 March 2015 at http://www.dawn.com/news/1171902.

33. Ibrahim Shinwari, "Security forces claim major success in Tirah valley", *The Dawn*, 29 April 2015 at http://www.dawn.com/news/1178827, also see "Operation Khyber-II: 27 militants killed in fresh Tirah fighting", *The Express Tribune*, 30 April 2015 http://tribune.com.pk/story/878734/ operation-khyber-ii-27-militants-killed-in-fresh-fighting/.

34. Kamran Yousaf, "Rajgal cleansed of terrorists as military concludes Operation Khyber-IV", *Daily Tribune*, 21 August 2017 at https://tribune. com.pk/story/1487260/army-announces-completion-operation-khyber-4.

35. "Pakistan Army launches 'Operation Radd-ul-Fasaad' across the country", *The Dawn*, 22 February 2017 at https://www.dawn.com/news/1316332.

36. For details about ASP, see "The rise and 'fall' of Ansarul Sharia Pakistan", *The Dawn* 9 September 2017 at https://www.dawn.com/news/1356467/ the-rise-and-fall-of-ansarul-sharia-pakistan.

37. Patronised by the PPP, especially its leader, Asif Ali Zardari, Rao Anwar's rise from a departmental clerk in Karachi police to SSP, Malir can easily beat any Bollywood crime thriller. Known for his bias against Muttahida Quami Movement (MQM), he was seconded by non-MQM Sindhi as well as other mainstream political parties and leaders and he played his part in conducting operations against MQM during 1992-1999, which broke the back of MQM to a large extent. Even if he was demoted by the Supreme Court in 2012 President Zardari, using his special powers, got him reinstated as SSP, Malir. In 2013, 2015 and 2016, Anwar was suspended for misusing his authority but was reinstated by the judiciary. For more details see Naziha Syed Ali, Fahim Zaman. "Rao Anwar and the killing fields of Karachi", *The Dawn*, 18 February 2018 at https://www. dawn.com/news/1389719.

38. "Rao Anwar's trial", Editorial, *The Dawn*, 2 November 2020 at https:// www.dawn.com/news/1588142.

39. See tweet at https://twitter.com/OfficialDGISPR/status/1007670089 192214530?s=20.

40. "Two 'highly educated' militants among three arrested by CTD in Karachi", *The Dawn*, 11 June 2018 at https://www.dawn.com/news/1413472.

41. "Mastung suicide bomber identified as Hafeez Nawaz from Abbottabad", *The Tribune*, 19 July 2018 at https://tribune.com.pk/story/1761755/1-high-level-committee-informed-progress-peshawar-mastung-attack-cases.

42. "Mastermind of Mastung carnage killed in Kalat", *The Dawn*, 21 July 2018 at https://www.dawn.com/news/1421460.

43. "Two 'accomplices' of Mastung bomber held", *The Dawn*, 11 August 2018 at https://www.dawn.com/news/1426207/two-accomplices-of-mastung-bomber-held.

44. "Five terror suspects held, weapons recovered: ISPR", *The Nation*, 17 July 2018 at https://nation.com.pk/17-Jul-2018/five-terror-suspects-held-weapons-recovered-ispr.

45. "Banned outfits adopt new methods to stay under the radar", *The Dawn*, 28 July 2018 at https://www.dawn.com/news/1423121.

46. "Missing KP SP found dead in Afghanistan?", *The News*, 14 November 2018 at https://www.thenews.com.pk/print/393533-missing-kp-sp-found-dead-in-afghanistan.

47. "Blast in Orakzai Agency", *The Newsweek*, Pakistan, 28 November 2018 at https://www.newsweekpakistan.com/blast-in-orakzai-agency/.

48. "Interior ministry to unveil a new version of National Action Plan", *The Dawn*, 28 November 2018 at https://www.dawn.com/news/1448119.

49. The report compiled by the Pakistan Institute for Conflict and Security Studies (PICSS) was cited in *The Dawn*, 1 November 2019 at https://www.dawn.com/news/1380001.

50. Annual Pakistan Security Report by Pakistan Institute for Peace Studies (PIPS), cited by *The Express Tribune* , 6 January 2019 at https://tribune.com.pk/story/1882804/1-595-martyred-262-terrorist-attacks-2018.

51. "Pak-Afghan border fencing to be completed by end of 2019: DG ISPR", *The Tribune,* 15 December 2018 at https://tribune.com.pk/story/1867668/1-pak-afghan-border-fencing-completed-end-2019-dg-ispr.

52. Ghulam Qadir Khan, "Pakhtun resistance", *The Dawn*, 3 March 2018 at https://www.dawn.com/news/1399271.

53. "Tribulations the families of missing persons face", *The Dawn*, 7 March 2018 at https://www.dawn.com/news/1393572.

54. "3 people killed, 5 soldiers injured in exchange of fire at check post in North Waziristan", *The Dawn*, 27 May 2019 at https://www.dawn.com/news/1484709 & "3 killed, 15 injured in 'PTM-Army clash' in North Waziristan", *Pakistan Today,* 27 May 2019 at https://archive.pakistantoday.com.pk/2019/05/26/3-killed-15-injured-in-ptm-army-clash-in-north-waziristan/.

55. Abubakar Siddiqui, "The Pashtuns' Year of Living Dangerously", *The American Interest* 3 August 2019 at https://www.the-american-interest.com/2019/03/08/the-pashtuns-year-of-living-dangerously/.

56. "'Engineered protests' won't be allowed, says army chief", *The Dawn*, 13 April 2018 at https://www.dawn.com/news/1401345.

57. "'Hybrid war' imposed on country to internally weaken it, says Bajwa", *The Dawn*, 15 April 2018 at https://www.dawn.com/news/1401747.

58. "Three officers, soldier martyred in North Waziristan IED attack", *The Dawn*, 8 June 2019 at https://www.dawn.com/news/1486779.

59. "3 soldiers martyred in Afghan cross-border attack in North Waziristan: ISPR", *The Dawn*, 1 May 2019 at https://www.dawn.com/news/1479605.

60. "Security forces arrest 4 from Lahore in connection with Data Darbar bombing", *The Dawn*, 10 May 2019 at https://www.dawn.com/news/1481431.

61. "'Facilitator' of Data Darbar suicide blast captured", *The Dawn*, 21 May 2019 at https://www.dawn.com/news/1483551.

62. "Deadly blasts hit Sufi shrine in Lahore", BBC News, 2 July 2010 at https://www.bbc.com/news/10483453.

63. "Terrorist killed, another arrested in DI Khan attack", *Daily Times*, 24 June 2019 at https://dailytimes.com.pk/417373/terrorist-killed-another-arrested-in-di-khan-attack/.

64. "Six cops among nine martyred in DI Khan gun and bomb attack", *Daily Times*, 22 July 2019 at https://dailytimes.com.pk/434680/six-cops-among-nine-martyred-in-di-khan-gun-and-bomb-attack/.

65. "One Year In: A Conversation with Pakistani Prime Minister Imran Khan", embedded video at the website of United States Institute of Peace, Washington at https://www.usip.org/events/one-year-conversation-pakistani-prime-minister-imran-khan (look for Khan's deliberation especially from 36.54 minutes to 37.05 minutes in the video).

66. "TTP warns against playing music, women going out alone in Miramshah", *The Dawn*, 1 August 2019 at https://www.dawn.com/news/1497395.

67. Ehsanullah Ehsan, "ISI chief begged for Taliban's help in Kashmir: Ehsanullah Ehsan", *The Sunday Guardian Live*, 6 September 2019 at https://www.sundayguardianlive.com/news/isi-chief-begged-talibans-help-kashmir-ehsanullah-ehsan.

68. Ehsanullah Ehsan, "Pak Army deceiving world, plans to use TTP as a pawn domestically, globally", *The Sunday Guardian Live*, 28 November 2020 at https://www.sundayguardianlive.com/world/pak-army-deceiving-world-plans-use-ttp-pawn-domestically-globally.

69. "TTP men who beheaded Polish engineer held", *The Dawn*, 11 June 2020 at https://www.dawn.com/news/1562716.

70. Annual Pakistan Security Reports (2008-2020), Pak Institute for Peace Studies Pvt Ltd. (PIPS) at https://www.pakpips.com/publications#1512730923805-d52fde57-07fa.

71. South Asia Terrorism Portal at https://satp.org/datasheet-terrorist-attack/fatalities/pakistan.

72. Month-wise break-up was: January-11, February-7, March-3, April-19, May-18, June-17, July-19, August-14, September-23, October-22, November-16, December-8.

5.   What Propels Talibanisation

The roots that sustain Islamist demands for establishment of the rule of Sharia in Pakistan lie, ironically, in the official Islam championed by the Pakistani state, which has been under pressure from the right wing ulema (religious scholars) right since its inception to convert the western-style Pakistani statecraft to a Sharia-based Islamic system. The modernist elite in Pakistan has, over time, conceded space to the Islamist demands with a view to co-opting the Islamists and stealing the thunder from their populist campaign. However, in the bargain, the state has been progressively Islamicised.

Pakistan was carved out of British India for the minority *Mussalmans* (Muslims) who felt insecure about the prospect of being marginalised in a democratic set up by the majority Hindu population. The leadership of the movement for Pakistan, mostly from northern India, and elitist and feudal in outlook, used Islam in their mobilisation strategy to attract the Muslim masses. During the course of the movement, the bogey of Islamic-culture-in-danger was also raised to elicit stronger mass support, and by the time of the creation of Pakistan, Islam had figured as a binding principle, a natural adhesive to bind the Muslims together. However, once the state of Pakistan came into being, its main architect, and its 'sole spokesman', Muhammad Ali Jinnah, who claimed to have carved it out with the help of a type-writer, underplayed the Islamic dimension and defined the core of the statecraft in liberal and secular terms. Jinnah passed away exactly 1 year and 24 days after Pakistan was created, on 9 September 1948, before the constitution was drawn up, without ensuring enshrinement of the principles he outlined in his oft-quoted address to the nation on 11 August 1947.[1]

Even when Jinnah was alive, there were differences in approach between him and his close colleagues on what would be the nature of the Pakistani state. For example, it is now quite well known now that his right-hand man, Liaqat Ali Khan, who was assassinated, three years after Jinnah died, by an assailant about whom not much is known, had instructed his secretary Mazid Malik not to publicise Jinnah's much-quoted speech emphasising on the secular character of the Pakistani state cited above. Even the first edition of the official biography of Jinnah authored by Hector Bolitho did not carry this speech.

There was a huge gulf of difference between Jinnah and Liaqat on how to approach secularism. For Jinnah, it was, definitionally, of the Western type, leading to separation of the church from the state, much at a notional level, because he himself laid emphasis on Islamic principles while building institutions for the Pakistani state, even if he lived a largely secular life, unbound by the shackles of Islamic principles—he did not pray regularly, leave alone praying five times a day, relished ham, perhaps never went on a *Haj* or *Umra*, enjoyed his drinks, loved his pets, his western attire and could hardly speak Urdu or Arabic. For Liaqat, secularism meant establishment of a non-theocratic state for the Muslims, where the non-Muslims were to be, for all practical purposes, unequal (if not second-class) citizens. The non-specificity of the attributes of the Pakistani state, beyond what Jinnah implied in his 11-August-address, and the deliberate neglect of the leadership to enumerate the principles that would lay down the foundations of the Pakistani state led the Ulama to clamour for Islamisation. As it has been argued by the author in one of his previous works[2], the "*pirs, sajda nashins* and the *mullahs*, who had stirred up a huge popular wave of Islam in favour of the dream project called 'Pakistan' and were more rooted in local politics, now sought to take the mantle of Islam further ahead. They were not to be discouraged either by Jinnah's famous interview where he snubbed the interviewer for asking him whether Pakistan would be a theocratic state by saying he did not know what a theocratic state meant, or by Liaqat's statement in the Pakistan Constituent Assembly while passing the Objective

Resolution in March 1949, that the people were "the real recipients of power" and the resolution, inasmuch as it was drafted by the representatives of the people 'naturally' eliminated "any danger of the establishment of a theocracy."

The leaders succeeding Jinnah and Liaqat were unable to contend with the Islamist forces that were encouraged during the movement for Pakistan. "What was the need of founding Pakistan if it were to be a secular one?",[3] some of the conservative right-wing leaders asked. As the debate on the nature of the Pakistani state gathered momentum in the Pakistani constitutional assembly, it soon came to notice that in the "Objective Resolution"[4] of the Pakistani constitution in 1949, Islam had already entered the Constitution, as an unalterable frame of reference.[5] Even secular leaders like Ayub Khan and Z.A. Bhutto had to insert 'Islamic provisions'[6] in the separate 'Constitutions' enacted during their rule. The 'Objective Resolution' was inserted into the Constitution as a "part of substantive provision" in March 1985 during Zia-ul-Haq's rule (Article 2A) which made it legally enforceable. Over the years, the Islamist impulse has only gained in strength rather than losing its momentum in the democratic processes that have had a chequered run in Pakistan. The frequent interventions by the military since 1950s and its *de facto* subsumption of power in the vital domains of the statecraft (like defence, security, foreign policy and economy) has led to a hybrid system, where democracy and praetorianism (read military preponderance) have existed together, with the latter using the conservative constituency at will (what is known as Mullah-Military nexus) to buttress its hold on power. In the process, Islamism has assumed enormous importance as a negative frame of reference, more for de-legitimisiation of authority than as a cohesive agent for building an effective nation-state.

Islamisation and Talibanisation

Article 2 of the 1973 constitution declares Islam as the official state religion and right in the beginning, the preamble emphasises the point that sovereignty belongs to Allah. Article 227 very clearly states that all "existing laws shall be brought in conformity with the injunctions of Islam as laid down in the holy Qur'aan and Sunnah ... and no law shall be enacted which is repugnant to such injunctions (Article 227). The ulema (Islamic scholars) have played an officially recognised role in shaping the Pakistani polity, including the writing of legislation.

The clergy has also been accorded a constitutional place through the establishment of the Council of Islamic Ideology (CII). The CII was first introduced by Ayub in his 1962 constitution and Ayub used his influence and discretion to select only conformist clerics who would adopt a modernist line and attest his policies. The constitution of 1973 also made constitutional provision for CII with a constitutional mandate to examine existing laws and recommend ways of bringing them into conformity with Islam's injunctions. The constitution had even promised to make all laws conform to the principles of Islam within ten years from the promulgation of the constitution. It is another thing that Z.A. Bhutto did not make any effort in this regard. But the damage had been done and CII has served as a body prescribing conservative steps to be taken by the governments from time to time. This has exerted unnecessary pressure on the government and at times government has made use of the recommendations of the CII to demonstrate their Islamic credentials.

During Zia-ul-Haq's rule CII worked most enthusiastically and served as Chief Advisory Council to the President entrusted with the responsibility of examining whether federal and provincial laws were in line with Islamic principles. So far CII has recommended repeal of 829 federal laws passed till 1977.[7] Many more laws are currently under review. As a result of their influence, Islamisation is, at least formally, the ultimate objective of the constitution and the basis of the state's legitimacy.

The attempt at Islamisation did not stop there. Zia-ul-Haq added Sharia benches to Provincial courts and a Sharia appellate bench to the Federal Supreme Court to decide matters concerning Islamic laws. These came to be known together later as Federal Shariat Court. Sharia education was added to university education and an International Islamic University was established to offer judges crash courses on Islamic jurisprudence, to train official mullahs, and to emphasise on research on Islamic history, politics and economics. During Zia's time, Islamisation efforts even spread to criminal justice system. The Penal laws, Criminal procedure and Evidence Act were also amended through Presidential decrees/ordinances demoting the legal status of women.

Zia's infamous Hudood ordinances sought to introduce medieval forms of punishment like flogging, amputation, public stoning, etc. into the criminal justice system of Pakistan. With such symbolic but pervasive Islamisation efforts the non-Muslim minorities were reduced to '*dhimmis*'[8] of the medieval age. Even if the constitution gave them right to profess and practice their religion, in practice there was an overwhelming majoritarian bias against minority sects like Ahmadiyas.[9] In many cases, over the years, the Christians and other minorities have been targeted through blasphemy laws brought in by Zia. The most prominent of this was the case of Asia Bibi, which demonstrated the abiding contradictions pertaining to the nature of the society and state in Pakistan. In this particular case, a sitting Governor, Salaman Taseer, was assassinated by his own body guard on 4 January 2011 for opposing the blasphemy laws, and the assassin, Mumtaz Qadri, of Sunni Barelvi persuasion, upon his execution on 29 February 2016, has been declared a martyr and a mosque has been raised in his honour in the capital city of Islamabad itself. An unbelievably large throng of people joined his funeral procession in a rare show of spontaneity, and the anniversary of his death, even if it was on 29 February, (which comes once every four years) is observed with great gusto every year in end February. Qadri was compared to Ilm-ud-din, who, in 1929, had killed a Hindu publisher for publishing "*Rangila Rasul*", a damning treatise on the Prophet's private life. Many people even visited him in jail, when he was in prison, and sought his blessings. The nation-wide protest by Barelvi leader, Khadim Hussain Rizvi following Pakistan Supreme Court's acquittal of Asia Bibi on 31 October 2018, buzzed with calls of 'death-to-the-judges'. The Pakistani judiciary did show unprecedented nerve over the issue and the state managed to send Asia Bibi out of Pakistan, but the extreme sensitivity about blasphemy remains.

In fact, similar cases abound in Pakistan. In a recent case on 13 April 2017, Mashal Khan, a student of Abdul Wali Khan University Mardan, was brutally lynched by the public over allegations of blasphemy. In Bahawalpur city, according to law enforcement officials, a student named Khateeb Hussain attacked his English professor, Khalid Hameed, with a knife in March 2019 at the Government Sadiq Egerton College for arranging a 'welcome party' which involved both boys and girls, which he viewed as anti-Islamic. Khateeb even recorded a video after the incident, bragging about his crime saying he had no remorse whatsoever for his action, which went viral on the internet in Pakistan.[10] In May 2019, a Hindu veterinarian named Ramesh Kumar Malhi, in Mirpur Khas district of Sindh, was arrested, charged with blasphemy, after a cleric alleged, he had delivered medicine wrapped in verses from the Quran.[11]

In the most recent case, an American citizen of Pakistani origin, Tahir Ahmad Naseem, was lured into Pakistan and a case of blasphemy was lodged against him for having posted some videos on youtube claiming that he was a *masih* (the chosen or the anointed one) as was conveyed to him by none other than Allah himself. Eventually, in a court room in Peshawar, in broad day light, Tahir Naseem was killed in a courtroom in Peshawar, on 29 July 2020 by a young boy named Faisal Khan. The perpetrator of the murder-in-cold-blood was hailed as a 'Ghazi' (a holy warrior) and as per the account of a human rights activist, Gulali Ismail, who has herself fled Pakistan under threat to her life for having spoken up against army excesses in the tribal belt as a supporter of PTM, put out a photograph of a cop from the Peshawar's elite police force, clicking a selfie with him after lawyers were done with selfies in the precincts of the court itself.[12] In the photograph, Fasial is beaming with an undying smile on his face, as if he was a hero who had accomplished a great task and was being feted for it. A large number of followers of a local cleric named Mufti Shahabuddin Popalzai, Khatib and head of the local moon-sighting committee at Qasim Ali Khan Mosque, Peshawar, poured out on the streets of Peshawar chanting slogans in favour of Fasial denouncing the alleged act of blasphemy. The slogans revealed the mood of the Pakistani believer:

"*Hurmat-e-Rasul par, jaan bhi qurban hai*" (We can sacrifice our life for protecting the dignity of the Prophet); *Gustakh-e-Rasul ki phansi do* (Hang those who disrespect the Prophet), *Khilafat ke liye muttahid ho jao, ab nahin to kab, aap nahin tau kaun?* (Stand united for *Khilafat*-loosely understood as Islamic rule—If not now, then when? If not you, then who?). Even if Pakistan is yet to execute anybody for blasphemy, there are about 75 people who have been killed extrajudicially in connection with blasphemy since 1990[13] and there are about 1,500 people who have been accused of having committed acts of blasphemy during 1987-2017.[14] Between 1947 and 1986, there were only 14 cases registered in Pakistan for blasphemy.[15]

It has been very difficult to repeal regressive provisions in Pakistan in the name of protection of Islam, as can be seen in the efforts by Musharraf to moderate some provisions of the Hudood ordinance to protect the rights of the women. It required Musharraf almost eight long years to venture into the terrain of the Mullahs over the issue of restoring some of their genuine rights encroached upon by the Islamist incursions during the Zia era. All this, in many ways, signals a gradual Islamisation of the Pakistani state and society and gradual societal acceptance of the Pakistani Taliban's ideology of Sharia rule in Pakistan.

The Islamist Impulse[16]

Islam has been successfully tried by almost all the Pakistani rulers as a potent crutch for ensuring their hold on power. In times of crises, there is tendency to attribute all problems to the sinking standards of Islam in the society and an overwhelmingly illiterate populace is easily persuaded into believing that nothing short of a bold step forward to bring Islamic rule to Pakistan can reverse trend of decline. Islam has so closely woven into warp of Pakistan identity that it has assumed a life of its own. Even if overemphasis on Islam has 'militantised' different versions of Islam and pitted them against each other in a spiral of violence spelling havoc for the internal security and very existence of the country, the ritual invocation of Islam forms an inalienable part of Pakistan's identity. What could explain this extreme sense of insecurity about its identity and existence? Waheed-uz-Zaman, would say: "If we let go the ideology of Islam, we cannot hold together as a nation by any other means.... If the Arabs, the Turks, the Iranians, God forbid, give up Islam, the Arabs yet remain Arabs, the Turks remain Turks, the Iranians remains Iranians, but what do we remain if we give up Islam?"[17]

All through the history of Pakistan, civilian rulers with liberal credentials felt it necessary, and perhaps harmless, to use Islam for reaching their political goals, while the world outside may find the whole business quite farcical. For the people of Pakistan, however, every move in the name of protection of Islam has falsely been projected as an existential necessity. However, in reality, extrapolating on the legitimacy and importance given to Islam on the state and political system in Pakistan, different Islamist groups have tried to interpret Islam-friendly measures differently, refracting them through their narrow prisms of Islamic thinking, approaching them from their own sectarian perspectives. Therefore, love for Islam has meant different things to different sects. In the process, all the sects in Pakistan have sought to demonstrate their love for Islam in their own separate ways, often in a militant manner, weakening the law-enforcing capacities of the state.

In an earlier research article, this author referred to 'many Pakistans within Pakistan'[18] especially in the context of different exclusive conceptions of Islam being floated in Pakistan in the name of introducing Islamic sharia in Pakistan. As famously written by the Justice Munir in his report in 1953, as the head of a Commission set up to investigate into the anti-Ahmadiya riots of the 1950s, the "phantom of an Islamic State has haunted the Mussalman throughout the ages" and "Pakistan is being taken by the common man, though it is not, as an Islamic State. This belief has been encouraged by the ceaseless clamour for Islam and Islamic State that is being heard from all quarters since the establishment of Pakistan." He then goes on to make a profound observation that has defined politics of religion everywhere but applies more specifically to Pakistan because of the lasting enthusiasm among a vocal and orthodox section of the people for introducing Islamic Sharia based rule in Pakistan. He writes:

If there is one thing which has been conclusively demonstrated in this inquiry, it is that provided you can persuade the masses to believe that something they are asked to do is religiously right or enjoined by religion, you can set them to any course of action, regardless of all considerations of discipline, loyalty, decency, morality or civic sense.[19]

Keeping in view the opinions of leading Mullahs of his time about Islam informed by their knowledge of scriptures and Islamic theology the Munir found that despite their overwhelming consensus on the need to excommunicate Ahmadiyas from the fold of Islam, their views on who was a Muslim were remarkably dissimilar and contradictory, which led Munir to write:

Keeping in view the several definitions given by the ulama, need we make any comment except that no two learned divines are agreed on this fundamental. If we attempt our own definition as each learned divine has done and that definition differs from that given by all others, we unanimously go out of the fold of Islam. *And if we adopt the definition given by any one of the ulama, we remain Muslims according to the view of that alim but kafirs according to the definition of every one else.*[20]

These are observations that have been quoted and requoted over the years to acknowledge sagacity of Justice Munir but nobody has taken any clue from it to try to reform the society in light of such brilliant remarks. It is quite another thing that Justice Munir himself was greatly responsible for setting off the tradition of military rule which undermined the process of consolidation of democracy which could have absorbed such sentiments and encouraged genuine pluralism and tolerance. In fact, such sentiments have survived because of failure of democracy and good governance because of regular intervention of the army in politics facilitated by judges like Munir, who referred to the clause of necessity to legitimise Ayub Khan's takeover.

Ever since, all rulers have invoked Islam to lend legitimacy to their rule and perpetuation in power. In the process they have legitimised role of religion in politics to such an extent that it has divided people and set them up at each other's throat—all for the sake of exaltation of one's own sectarian version at the cost of everyone else's. The inert-sectarian as well as intra-sectarian clashes that take place almost on everyday basis have let Pakistani society to acute violence and destabilised economy and politics of Pakistan. As Pakistan has journeyed through coups and self-aggrandising politics, an overall environment conducive to orthodoxy and intolerance has replaced the liberalism and openness that characterised the first few decades of Pakistan's existence. Progressive incursion of degenerate and primitive thought process into the political mainstream has legitimised the role of religion in politics in a regressive manner. The assertive presence of Pakistan Taliban points to an extreme form of such degeneration. The entire society is concerned about it, but does not know how to contend with it.

The virus of radicalisation has entered body politic so deep that leave alone politicians and the military rulers, even the judiciary of Pakistan is afflicted with it. This was most conspicuous when a top judge who was lapped up by the people as the conscience keeper of the nation and emerged as the nemesis of a military dictator—Iftikhar Muhammad Chaudhry—in August 2010 made an impromptu remark while hearing a case involving the issue of parliamentary sovereignty dragged in the issue of centrality of Islam in Pakistan and commented "should we accept if tomorrow parliament declares secularism, and not Islam, as the state polity?" Another judge quickly joined him in asking "Will it be called a rightful exercise of authority if tomorrow parliament amends Article 2 of the Constitution which states that Islam will be the state religion?"[21] Such comments drew instant criticism from a section of the media. *The News on Sunday* wrote editorially, "What is worrisome is that these were not off the cuff remarks but a considered view shared by a majority of the country's educated elite."[22] It went on to quote a Pakistani analyst who said that "Islam in Pakistan ... has ceased to be a religion and world-view; it has become an obsession, a pathology. It has been drained of all ethics and has become a mechanism for oppression and injustice."[23]

The judiciary was not alone in the act. Around this time, in the face of Islamic radicalism raising its ugly head in the tribal areas, the then army chief loudly proclaimed that Pakistan was not only a geographical entity but an ideological one as well and it was a fortress of Islam. While addressing a gathering in police line, Peshawar, on 25 November 2009, Gen Kayani said: 'Pakistan was founded by our forefathers in the name of Islam and we should work to strengthen the country and make committed efforts to achieve the goal of turning it into a true Islamic state'.[24] Few days later, while responding to a suicide attack claimed by TTP, on a mosque in Rawalpindi on 4 December 2009,[25] he repeated: "Pakistan is our motherland. It is the bastion of Islam and we live for the glory of Islam and Pakistan ... Our faith, resolve and pride in our religion and in our country is an asset, which is further reinforced after each terrorist incident".[26]

The power elite of Pakistan have thus succumbed to the Islamists and allowed the latter to dictate the terms of popular discourse. Rather than encouraging moderation, they have invoked 'Islam' to convince the masses that they too are ardent exponents of Islamic principles and Islamic state. The elite does not realise that it is indirectly legitimising the demand of the radical elements for the establishment of an 'Islamic state' in Pakistan and in a theological debate they cannot contest the rhetorical competence of a mullah to sell his point of view as more apt and genuine. On a whole, it does not realise that it is fighting a losing battle and is ultimately left with the choice of being co-opted by the orthodox section.

Pakistan has long debated whether it should be a Muslim state or an Islamic one, whether it was created for the Muslims of India or to preserve and protect Islam. Perhaps the truth lies somewhere in the middle. The debate over whether Pakistan should be 'a Muslim state' (for the Muslims of India) or an 'Islamic state' has a long history of its own. It had started in the womb of the Pakistan movement itself. In the Karachi Session of the Muslim League in 1943, Nawab Bahadur Yar Jang, an important member of the League had clearly stated in the presence of Muhammad Ali Jinnah, the founder of Pakistan, "There is no denying the fact that we want Pakistan for the establishment of Quranic system of government. It will bring about a revolution in our life, a renaissance, a new fervour and zeal, and above all, a resuscitation of pristine Islamic purity and glory." Addressing Jinnah who was presiding over the session, he had stated, "Quaid-i-Azam (the great leader) we have understood Pakistan in this light. If your Pakistan is not such, we do not want it." In his submission later, Jinnah had endorsed these views and held that "Islam was the bed-rock of the community" and went on to add "It is the Great Book, the Quran that is the sheet-anchor of Muslim India," he said. "I am sure that as we go on, there will be more and more oneness—one God, one Book, one Qibla, one Holy Prophet and one Nation."[27]

As a leader of a mass movement, Jinnah was aware of the appeal of Islam amongst the Muslim masses and did not hesitate to use it to his advantage. For example, he urged the students of Islamia College Peshawar in 1946 that the League stood for carving out a separate state and turning it into a "laboratory of Islam", where Muslims were in numerical majority to rule there under Islamic Law. He used Islamic symbols to sell his idea of liberal democracy on many occasions. He had also famously snubbed and chastised Mountbatten for having counselled him to take Akbar, the medieval Mughal ruler of India known for his toleration, as his role model while taking over the mantle of Pakistan as its first Governor General. He had responded by saying that if he were to go back into history, he would go all the way back to the Prophet (Muhammad) rather than stop at Akbar!

Soon after his famous address to the Pakistan constituent assembly on 11 August 1947, where he asked his colleagues to work towards a system where 'citizenship' of the state would be more important than the religion of a person, he would ask each Pakistani to "take [a] vow to himself and be prepared to sacrifice his all, if necessary, in building up Pakistan as *a bulwark of Islam*", "to develop *the spirit of Mujahids*" and be unafraid of death because "our religion teaches us *to be always prepared for death*. We should face it bravely to save the honour of Pakistan and Islam. There is *no better salvation for a Muslim than the death of a martyr for a righteous cause*" (italicised for emphasis by the author).[28]

Using Islam for Political Purposes Backfires: Jinnah and his Successors

Jinnah also used Islam as a unifier to stitch together disparate ethnic and sectarian identities which had started raising their heads soon after partition. In his speech on the occasion of the opening of the State bank of Pakistan in July 1948, he even went to the extent of criticising "the economic system of the West" for creating "almost insoluble problems for humanity" and urged the audience "to work our destiny in our own way and present to the world an economic system based on true Islamic concept of equality of manhood and social justice" and evolve "banking practices compatible with Islamic ideals of social and economic life".[29]

Jinnah's efforts to sell his idea of a liberal democratic Pakistan based on basic Islamic principles of equality and social justice sought to bridge the gulf between liberal democracy, which he wanted Pakistan to adopt as a system of governance, and a Sharia-based Islamic system, which many of his followers instinctively gravitated towards. He was perhaps aware of the contradictions he had to deal with in the process. At one breath he would dismiss the idea of Pakistan becoming a theocracy, while at another, he would comfort the clergy, which was vocal about Sharia, by saying that the Constitution will not be in conflict with the Sharia laws. He did not live longer to resolve these contradictions. The constant tussle between the moderates and the conservatives would mark the political landscape of Pakistan heretofore.

The rulers of Pakistan who succeeded him inherited this legacy of unresolved contradictions. They employed the same tactics to justify their actions. The liberals like Ayub Khan (1958-1969), Zulfikar Ali Bhutto (1972-1977) used Islam to justify their actions, legitimise their rule and even to undermine their political opponents. The years of military dictatorship under Zia-ul-Haq (1977-1988), which coincided with Afghan Jihad, saw the balance shifting towards the Islamists. It was during this time that Islamic content of Jinnah's speeches were isolated and served as proof of his Islamist rather than secular orientation. Democratic leaders like Nawaz Sharif who followed Zia even tried unsuccessfully to introduce Islamic provisions into the constitution through legislation (15th Amendment, that could not be adopted by both houses of the parliament).

The influence of the radical elements has grown manifold in Pakistan over the years despite the much-advertised efforts of Pervez Musharraf (1999-2008), a military dictator, to bring 'enlightened moderation' to Pakistan. He had also unsuccessfully tried to mainstream the madrassa education system as much as his successors tried to register them and bring in governmental control on them. Musharraf's attempt to appropriate Islamic symbols, much like Jinnah's, and the efforts of his successors to use Islam symbolically for political purposes could not make much dent into the radical Islamic constituency that is threatening to swamp Pakistan today.

Army's recent Experiments

In recent times, the use of Islam as an electoral/political tool was evident in the last elections of July 2018. On the eve of the elections, there was a bid by the deep state, apparently, to mainstream some jihadi/Islamist groups. One of these was a Barelvi oufit, led by Tehreek-i-Labbaik Ya Rasool Allah Pakistan (TLYRAP) which registered itself as a political party named as Tehreek-i-Labbaik Pakistan (TLP) in May 2017 but launched in June 2017. The other Islamist group was Jamaat-ud-Dawa (parent organisation of the militant LeT) which tried to register itself as a political party named Milli Muslim League (MML) and upon being turned down by the Election Commission of Pakistan (ECP) fielded its followers as independent candidates in the 2018 elections. The TLYRA organised a massive sit-in protest in November 2017, shortly after Nawaz Sharif was removed from prime ministership by the apex court in (August 2017), at the Faizabad Interchange near the capital city of Islamabad for three weeks, demanding rolling back of the Elections Act of 2017, which allegedly diluted the Khatm-e-Nabuwwat (Finality of Prophet) oath taken by candidates during filing of nominations (from 'I solemnly swear' to 'I believe'),[30] and removal of the then law minister Zahid Hamid for such an anti-Islamic act. That the leaders of the protest were amenable to mediation by the army and a six-point accord[31] was drawn up which was signed by an ISI officer, then Major General

Faiz Hameed (now Lieutenant General, and Director General of ISI) indicated the hold of the army on the protesting groups—all conservative Barelvi outfits, TLP, Tehrik-e-Khatm-e-Nabuwwat (led by Pir Afzal Qadri) and Sunni Tehrik. As per the terms of the agreement, Zahid Hamid had to tender his resignation signalling the power of the Islamic groups taking to the streets.[32]

The TLP's election posters openly invoked Islam with call for sacrificing one's life for the sake of religion—"*Vote ki kya haisiyat hai, Deen ke liye tau gardanain bhi hazir hai*" (What value does votes carry for us? We are ready to sacrifice our lives for our religion). It fought elections in 175 National Assembly (NA) seats—122 in Punjab, 29 in Sindh, 16 in KP, five in Balochistan and three in Islamabad. TLP surprised all pollsters by bagging 4.2 per cent of the popular votes which amounted to 2.234,316 votes. It was argued by many in Pakistan that there was a clever bid to encourage TLP to fight the elections to wean away votes from PML-N candidates in Punjab and help Imran Khan win the elections. Imran Khan's PTI openly blamed Nawaz Sharif government for the hanging of Mumtaz Qadri, the assassin of Salman Taseer, who had allegedly defended a blasphemer (Asiya Bibi). In the election posters, PTI candidates asked the voters: "*Ae Musalmanon Jago, PTI ko vote de kar Insaaf karo … Kya Aap Ashiq-e-Rasool Mumtaz Qadri ko Phansi dene wale ko vote de kar Allh ko kya jawab dogey?*" (Oh, Muslims, Wake up, Vote for PTI; Will you be able to face the Allah, if you vote for people who hanged Mumtaz Qadri, who in turn sacrificed his life for his love for the Prophet?).

It was evident that Islamic parties were covertly encouraged to whip up a political bogey against the ruling dispensation in the name of Islam in the run-up to 2018 elections. Such quiet prodding of the Islamist groups often lead to unintended consequences, as could be seen in the November 2018 demonstrations in the wake of the Supreme Court's verdict in October to release Asiya Bibi, accused of blasphemy. As TLP and other, mostly Barelvi outfits took to the streets, the army geared up into action and had to arrest the leaders of the protest who had started raising slogans against the army, the judiciary and the government. Khadim Hussain Rizvi of TLP and

Pir Afzal Qadri of Majlis-e-Khatm-e-Nabuwwat were among them. Under pressure from the military, Afzal Qadri decided to retire from politics and apologised for "hurting the sentiments of the government, the judiciary and the Army chief".[33] Khadim Hussain Rizvi kept on inspiring the youth to take on alleged blasphemers until his death in November 2020.[34] The strategy of the Pakistani army to use Islamic groups at will for political purposes and then use coercion to keep them under control, as can be seen in this particular case, has led to gradual assertion of such elements in Pakistani society. It has reached a stage where sentiments in favour of Islamic rule is seeping into the society at various levels making people insular to Islamist radicalism in some ways. There are many in Pakistan who would say that lower ranks of the Pakistan army are very conservative in their outlook by now, which might affect the army's efforts against Islamist militants in the long run.

Crisis of Identity

The inability of the elite to define Pakistani nation in non-religious geo-cultural terms has allowed Islam to endure as the most important marker of the Pakistani identity. This sense of identity-crisis persists even after almost seven decades of Pakistan's sovereign existence as an independent entity in the comity of nations. Ironically, as long as Islam remains the most potent referent, it is certain to emit strong Islamist impulses, which will continue to legitimise the operation of radical Islamic groups in Pakistan.

Rather than leading to a consensus, the increasing accent of the state on Islam has hardened the boundaries between different sects and groups within Islam. Each of these groups have tried to define Islam in narrow and exclusivist terms and sought to impose their world-views on others in militant ways. If one goes by their separate versions of Pakistan, one will find many Pakistans within Pakistan competing for influence and legitimacy.[35] Rather than fighting them or trying to transcend such fissiparous tendencies by promoting a progressive version of Islam, the state apparatus has collaborated with the Islamists and even granted them their mini-emirates in far-flung areas. Inevitably, the Islamist discourse has been dominated by sectarian and regressive *maulanas* of all shades, pushing the resultant vector in the direction of growing Islamisation of Pakistani society with each passing day. The trend is too obvious to be ignored and appears irreversible in present circumstances.

The Malaise and the Remedy

The failure of democracy, prolonged periods of military rule, persisting crises of governance and a self-perpetuating highly exploitative and inegalitarian socio-economic structure have created the ideal context for radical forces to thrive in the name of Islam, which—the radical and orthodox elements argue—could provide the panacea for all the ills Pakistan is suffering from at the moment. For example, in an article in a vernacular daily, coincidentally on 16 December 2014, anniversary of formation of Bangladesh and the day the Pakistani Taliban attacked the army school in Peshawar, the leader of one of the 'good' jihadi outfits, the Pakistani establishment has nurtured as almost its paramilitary arm for waging asymmetrical war against India, wrote indulgently on the issue of creation of Bangladesh:

> The nation which forgets history is condemned to repeat it.... A nation which forgets is past loses its memory ... the loss of East Pakistan is one such incident, which we should never forget.... The people of *Bangaal* and Bihar made supreme sacrifices for the formation of Pakistan; however, as soon as it came into existence, we forgot the value of Islam. Rather than establishing Islamic rule, we were busy building, decorating and populating the city of Islamabad. As a result, the sense of unity among the two halves was lost. In the absence of the glue of Islam, smaller issues like language, ethnicity, regional autonomy started assuming gigantic shapes. India took full advantage of our disunity and divided us. The answer lies in establishing Islamic rule in Pakistan.[36]

The Pakistani strategy of using some of these elements against India has strengthened the hold of the militant constituencies further and led to unintended consequences at the internal level. The rising incidence of sectarian violence and the spread of Taliban into the hinterland amply demonstrate this trend. Pakistan is thus likely to countenance prolonged period of chaos and turmoil. It will require a total transformation of Pakistani society to lift Pakistan out of the mess it is in today. Pakistan can arrest its decline and reverse the trend by de-emphasising its Islamic identity, reconstituting itself as a liberal democracy, bringing about people-centric socio-economic reforms, and define itself in geo-cultural rather than religious terms.

One way of comprehending the present radical environment that obtains in Pakistan and has made TTP a forbidding reality is to recognise the unintended consequence of overemphasis on Islam in the electoral process as well as in the business of the state and enable a forward-looking interpretation of Islam by engaging with and promoting religious scholars, academics and intelligentsia who can evolve an antidote to the abhorrent and regressive version of Islam that the TTP seeks to establish by all means.

Notes

1. In his inaugural address on 11 August 1947, Jinnah promised equal rights for all citizens regardless of religion, caste or creed. He famously said: "If we want to make this great State of Pakistan happy and prosperous, we should wholly and solely concentrate on the well-being of the people, and especially of the masses and the poor ... you are free—you are free to go to your temples mosques or any other place of worship in this state of Pakistan. You may belong to any religion, caste or creed that has nothing to do with the business of the state ... in due course of time Hindus will cease to be Hindus and Muslims will cease to Muslims—not in a religious sense for that is the personal faith of an individual—but in a political sense as citizens of one state" at http://www.pakistan.gov.pk/Quaid/governor_g.htm, accessed on 18 August 2007.

2. Ashok K Behuria, "Myth of the Monolith". *Strategic Analysis*, January-March 2005, p. 64.

3. Maulana Maududi, founder of Jamat-i-Islami had argued this way.

4. On 12 March 1949, the Constituent Assembly of Pakistan adopted a resolution moved by Liaquat Ali Khan, the then Prime Minister of Pakistan. It was called the Objectives Resolution. It proclaimed that the future constitution of Pakistan would not be modeled on European pattern, but on the ideology and democratic faith of Islam. Liaquat called it "the most important occasion in the life of this country, next in importance only to the achievement of independence".

5.   An interesting analytical piece titled "Talibanization of Pakistan", by Rafi Aamer, came up recently in *The Dawn* (Karachi), 12 August 2008, which also argues out the same.

6.   Ayub had to include Islamic clauses in the 1962 Constitution. These could not be challenged in any court of law. The state was originally named the Republic of Pakistan, but the first amendment added the word "Islamic" to the name. The word "Islam" and not "Quran and Sunnah" was used in the Islamic clauses to give a liberal touch to the Constitution. The Advisory Council of Islamic Ideology was introduced whose job was to recommend to the government ways and means to enable Muslims to live their lives according to the teachings of Islam.

7.   ICG Asia Report N°49, "Pakistan: The Mullahs and the Military", Islamabad/Brussels, 20 March 2003.

8.   Non-Muslim minorities in an Islamic state were called Dhimmis and they were treated differently and were discriminated against by the rulers.

9.   Ahmadiyas regard Mirza Ghulam Ahmed of Qadian (in present day India) as a later day Messiah who brought the message of Prophet Muhammad forward. Mainstream Islamic sects like Sunni and Shia consider it heretical to accept anybody as a Messiah after Muhammad because the Holy book accords the status of final Prophet to Muhammad alone. Hardline Sunnis and Shias came together in 1950s and then in 1970s and launched a movement in honour of the 'finality of prophethood' (Khatm-e-Nabuwat) and demanded expulsion of Ahmadiyas from the fold of Islam. Bhutto brought about a constitutional provision to deny Ahmadiyas the right to call themselves Muslims.

10. "Bahawalpur student stabs professor to death over 'anti-Islam' remarks— Pakistan", *The Dawn*, 20 March 2019 at https://www.dawn.com/news/1470814.

11. Salman Masood, "Hindu Veterinarian Is Latest to Face Blasphemy Charges in Pakistan", *New York Times*, 30 May 2019 at https://www.nytimes.com/2019/05/30/world/asia/pakistan-blasphemy-law.html.

12. See the tweet by Gulalai Ismail at(@Gulalai_Ismail on 4 August 2020 at https://twitter.com/Gulalai_Ismail/status/1290368970009313280?s=20.

13. Asad Hashim, "Sentenced to death for blasphemy: Surviving Pakistan's death row", Al Jazeera, 21 February 2020 at https://www.aljazeera.com/features/2020/2/21/sentenced-to-death-for-blasphemy-surviving-pakistans-death-row.

14. "More than 1,500 people—most of them Christian or members of the Ahmadi Muslim minority—were charged under Pakistan's blasphemy law from 1987 to 2017, according to the Centre for Social Justice, a Lahore-based religious-minority rights group", cited in Salman Masood, "Hindu Veterinarian Is Latest to Face Blasphemy Charges in Pakistan", *New York*

Times, 30 May 2019 at https://www.nytimes.com/2019/05/30/world/asia/pakistan-blasphemy-law.html.

15. "Timeline: Accused under the Blasphemy Law", *The Dawn*, 19 September 2019 at https://www.dawn.com/news/750512/timeline-accused-under-the-blasphemy-law.

16. This section draws heavily upon an earlier work of the author "Islamist Impulse Haunting Pakistan", *Strategic Analysis* Vol. 35, No. 1, January 2011, pp. 12-16.

17. Waheed-uz-Zaman, wrote this in his editorial note to the book *In Quest of an Identity, Proceedings of the First Congress on the History and Culture of Pakistan*, p. iv. This congress was held at the University of Islamabad in April 1973. Quoted in Edward Mortimer, *Faith and Power: The Politics of Islam*, London, Faber and Faber, 1982, p. 216.

18. Ashok K Behuria, "Many Pakistans within Pakistan: The Case of Sectarian Conflicts in a Talibanised Context", Omprakash Mishra and Sucheta Ghosh, eds., *Terrorism and Low Intensity Conflict in South Asian Region*, Manak Publications, New Delhi, 2003.

19. *Report of the Court of Inquiry Constituted under Punjab Act II of 1954 to Enquire into the Punjab Disturbances of 1953*, Printed by the Superintendent, Government printing, Punjab, Lahore, 1954, p. 231.

20. Ibid., p. 219.

21. Quoted in *The Dawn*, 16 August 2010.

22. Special Report on *The News on Sunday*, 29 August 2010 at http://jang.com.pk/thenews/aug2010-weekly/nos-29-08-2010/spr.htm, accessed on 30 August 2010.

23. Ibid. Interview with Ziauddin Sardar at http://jang.com.pk/thenews/aug2010-weekly/nos-29-08-2010/spr.htm#5.

24. *The Dawn*, 25 November 2009.

25. Forty people including a including a major general, a brigadier, two lieutenant colonels and two majors were killed in the attack. Report by Mohammad Asghar, "Carnage in Pindi army mosque as Taliban breach security", *The Dawn*, 4 December 2009.

26. See report by BBC, "Pakistan buries victims of Rawalpindi mosque attack", 5 December 2009 at http://news.bbc.co.uk/2/hi/8397598.stm.

27. Nazariat Trust which dug out Jinnah's less known speeches endorsing Islam as the sheet anchor of the ideology of Pakistan led to assertions during Zia-ul-Haq's time that the liberal secular Jinnah that the world talks about was not the whole truth about the personal predilections of Jinnah. See Sarfaraz Hussain Mirza, "Quaid and Pakistan" at http://www.nazariapak.info/Quaid-e-Azam/Quaid-Pakistan.php.

28. "The Tasks Ahead", Speech at a Rally at the University Stadium, Lahore on 30 October 1947 at http://www.mofa.gov.pk/Pages/Qua_Speeches/THE_TASKS_AHEAD.htm.

29. "The State Bank of Pakistan: A Symbol of our Sovereignty", Speech on the occasion of the opening of the State Bank of Pakistan on 1 July 1948 at http://www.mofa.gov.pk/Pages/Qua_Speeches/THE_STATE_BANK_OF_PAKISTAN.htm.

30. "How the Islamabad protests happened", *The Dawn*, 25 November 2017 at https://www.dawn.com/news/1372800.

31. "List of demands put forward by TLY and accepted by govt for ending the Faizabad protest", *The Dawn*, 28 November 2017 at https://www.dawn.com/news/1373197.

32. In 1979, the Shias took to streets and staged a dharna in front of the GHQ over the Zakat ordinance promulgated by Zia-ul-Haq, forcing him to retreat on the issue. During Musharraf's rule also there were sit-ins in front of the GHQ demanding protection of Islam. Islamic groups have periodically taken to streets to pressurise the governments to frame their policies to conform to their version of Islam.

33. "TLP patron-in-chief Pir Afzal Qadri quits party citing health issues", *The Dawn*, 1 May 2019 at https://www.dawn.com/news/1479593, Also see the video on Youtube at https://www.youtube.com/watch?v=E874O02pU5E.

34. A student in Charsada killed the principal of his college in January 2018. Similarly, another student in Bahawalpur stabbed his professor to death in March 2019 on allegations of blasphemy. Both of them said that they were inspired by Rizvi.

35. Ashok K Behuria, "Many Pakistans within Pakistan: The Case of Sectarian Conflicts in a Talibanised Context", Omprakash Mishra and Sucheta Ghosh, eds., *Terrorism and Low Intensity Conflict in South Asian Region*, Manak Publications, New Delhi, 2003.

36. Hafiz Saeed, "How did Bangladesh come into being?", *Roznama Ummat*, 16 December 2014.

Conclusion: Prognosis

The Pakistani state with its modern democratic trappings has found it difficult to fight the menace of Islamic radicalism and it has progressively allowed the conservative lobby to prosper and advance slowly, but consistently. One of the reasons for all this to happen may be attributed to the minority elite group consisting of political, military and bureaucratic elite, largely drawn from the feudal class or as Hamza Alavi has called it, from the elite *salariat*,[1] which has dominated Pakistani politics ever since it was created, and has been responsible for driving the country into the current mess. Due to the slow pace of socio-economic development of the Pakistani society and the apathy of the ruling elite towards the issue of creating equal conditions for people to make social, economic and political mobility possible for the people at all levels aspiring for political power. The ruling elite of Pakistan has, both through its acts of omission and commission, left the ideological contours of the state underdefined, and through its incremental capitulation to the growing constituency of conservatives, it has conceded space to the Islamists to define Pakistan in overtly Islamic terms. It has been but natural for a state run by an elite constantly swearing in the name of Islam to contend with the passionate belligerence of an assertive lobby of the mullahs seeking to bring in a Sharia-based system dismissing the current system of democracy as an anti-Islamic one. The elite of Pakistan has raised the ambivalence of Jinnah and other founding members of the Pakistan movement (regarding whether Pakistan will be a state for the majority Muslims, secular and liberal, or an Islamic state run according to the principles of Islam) to an unsustainable level. The rise, decline and re-emergence of TTP signals a failure of the state and its capacity to transform itself.

In this context, what explains the persistence of the threat of Islamic radicalism in Pakistan? In the chapter earlier, it has been argued that exaggerated emphasis on Islam by the power elite in Pakistan has created the conditions for gradual growth of hardline Islamic sentiments, which have helped the evolution of a constituency which has backed Islamisation by force. The TTP is a manifestation of such a trend which threatens to engulf Pakistan and slowly turn it into an Islamic theocracy. Despite its de-legitimation, in some ways, by its act of terrorism in Peshawar in December 2014 and comprehensive kinetic action by the Pakistani military, it has slowly spread out into other areas of Pakistan, as can be seen in the arrests of hardcore militants professing loyalty to either TTP or its ideological mutants parading as affiliates of Al Qaeda and ISIS, from Punjab, Sindh and Balochistan. There is also news of these militants attacking the security forces on an everyday basis. The ruling elite is mainly looking at it as a law-and-order issue, or as the result of a well-oiled conspiracy hatched by external powers and agencies to weaken Pakistan. The ruling elite has enabled a system, which some observers have called 'a hybrid-theocratic state'[2] where the military and the mullahs have kept each other relevant both by colluding with each other and sometimes by fighting each other.

Democracy in Distress

One plausible cause of Islamic forces competing for power by different means could be deduced from the nature of their social composition. Ever since Pakistan was established, large majority of the clergy came from lower social classes unlike the ruling elite which invariably came from the feudal class. Famous Pakistani economist Late Mahbub-ul-haq estimated that the ruling class in Pakistan was an exclusive class confined to about 500 families of Pakistan in mid-1980s. Apart from few leaders like Qazi Hussain Ahmed, most of the mullahs have humble origins and come from poorer areas of Pakistan. Moreover, the foot-soldiers in the jihadi outfits also come largely from the underclass. An American scholar analysing the issue writes:

Whereas wealthy Pakistanis would rather donate their money than their sons to the cause, families in poor, rural areas are likely to send their sons to "jihad" under the belief that doing so is the only way to fulfil this spiritual duty. One mother whose son recently died fighting in Kashmir told me she would be happy if her six remaining sons were martyred. "They will help me in the next life, which is the real life."[3]

Due to unavailability of a legitimate system of elite circulation, the sprawling underclass has found political and economic mobility very difficult for itself. The mullahs/leaders championing religious orthodoxy representing this section find in 'appeal to Islam' a lever to make them relevant in the society and wield informal power. Given the backwardness of the constituency they seek to represent the louder they would pitch their demand for Islam and Islamisation the more acceptable they are for the people they are addressing. However, this is not to deny such leaders with their nuisance value and coercive power also tend to ally themselves with the military elite symbolising legitimate power of the state. Such connections have whetted the ambition of these elements and led to the present crisis.

The Stakes of the Mullah

The idea of a mullah-military nexus[4] which has been the theme of extensive research in Pakistan and outside, holds that it has been tempting for the military elite, which has been one of the important constituents of state power, to make use of the militant religious constituency to keep itself relevant in the power politics in the country. During the post-Afghan-Jihad days the use-value of this constituency even increased substantially and the military-dominant Pakistani state forged it into their Kashmir policy vis-à-vis India and in the bargain tolerated the intense Sunni-Deobandi sectarian manifestations at the domestic level. There was little realisation that these elements would turn against their mentors. By 1990s it was seen that they had indeed made their presence felt in the tribal belt in Pakistan and by 2005 they had taken it by storm.

There is another element to the militant Islam that has adopted the Taliban model in Pakistan in the last decade. It has nested itself in the Pashtun majority tribal areas, in and around the Tribal Areas of Pakistan and northern Balochistan. They have managed to spread to areas adjoining these areas in the so called settled areas. They have even penetrated into Punjab and Sindh—especially into Karachi—through their sectarian cousins and have had presence in Islamabad, as the Red Mosque episode showed. Moreover, majority of the leaders of orthodox religious outfits, both militant and moderate ones, have come from one ethnic group, i.e., the Pashtuns. There have been apprehensions that if Pakistan does not resolve its internal Taliban problem it may even encounter a Pashtun-religious opposition in Khyber-Pakhtunkhwa and northern Balochistan.

Military-militant Dynamics

It is well-known that the military has enabled the religious forces over time to serve its interests in Pakistani politics. Both in 1988, and in 2002, the military played a big role in bringing disparate conservative political groups together to form political alliances like Islamic Jumhoori Ittehad (IJI) and Muttahida Majlis-e-Amal (MMA). Such grand coalitions of religious-political parties including Deobandi, Barelvi and Ahl-e-Hadith (AeH) Sunni groups as well as Shias were made possible at military's behest in the past to enhance its relevance in Pakistani politics. However, building such alliances has been easier than controlling the agenda of Islamists in Pakistani politics. Moreover, the radical Islamist constituency demanding Islamic rule in Pakistan has separated itself from the religious political forces and aims at establishing an Islamic state in Pakistan through an armed struggle holding the army as its main enemy in the bargain.

This has taken the wind out of the moderate Islamic leaders who were looking at adopting a gradual approach. In the past, the religious forces brought together by Musharraf as MMA had insisted on Sharia-based rule through democratic means. Its leaders had argued that unlike the "Taliban which had gained power after a bloody conflict" they would "employ a gradual approach to total

Islamisation of society as recommended by the Shariat Council".[5] Given their proximity to the military the so called democratic religious forces had sought to bring in Islam through peaceful and democratic means. However, in the changed circumstances, the TTP and its affiliates have outpaced and overshadowed these forces. Ironically, their efforts to bring Islamic rule to Pakistan through armed jihad has been backed by a cross-section of the jihadi constituency raised by the Pakistan military for strategic purposes in the past.

India Factor

Due to the maturity shown by the democratic political forces Pakistan witnessed a smooth democratic transition in May 2013, for the first time perhaps in its entire history. Despite the efforts by certain political forces allegedly linked to the military to destabilise the process, the leaderships of the two main political parties, PML-N and PPP as also leaders of main religious parties managed to avert the crisis created by the so-called Tsunami march and subsequent sit-in in Islamabad in August-September 2014. In the bargain for obtaining the army's endorsement for continuation of the democratic process the government allegedly conceded army's veto in these spheres and the military assumed lot of salience designing the security policy to respond to the challenge posed by the TTP and its affiliates. Feeding the army with more power and enhancing its salience, however, could not endear either PPP or PML-N to the establishment, as could be seen in the army's approach towards both once they would work towards improving relations with India. With PPP and PML-N sticking to their understanding not to bring in the army into their power struggles, the army was on the look out for a political force that could be used to advance its agenda in the realm of foreign policy. Zardari's bid to repair relations with India as well as Nawaz Sharif's bid to attend the Indian Prime Minister Narendra Modi's swearing in July 2014 did not go down well with the army. Imran Khan's Tsunami march from 14 August to 17 December 2014 which followed Nawaz's Delhi visit was just indicative of the shape of things to come. The capital city of Islamabad was under a virtual siege and Imran's reference to the 'umpire' who would raise his finger if Nawaz did not leave, only indicated possible back-room political engineering that was perhaps being attempted behind the scene to punish Nawaz Sharif.

Later, the army was visibly upset when Cyril Almedia of the daily *Dawn* leaked out to the media, based on information that he gathered after a high-profile national security meeting in October 2016, that "in a blunt, orchestrated and unprecedented warning, the civilian government [had] informed the military leadership of a growing international isolation of Pakistan and sought consensus on several key actions by the state", including then Prime Minister Nawaz Sharif's direction that "fresh attempts be made to conclude the Pathankot investigation and restart the stalled Mumbai attacks-related trials in a Rawalpindi antiterrorism court".[6] Nawaz Sharif's political fortunes declined very fast in the aftermath of this leak. He had to sacrifice some of his close associates who had to resign for disclosing the details of a closed-door meeting involving national security issues. Subsequently, it was Imran again who filed a case in the Supreme Court on the Panama Leaks case (in April 2014) to see whether Nawaz Sharif was *"sadiq and ameen"* (honest and righteous) as per Article 62(1)(f), which sets the precondition for a member of parliament to be eligible for the post. The judicial drama that followed with the judiciary first giving Nawaz benefit of doubt in April 2017, but subjecting his case to be enquired by a Joint Investigation Team (JIT) which included one member each from ISI and Military Intelligence (MI). Based on the JIT report, the Supreme Court announced a unanimous decision on 28 July 2017 that Nawaz was not *sadiq* and *ameen* and hence unqualified to hold any public office.

The politics of Pakistan, in the aftermath of Nawaz's disqualification, revolved around the case involving the families of Nawaz Sharif and people close to him in his cabinet in the National Accountability Bureau (NAB) and Imran capitalised on it and reaped a good political harvest. It was common knowledge in Pakistan that Imran was riding the crest of a political wave curated by the military establishment (which is called *miltablishment* by Najam Sethi, a seasoned Pakistani commentator) during this time (July 2017-July

2018), finally resulting in his assumption of power after elections in 2018. With Imran Khan coming to power, the army, it seems has regained its primacy in the power-architecture of Pakistan. With all possibility of threat of opposition to its security policy removed, the army is comfortably ensconced at the apex of Pakistan's power matrix. However, even then, the threat of forces like TTP has not reduced, as one can see from the discussion below.

It is important to note that Nawaz suffered this fate because of his efforts to get the army off his back while reshaping Pakistan's foreign policy, especially recasting Pakistan's approach to India. It is also true that the military's bid to generate exaggerated and often convoluted fear of India among the population is a function of its penchant for power, because it is that fear that legitimises its continued salience in Pakistani society. However, the strategy that it has adopted to balance that fear through nurturing militant constituencies has had a blowback and this has created the context for TTP-like elements to rise.

Army's Resolve has not Worked

There is a perception in Pakistan now that ever since Gen Kayani demitted office, the army under the leadership of Raheel Sharif and then Gen. Qamar Javed Bajwa has shown much more resoluteness in its fight against the TTP. The move for dialogue with the TTP was also allegedly aborted because of the army chief's disinclination to pursue the process when the civilian government of Nawaz Sharif was intent to engage the TTP despite its provocations. The TTP alleged that the army forced them to end the ceasefire and provoked them to do so by resorting to extra-judicial extermination of many of its cadres during the process of engagement. There was another view also that the TTP wanted to buy time by prolonging the process and was internally divided over the issue. Whatever it is, the strain between military and militants has become too obvious now and therefore the confrontation is likely to be a protracted one, even if it is widely believed that the Zarb-e-Azb together with operation Khyber (I & II) have dismantled the infrastructure of the militants especially that of the TTP and its patron Haqqani group.

It is being reported that the Pakistan military undertook the operations after conveying the Haqqani group about it in advance and, therefore, the leadership of the group melted away into Afghanistan before the operations. Since the TTP was also watching the behaviour of the army very closely and could have easily sensed its decision to attack its facilities, most of its top commanders also went across the Durand line and managed to survive. As per ex-TTP spokesperson Ehsan-ul-Ehsan's account (discussed in detail earlier) suggests, the army was constantly trying to cut deals through the Haqqanis with the TTP to turn their attention towards India. However, this tactic of using India as an alibi has not succeeded so far. The Pakistan army's strategy of using terror for maximising its influence in the region, and dealing with India and Afghanistan more effectively has backfired. While it still has a large bevy of militants to serve almost as its paramilitary arm to annoy India through subversive terror acts, growing number of such trained cadres share their frustration with forces like TTP and argue that the Pakistan army is anything but Islamic and the jihad they have been trained to wage against India must be waged against Pakistan army as well, because it is not fully Islamic in its orientation.

Pakistani state is in for a long haul, as far as fighting these elements are concerned. It may be true that such militancy may not pose a disintegrative pressure on the Pakistani state. However, given the close nexus between Taliban and other types of extremists like Deobandi Sunni sectarian elements and Kashmir-focused militants within Pakistan, the very possibility of such autonomous but inter-connected armed militant groups operating within Pakistan—even if they were to stay largely localised in the Pashtun belt—will be counterproductive for long-term security interests of Pakistan. Such forces may engage the state in a perpetual confrontation as a regressive force, and contribute to the fragility of the state machinery. This would make the army play a more central role and further strengthen its hold on power in Pakistan.

It has to be remembered that even if TTP has made religious political parties like JUI and even JI look like moderates, there is a basic agreement among all these groups regarding the need to have Islamic Sharia-based rule in Pakistan. The moderation induced by participation in the democratic political process wears off once the leaders of such moderate religious parties go out of governmental patronage. The temptation to bring in Islamic rule through coercion is always there among their enthusiastic supporters at the grassroots level and this constituency will continue to provide the necessary oxygen for the pro-Taliban Islamist militancy in the tribal belt.

Can the Process be Reversed?

After the last four years of high-voltage kinetic operations, the army has managed to kill some Al-Qaeda operatives, apprehended few local Taliban leaders and wrested control of the notorious Shawal and Tirah valleys apart from Miramshah, Mir Ali and Wana. The army has claimed that it had cleared the area of the militants, and the next logical step would be to demonstrate the willingness and capability to hold the terrain and bring in responsive and accountable administration with promise of good governance to transform the local socio-cultural and political dynamics to be able to reverse the trend of radicalisation. The case of large-scale displacement of the people due to the operations, according to some reports, if left unattended for long, has the potential to turn into a sympathetic constituency and a recruitment ground for terror outfits again.

Many analysts in Pakistan would argue that, after the Peshawar tragedy, orchestrated by the TTP, there is a national resolve in Pakistan to put an end to such phenomenon forever. There is also a liberal argument that the silent majority of Pakistan is against a militant version of Islam and the plurality within Islam in Pakistan would always act as a defence against any move by any one version to dominate the political scenario in Pakistan. Moreover, the largest province of Pakistan, Punjab, will not, in all likelihood, come under the sway of any such regressive force. However, all such sanguine analysis would come to naught, if the state does not take measures to protect diversity and deemphasise on Islam as a major referent in the conduct of state affairs. It has to ensure that while dealing with TTP's call for jihad with an iron hand, it is not encouraging calls for jihad by other groups being developed as force multipliers for Pakistan's approach towards Afghanistan and India.

To make a beginning, the dominant elite of Pakistan may have to define the state-craft in liberal terms, keeping Islam out of the affairs of the state and stop sponsoring jihad in neighbouring countries to retain their hold on power and invest in normalisation of relations with India rather than project it as an existential threat and force India's hand against it, turning its unreasoned fear into a self-fulfilling one. The state, rather than working on how to make good Muslims, allowing constituencies of jihadis to grow inside as recruitment ground for its asymmetric war vis-à-vis India and Afghanistan, ought to devote more time to liberal education, genuine reform of existing madrassas and open up the political domain to allow the militant forces to battle it out in the game of electoral politics, which will effectively deter their enthusiasm and appeal. A closed political system with doctored elections and unrepresentative set of rulers would be recipe for disaster. If the state makes an effort to contain the militant groups through force alone, it may not work as can be seen in many other Muslim countries of the world.

Moreover, various institutions of the state may have to act in concert while dealing with forces averse to representative democratic rule (*jumhoori nizam*), based on their allegations of corruption, nepotism, immoral and self-serving politics and slavish attitude of the rulers towards external forces. Inter-institutional struggle for power often weakens the system and provides the fuel for conservative forces, who in alliance with one or more institutions find an opportunity to infect the system with their regressive ideas and sap its energies further. Looking at the political scenario today, with the Pakistan Democratic Movement (PDM) and the ruling party/coalition fighting a pitched political battle, and also with the army losing its appeal because of its over-identification with the ruling elite, there is a cumulative apathy for the existing system of democracy, which has the potential to shift popular attention towards the conservative narrative of Sharia rule, as a healthier alternative, stimulating Islamist discourses further, creating a conducive atmosphere for outfits like TTP to penetrate into the heartland of Pakistan. Even mainstreaming of Islamists may not provide the panacea for dealing with threats like TTP.

The world at large can only be of help to Pakistan if it is willing to help itself. This can be achieved if Pakistan ensures a participative political process, where people with radical mindsets would be compelled to try out their strength in the theatre of electoral politics. Simultaneously, Pakistani state should initiate a process of integrating the far-flung tribal areas by promoting connectivity through all-weather road networks, through greater penetration of political parties to these areas, heeding the appeals of the people from the region to deal with them fairly and equitably rather than branding civil society activism (like that of PTM) as externally-sponsored sedition, and by providing the people with access to liberal education and by reforming the madrassa education system, if it is serious about reversing the tide of Talibanisation.

Notes

1. The salary earning class that emerged during the colonial period has been called as 'salariat' by eminent political scientist from Pakistan, Hamza Alavi.

2. Ayesha Siddiqa, "Pakistan's modernity: Between military and militancy", *The Friday Times*, 9-15 March 2012, Vol. XXIV, No. 04 at http://www.thefridaytimes.com/beta2/tft/article.php?issue=20120309&page=2.

3. Jessica Stern argues correctly in her piece, "Pakistan's Jihad Culture", *Foreign Affairs*, November-December 2000.

4. See Hussain Haqqani, *Pakistan: Between Mosque and Military,* Washington: Carnegie Endowment for International Peace, 2005, Zahid Hussain, *Frontline Pakistan: The Struggle with Militant Islam,* I.B. Tauris, distributed by Palgrave Macmillan, 2006, Hassan Abbas, *Pakistan: Drift into Extremism.*

5. See the discussion on 'Implementing Sharia', in ICG Report, note 15, See the quote from the ICG interview with Hafiz Akhter Ali, NWFP minister for Religious Affairs and Auqaf, Peshawar, 3 January 2003, p. 29.

6. Cyril Almeida, "Exclusive: Act against militants or face international isolation, civilians tell military", *The Dawn*, 6 October 2016 at https://www.dawn.com/news/1288350.

Select Bibliography[*]

Books/Monographs/ Articles/Reports/Briefs

Abbas Hassan, *The Taliban Revival: Violence and Extremism on the Pakistan-Afghanistan Frontier*, New Haven, CT, Yale, University Press, 2014, pages. 296.

Abbas, Hassan, *Pakistan's Drift into Extremism Allah, the Army, and America's War on Terror*, Routledge, New York, 2005, pages.305.

Acharya, Arabinda, Syed Adnan Ali Shah Bukhari and Sadia Sulaiman, "Making Money in the Mayhem: Funding Taliban Insurrection in the Tribal Areas of Pakistan", *Studies in Conflict & Terrorism*, Vol. 32, 2009, pp. 95–108.

Ahmed, Khaled, *Sleepwalking to Surrender*, Penguin India Viking, 2016, pgs. 472.

Al-Libi, Sheikh Abu Yahya, *Shamsher Beniyam, Yaani Pakistani Hukumat aur Afwaz ke khilaf Qitaal ki Sharia'i Haisiyat*, (The Sheathless Sword: Killing of Pakistani Rulers and Army men in light of Shariah), 2011, pages. 216.

Al-Swati, Sheikh Abu Darda, *"Khud Badaltay Nahi Quran Ko Badal Detey Hain* (They do not change, They change the Quran), Al Muwahideen, October 2013, pages. 219.

Anonymous, TTP, "Operation Manual for Mujahideen of Tehrik Taliban Pakistan", September 2018, 28 October 2018, at https://justpaste.it/ Laiha_TTP_Eng

Anonymous, TTP, "Tum log Amrika se kyun nahin ladte?" May 2017, available at https://justpaste.it/tum_america_ko_kiu_nahi_martay/pdf

Basit, Abdul, "Asim Umar - 'New Kid on the Block'?", *Counter Terrorist Trends and Analyses*, Vol. 6, No. 10 (November 2014), pp. 8-12

---

[*] These books/monographs/articles may or may not have appeared in the notes and references, however, they have certainly helped the author's understanding of the eco-system in which the TTP has emerged as an implacable adversary of the Pakistan state.

Burki, Khan Zeb, "Rise of Taliban in Waziristan", *The Dialogue*, Volume V, Number 3, July-September 2010, pp. 188-211 at http://www. qurtuba.edu.pk/thedialogue/The%20Dialogue/5_3/Dialogue_July_ September2010_188-211.pdf

Coll, Steve, "The Unblinking Stare: The drone war in Pakistan", *New Yorker*, 17 November 2014, at https://www.newyorker.com/ magazine/2014/11/24/unblinking-stare.

Dalrymple, "William, The Military and the Mullahs", *New Statesman*, 23 August 2010, pp. 26-29.

Dressler, Jeffrey A., "The Haqqani Network: From Pakistan to Afghanistan", Afghanistan Report 6, Institute for the Study of War, October 2010, at www.understandingwar.org/sites/default/files/Haqqani_Network_ Compressed_0.pdf

Dormandy, Xenia, "Reversing Pakistan's Descent: Empowering its Middle Class", *The Washington Quarterly*, Vol. 35 No. 2, 2012, pp.157-173.

Eijaz, Abida, "Pakistan Media Sphere and Public Sphere Negotiating the Concept of Taliban", *Pakistan Vision*, Vol. 12 No.1, 2011, pp.114-124.

Fair Christine C., "Who Are Pakistan's Militants and Their Families?", *Terrorism and Political Violence*, Vol. 20, No. 1, 2008, pp.49-65.

Fair Christine C. and Seth Jones, "Pakistan's War Within", *Survival*, Vol. 51, No 6, December 2009-January 201, pp. 161-188.

Farooq, Ustad Ahmad, "Aik Haath mein Talwar, Aik haath mein Bandhook", www.malhamah.tk, Hattin Media, 2009.

Farooq, Ustad Ahmad, *Pakistan Mein Jihad Jaari Rehna Chahiye*, www. malhamah.tk, TTP Media, Undated.

Filkins, Dexter, "Pakistan's Monster", *New Yorker*, 22 January 2016, at https://www.newyorker.com/news/news-desk/pakistans-monster.

Ghazi, Muhammad Abdul Aziz, "Jumhooriyat Aik Faraibi Taghooti Nizam" (Democracy is a Deceptive and Satanic System), Umar Media (TTP Publication) Undated, pages. 64.

Grare, Frederic, "Islamic Threat to Stability: How Real?", *Economic and Political Weekly*, Vol. 36, No. 48, 1-7 December, 2001, pp. 4461-4463.

Gunaratna, Rohan and Anders Nielsen, "Al Qaeda in the Tribal Areas of Pakistan and Beyond", *Studies in Conflict & Terrorism*, Vol. 31, Issue 9, 2008, pp.775–807,

Hassan, Maulana Muhammad Masni, *'Pakistan' Jarnailon ke Shikanje Mein*, TTP Publication Hattin, Undated, pages. 67.

International Crisis Group, "Pakistan's Tribal Areas: Appeasing The Militants", Asia Report No 125, 11 December 2006, pp. 1-38.

Iqbal, Khuram and Sara De Silva, "Terrorist lifecycles: a case study of Tehrik-e-Taliban Pakistan", *Journal of Policing, Intelligence and Counter Terrorism*, Vol. 8, No. 1, 2013, pp. 72-86.

Iqbal, Khurram, "Therik-e-Taliban Pakistan: A Global Threat", *Conflict and Peace Studies*, Vol. 3, No.4, October-December, 2010, pp. 1-10.

Jadoon, Amira and Sara Mahmood, "Fixing the Cracks in the Pakistani Taliban's Foundation: TTP's Leadership Returns to the Mehsud Tribe", *CTC Sentinel*, Volume 11, Issue 6, June/July 2018, at https://ctc.usma.edu/fixing-cracks-pakistani-talibans-foundation-ttps-leadership-returns-mehsud-tribe/.

Jamal, Arif, "Pakistani Taliban Widen the Civil War --- Against Fellow Deobandis", *Terrorism Monitor*, Volume IX, Issue 15, 14 April 2011, pp. 3-4.

Jamal, Sana and M. Ahsan, "TTP- Analyzing the Network of Terror", Report No 6, International Relations Insights and Analysis (IRIA), Bucharest, pp. 1-46.

Kaltenthaler, Karl and William Miller, "Ethnicity, Islam, and Pakistani Public Opinion toward the Pakistani Taliban", *Studies in Conflict & Terrorism*, Vol. 38, No. 11, 2015, pp. 938-957.

Kaltenthaler, Karl, William J. Miller, Stephen Ceccoli, and Ron Gelleny, "The Sources of Pakistani Attitudes toward Religiously Motivated Terrorism", *Studies in Conflict & Terrorism*, Vol. 33, 2010, pp.815–835,

Kaplan, Robert D., "The Lawless Frontier", *The Atlantic*, September 2000.

Khan, Adnan R., "The Rise of 'Talqaeda'", *Macleans,* 31 March 2009, at https://www.macleans.ca/news/world/the-rise-of-talqaeda/

Khan, Muhammad Khalil, and Lu Wei, "When Friends Turned into Enemies: The Role of the National State vs. Tehrik-i-Taliban Pakistan (TTP) in the War against Terrorism in Pakistan", *The Korean Journal of Defense Analysis*, Vol. 28, No. 4, December 2016, pp. 597-626

Khawaja, Asma Shalir, "Talibanisation of Pakistan: Myth or Reality", Online Working Paper No 6, Graduate School Asia and Africa in World Reference Systems, Martin-Luther-University Halle-Wittenberg, 2009, at http://wcms.itz.uni-halle.de/download.php?down=9047&elem=1986859

Lieven, Anatol, "A Mutiny Grows in Punjab", *National Interest,* March-April, 2011, pp. 15-23.

Lieven, Anatol, "How the Afghan Counterinsurgency Threatens Pakistan", *The Nation*, 3 January 2011, pp. 11-13.

Linschoten, Alex Strick van and Felix Kuehn, *An Enemy We Created: The Myth of the Taliban-Al Qaeda Merger in Afghanistan*, Oxford University Press, 2012

Mir, Amir, *Talibanisation of Pakistan From: 9/11 To 26/11 And Beyond*, Pentagon Press, 2010, pgs. 452.

Naseemullah, Adnan, "Shades of Sovereignty: Explaining Political Order and Disorder in Pakistan's Northwest", *Studies in Comparative International Development*, Vol. 49, May 2014, pp. 501-522 at https://doi.org/10.1007/s12116-014-9157-z.

Nawaz, Shuja, "FATA— A Most Dangerous Place", Center for Strategic and International Studies (CSIS), Washington DC, January 2009, pp. 1-57.

Norell, Magnus, "The Taliban and the Muttahida Majlis-e-Amal (MMA)", *China and Eurasia Forum Quarterly*, Volume 5, No. 3, 2007, p. 61-82.

Orr, Allan, "The Artful Dodger: On Pakistan, Reality Bites", *Defense & Security Analysis*, Vol. 26, No. 3, pp.243-260.

Peters, Gretchen, "Crime and Insurgency: in the Tribal Areas of Afghanistan and Pakistan", Combating Terrorism Center, 15 October 2015, pages. 95.

Qazi, Shehzad H, "An Extended Profile of Pakistani Taliban", Policy Brief No-44, August, 2011, Institute for Social Policy and Understanding, pp. 1-13.

Qazi, Shehzad H., "Rebels of the frontier: origins, organization, and recruitment of the Pakistani Taliban", *Small Wars & Insurgencies*, Vol. 22, No. 4, September 2011, pp. 574-602.

Roggio, Bill, and Thomas Joscelyn, "Discord Dissolves Pakistani Taliban Coalition", *Long War Journal*, 18 October 2014, at https://csc.asu.edu/2014/10/18/discord-dissolves-pakistani-taliban-coalition/.

Schmidle, Nicholas, "Migration Season: The Taliban and Their Expanding Influence in Pakistan", ICWA Letters, NES-4, Institute of Current World Affairs, June 2006, pp. 1-8, at http://www.icwa.org/wp-content/uploads/2015/10/NES-4.pdf.

Schmidt, John R., "The Unravelling of Pakistan", *Survival*, Vol. 51, No. 3, June–July 2009, pp. 29–54.

Shah, Niaz A., *Islamic Law and the Law of Armed Conflict: The armed conflict in Pakistan*, Routledge, London, 2011, pages.165.

Shahzad, Syed Saleem, *Inside Al-Qaeda and the Taliban: Beyond Bin Laden and 9/11*, Pluto Press, London 2011, pages. 260.

Shaikh, Farzana, "From Islamisation to Shariatisation: Cultural Transnationalism in Pakistan", *Third World Quarterly*, Vol. 29, No. 3, Developmental and Cultural Nationalisms, 2008, pp. 593-609.

Shehzad, Mohammad, "The State of Islamic Radicalism in Pakistan", *Strategic Analysis*, Vol. 37, No. 2, 2013, pp.186-192.

Sheikh Khalid Haqqani, *Jumhooriyat o Naam Nihad Islami Jumhooriyat ke Mauzoo Par Jabardast Mukalma* (A Great Discussion on Democracy and so-called Islamic Democracy), June 2018, Umar Media, pages. 164.

Sheikh, Mona Kanwal, *Guardians of God: Inside the Religious Mind of the Pakistani Taliban*, Oxford University Press, September 2016, pgs. 226.

Sheikh, Mona Kanwal, "Sacred Pillars of Violence: Findings from a Study of the Pakistani Taliban", *Politics, Religion & Ideology*, Vol. 13, No. 4, December 2012, pp. 439–454.

Siddiqa, Ayesha, "Pakistan's Counterterrorism Strategy: Separating Friends from Enemies", *The Washington Quarterly*, Vol. 34, Issue 1, Winter, 2011, pp. 149162

Siddique, Abubakar, *The Pashtuns: The Unresolved Key to the Future of Pakistan and Afghanistan*, Hurst, 2014, pgs. 256.

Siddique, Qandeel, "The Red Mosque operation and its impact on the growth of the Pakistani Taliban", Norwegian Defence Research Establishment (FFI), 8 October 2008, pp. 1-55.

Siddique, Qandeel, "Tehrik-e-Taliban Pakistan: An attempt to deconstruct the umbrella organization and the reasons for its growth in Pakistan's north-west", DIIS Report 12, 2010, pp. 1-74.

Smith, Greg, "The Tangled Web of Taliban and Associated Movements", *Journal of Strategic Security*, Vol. 2, No 4, 2010, Danish Institute For International Studies, Copenhagen, pp. 31-37.

Soherwordi, Hussain Shaheed, "A Theoretical Discourse on the Pakistani Taliban", *Pakistan Horizon*, Vol. 64, No. 1, January 2011, pp. 39-51.

Staniland, Paul, "Caught in the Muddle: America's Pakistan Startegy", *The Washington Quarterly*, Vol.41, No. 1, Winter 2011, pp. 133-148.

Stenersen, Anne, "Al-Qaeda's Allies: Explaining relationship between AL-Qaeda and various Factions of Taliban after 2001", Counterterrorism Strategy Initiative Policy Paper, New America Foundation, April 2010, pp-1-17.

Sullivan, Daniel P., "Tinder, Spark, Oxygen, and Fuel: The Mysterious Rise of the Taliban", *Journal of Peace Research*, Vol. 44, No. 1, 2007, pp. 93–108.

Sultana, Razia and Saira Aquil, "The Pakistani Pashtuns and the endgame in Afghanistan", *International Journal On World Peace*, Vol. XXIX No. 4, December 2012, pp. 13-36.

Syed, Jawad, Edwina Pio, Tahir Kamran, Abbas Zaidi, eds., *Faith-Based Violence and Deobandi Militancy in Pakistan*, Palgrave Macmillan, London, 2016, pp. 552.

Taj, Farhat, *Taliban and Anti-Taliban*, Cambridge Scholars Publishing, August 2011, pgs. 226.

Tankel, Stephen, "Beyond FATA: Exploring the Punjabi Militant Threat to Pakistan", *Terrorism and Political Violence*, Vol. 28, Issue 1, 2016, pp. 49-71.

Thames, Knox, "Pakistan's dangerous game with religious extremism", *The Review of Faith & International Affairs*, Vol. 12, No. 4, 2014, pp.40-48.

Umar, Maulana Asim, *Adiyaan ki Jung: Deen-e-Islam Ya Deen-e-Jumhooriyat?* (Clash of Religions: Religion of Islam or Religion of Democracy?), Umar Media, Shawaal, 1434, August 2013, pages. 201.

Umar, Maulana Asim, *Jumhoori Nizam Tabahi ke Dahane Par*, (Democracy on the verge of destruction), Hattin Media, Rajab, 1438, March 2017, pages. 142.

Williams, Brian Glyn, "Talibanistan: History of a Transnational Terrorist Sanctuary", *Civil Wars*, Vol.10, No.1, March 2008, pp.40–59.

Witter, David, "Uzbek Militancy in Pakistan's Tribal region", Backgrounder, Institute for Study of War, 27 January 2011.

Yasmeen, "Samina, Pakistan, militancy and identity: parallel struggles", Australian Journal of International Affairs, Vol. 67 No. 2, 2013, pp.157-175.

Yusufzai, Rahimullah, "The Impact of Pashtun Tribal Differences on the Pakistani Taliban", *Terrorism Monitor*, Volume: 6 Issue: 3, 11 February 2008 at https://jamestown.org/program/the-impact-of-pashtun-tribal-differences-on-the-pakistani-taliban/

Yusufzai, Rahimullah, "A Who's Who of the Insurgency in Pakistan's North-West Frontier Province: Part One – North and South Waziristan", *Terrorism Monitor*, Volume: 6 Issue: 18, 22 September 2008 at https://jamestown.org/program/a-whos-who-of-the-insurgency-in-pakistans-north-west-frontier-province-part-one-north-and-south-waziristan/#.VNJUrPmSySo.

Yusufzai, Rahimullah, "A Who's Who of the Insurgency in Pakistan's North-West Frontier Province: Part Two – FATA excluding North and South Waziristan", *Terrorism Monitor*, Volume: 7 Issue: 4, 3 March 2009, at https://jamestown.org/program/a-whos-who-of-the-insurgency-in-pakistans-north-west-frontier-province-part-two-fata-excluding-north-and-south-waziristan/

Zahid, Farhan, "Fragmented Yet Fatal: Tehreek-E-Taliban Pakistan", *Foreign Analysis*, No 15, January 2015, Centre Français de Recherche sur le Renseignement (CF2R) at https://www.cf2r.org/foreign/fragmented-yet-fatal-tehreek-e-taliban-pakistan-2/

Zaidi, Syed Manzar Abbas, "Hating the Taliban, Hating the United States: Trajectories of Pakistan's Anti-Americanism", *American Foreign Policy Interests*, Vol. 31, 200, pp. 376–388.

Zaidi, Syed Manzar Abbas, "Understanding the Appeal of the Taliban in Pakistan", *Journal of Strategic Security*, Vol 3, No. 3, Fall 2010, pp. 1-14.

Zenn, Jacob, "The Growing Alliance between Uzbek Extremists and the Pakistani Taliban", Terrorism Monitor, Volume XI, Issue 5, 8 March 2013, pp. 7-8.

Index